CATHOLIC
BOOK OF
THE DEAD

CATHOLIC BOOK OF THE DEAD

ANN BALL

Our Sunday Visitor Publishing Division
Our Sunday Visitor, Inc.
Huntington, Indiana 46750

Nihil Obstat: Reverend Frank H. Rossi, S.T.L.

Imprimatur: Most Reverend Joseph A. Fiorenza
             Bishop of Galveston-Houston, Texas
             October 28, 1994

Our Sunday Visitor Publishing Division
Our Sunday Visitor, Inc.
200 Noll Plaza
Huntington, IN 46750

ISBN: 0-87973-744-1
LCCCN: 94-68928

PRINTED IN THE UNITED STATE OF AMERICA

Cover design by: Rebecca Heaston

744

Dedication

I know that my Redeemer lives, And because He lives, I too shall live.

Job 19:25-26

You will be sorrowful, but your sorrow will be turned into joy.

John 16:20

This book is lovingly dedicated to the memory of my Father and Mother, and all my beloved dead. They live in Him and in my heart.

Ora • Julian • Ann • Charles • John • Viola • Robert • Robertha • Grace • Arthur • Bethel • Mary • Gus • Louise • Philip • Natalie • Peter • Louis • Bruce • Bill • Joanne • Matt • Angelita • Angelito • Jack • J.C. • Joe • Bob • Sister Bernadette • Brother Dan • Angie • Johnny • Santos • Andy

Contents

Part One: The Historical Perspective

Part Two: We Celebrate Our Dead

Part Three: Funeral Customs Around the World

Part Four: Praying for and to the Dead

Introduction

I am going to die. You are going to die. In accord with the natural process of our natural world, every person dies and the shell we call our body becomes nothing but dust or ashes.

I want to live forever. We can live forever. Christ died for us and through his death and Resurrection He has redeemed the world.

Sherwin B. Nuland, a surgeon and writer, pummels his readers with their mortality to get them to face the skull beneath the skin of life. In less than one-hundred years, the life expectancy of a child in the Western world has more than doubled, inciting the hope that there is no species-determined limit to our life span. Twentieth-century man pressures medical science in his vain attempts to stave off nature's inexorable tides. Nuland believes medicine has a job to do, but says "nature does too, and will do it, medicine be damned." He says that today life's final flickerings are, more often than not, messy and agonizing and devoid of dignity. Our obsession with longevity distracts us from our duty to live well, and acceptance of death is a prerequisite for rising above concern for mere bodily continuance. Today, eighty percent of Americans die in hospitals' intensive care units, too often tangled in webs of wires and tubes that Nuland calls the "purest form of our society's denial of the naturalness, and even the necessity, of death" (*Newsweek*, March 7, 1994).

Death, then, exists in the natural order. It is reasonable and even necessary, and we Americans most often do all that we can to deny it.

As Christians, we have the duty to accept death in the joyful light of our faith in the Resurrection. As humans we will also experience the sorrow of the loss of our loved ones, but our grief should not lead us to the sin of despair. And while we live on this earth, we have duties to perform for the sick, the dying, and our beloved dead.

As Christians, we are mandated to visit, assist, and comfort the sick and the dying, to console the bereaved, and to pray for the dead.

We must not bury the dead twice — in the grave and in our hearts. We may bury the body, but should keep alive the soul in our hearts, extolling it in brightness. Through our love for the departed souls, we honor them and our Creator and draw them, and ourselves, nearer to the great brightness that is Love.

I have taken a great deal of teasing from my friends while writing this book. We have all taken to referring to the fruits of my labor as the "dead book." My last birthday reinforced the humor. Amidst an office full of black balloons, my sister entered costumed as Lady Death, singing a funeral dirge. Our secretary and a priest friend both presented me with bouquets of dead flowers — one of roses, one of lilies. Amidst the laughter I meet the eyes of close friends, who wonder if my writing this book is in response to recent deaths in my family, some deep sense of personal sorrow, or merely morbid curiosity.

For myself, I struggled with the concept of human death many years ago. Sometimes I sat up at night in a cold sweat, afraid to die. Somehow, these fears went away after the birth of my daughter, and through the years the investigation of my faith has prevented their return. Fear of death is no longer part of my nature, and I pray that its shadow will never return.

I wish to thank Mr. Vincent De Santis of the Department of History of the University of Notre Dame for inspiring me to write this book. For me, the contemplation and celebration of death can bring a renewal of life and faith. For some years I have kept the Mexican custom of erecting a home *ofrenda* (altar) in November to honor the dead of my family. An article I wrote about it for *Our Sunday Visitor* brought me a handful of angry letters from persons accusing me of promoting cultism and a new child to love. It also brought me a letter from Mr. De Santis, who pointed out that for a religion like ours that puts so much emphasis on praying for the dead, we had very few books about the subject.

A favorite pastime of mine since childhood has been visiting cemeteries. I find it sad that today so many Americans ignore them. They are interesting, peaceful, and can help to unite us in the communion of saints. With my father, I traveled to the cemetery to clean around the grave sites of our family and to try and plant flowers as reminders of life in this garden of the dead. With my children I sought interesting and unusual markers, epitaphs, and art. With my brother, visiting cemeteries was a relaxing way to pass a visit, enjoying our drives into the East Texas countryside as well as our strolls through the resting places of the dead. By myself, I honored the memory of the dead, reminded myself of my mortality, and learned lessons for life, especially the lesson that this life should not be wasted.

In this book I have tried to give the reader a glimpse of the beauty and variety of the people of our Catholic heritage, even in light of so somber a subject. Our faith draws us together, past, present, and future, into the large communion of saints.

If even a single reader finds one word of peace or comfort in what I have gathered between the covers of this book, my goal is met. If one prayer is uttered for the benefit of a forgotten soul, my goal is exceeded.

Praying for the Dead — A Holy and Pious Thought

by Rev. J. Michael Miller, C.S.B.

Since the liturgical renewal after the Second Vatican Council, Catholic funerals are no longer such somber affairs. White vestments and alleluias have replaced black vestments and the mournful but beautiful *Dies Irae*. A spirit of paschal rejoicing prevails. An unfortunate result of this new style has been that prayers for the faithful departed have been increasingly eliminated from Catholic preaching and piety.

Crisis in Praying for the Dead

We need reminders of our supernatural solidarity with the deceased and their need for further purification, even after death. Although the Church's liturgical prayers continue to stress the reality of purgatory, without mentioning the term, adverse cultural forces now militate against the ancient Catholic custom of praying for the dead. The practice of Masses and other prayers for the faithful departed are no longer the stock-in-trade of everyday Catholic life.

In our desire to console the bereaved, moreover, it is all too tempting to "guarantee" the deceased's entry into heaven. Homily after homily assures the congregation that the dead are already at peace with the Lord. Sermonizers wax eloquently about the heavenly pleasures — from eternal golf games to reunion with loved ones — that the dead are now enjoying.

Unlike faith, which is certain, the object of hope is not inevitable. The *reason* for our hope, however, is certain. God *will* reward his faithful ones. In teaching about the destiny of the departed, we must not compromise the utter gratuity of salvation. Nor should we be presumptuous about identifying the victors with certitude. The Church's prayers give voice to our hope that God will admit the faithful departed to his kingdom, "and hope does not disappoint us" (Romans 5:5).

Why is it that we are never surer of God's ways than when comforting the mourning? If our dead are assuredly in heaven, it is not surprising that praying for them strikes us as useless and quaint.

Dare Catholics ignore centuries of tradition by putting purgatory aside and preaching immediate entry into heaven for all who die? Neglecting belief in purgatory undermines the Church's ancient faith and practice concerning the faithful departed.

Who First Prayed for the Dead?

Witness of Scripture

Sacred scripture provides the foundation for the Catholic custom of praying for the dead. In the second century before Christ, the Jews came to believe that, even if someone died in a state of sin which merited punishment, the destiny of the deceased could be altered by the prayers of the living.

The Second Book of Maccabees recounts that Judas Maccabeus and his men arranged for the burial of fellow soldiers who had died in sin. Because they were wearing amulets forbidden by the Mosaic Law, God justly struck them down. Judas, however, believed that the deserved punishment in the afterlife was not definitive. He and his warriors "turned to supplication, praying that the sin which had been committed might be wholly blotted out" (2 Maccabees 12:42).

Judas collected money for sacrifice in the temple and had prayers offered for the dead. "For if he were not expecting that those who had fallen would rise again, it would have been superfluous and foolish to pray for the dead. But if he was looking to the splendid reward that is laid up for those who fall asleep in godliness, it was a holy and pious thought. Therefore he made atonement for the dead, so that they might be delivered from their sin" (2 Maccabees 12:44-46).

According to this inspired author of the Old Testament, those who had led good lives, despite occasional sin, could still be purified after their death. Through the prayer and sacrifice of others they could be rewarded with resurrection from the dead.

In the New Testament, the single specific reference to the apostolic practice of praying for the dead is St. Paul's entreaty for Onesiphorus: "may the Lord grant him to find mercy from the Lord on that Day" (2 Timothy 1:18). Here a living Christian intercedes for a deceased brother, asking God to be merciful to him on judgment day.

Testimony of Immemorial Tradition

Christians acquired the habit of praying for the dead from a very early date. Unlike their pagan neighbors who prayed *to* the dead, Christians prayed *for* the dead.[1] The ancient Church did not believe that everyone made it to heaven right away. That privilege was reserved to the apostles and martyrs. Ordinary Christians were not with Christ immediately after judgment. No one could enter the kingdom of God who was tarnished with any stain of sin. Consequently, our early forebears thought that most of the faithful departed were at least temporarily detained on their journey to heaven.

The few scriptural statements about praying for the dead are best understood in light of the later witness of tradition. Aristides of Athens provides the earliest testimony to this pious custom. About the year A.D. 140, he gave this advice to believers: "If one of the faithful dies, obtain salvation for him by celebrating the Eucharist and by praying next to his remains."[2]

A half-century later, *The Passion of Perpetua and Felicitas* (LeGoff, p. 49) relates a story describing the practice of praying for the departed. Condemned to death, Perpetua had a vision of her dead brother Dinocratus, who was experiencing great suffering. Because of her faith, she was confident that she could relieve him from his state of pain. Perpetua "prayed for him night and day, wailing and crying that [her] prayers be granted." A few days later, in a second vision, she saw that her brother had been delivered from his torment. Not only had she prayed for her brother, her prayers for him had been instrumental in alleviating his suffering.

By the fourth and fifth centuries, witnesses to offering prayers for the faithful departed abound. St. Cyril of Jerusalem (d. 444) wrote about the well-established custom of praying for the deceased during the Eucharistic Prayer. Explaining this practice to the newly baptized, he said: "We believe that it will be of very great benefit to the souls of those for whom the petition is carried up, while this holy and most solemn sacrifice is laid out" (*Catechetical Lectures*, 23.9-10).

In describing his last conversation with his mother, St. Augustine (d. 430) records her last request to her two sons: "Bury my body wherever you will; let not care of it cause you any concern. One thing only I ask you, that you remember me at the altar of the Lord wherever you may be" (*Confessions*, Book 9.11).

St. Augustine's own entreaty for his holy mother is a touching example of the believer's trust in the effectiveness of prayers for the faithful departed: "Forgive her too, O Lord, if ever she trespassed against you in the long years of her life after baptism. Forgive her, I beseech you; do not call her to account. Let your mercy give your judgment an honorable welcome, for your words are true and you have promised mercy to the merciful" (*Confessions*, Book 9.13). Though Augustine left Monica's destiny to God alone, he was convinced that his prayers could hasten the day when his mother's soul would enter the heavenly Jerusalem.

Innumerable graffiti and markings in the catacombs and other ancient places of Christian burial confirm the antiquity of the custom of praying for the dead.[3] Engraved on these ancient stones are supplications in which the departed beg for the prayers of their loved ones who are still alive. These inscriptions give expression not only to faith and hope in eternal life, but also show the belief that union with God is impeded by sin. The prayers of the living express the confidence that God will purify the departed according to their need.[4]

According to our historical sources, this practice of praying for the dead began even before the reasons for doing so were clearly formulated. Christians assumed that the departed could be aided by the prayers of the faithful on earth. This custom necessarily implied belief in the possibility of some purification for the soul after death. "The early Church," writes Edmund Fortman, "did not seem to be very clear about *where* these were or *how* prayer would help them, but she definitely knew that prayer and the Mass could be of benefit for these faithful Christians" (*Everlasting Life Towards a Theology of the Future Life*, New York: Alba House, 1986).

Authoritative Teaching

Official Church teaching on praying for the dead is most fully summarized in statements of the Council of Florence (1439) and the Council of Trent (1563). At Florence the Church formulated her teaching on the value of praying for the faithful departed, linking this practice with the doctrine of purgatory. "But if they die [after Penance] truly repenting in charity before making satisfaction by worthy fruits for what they have done or omitted to do, their souls are purged after death ... by the punishments of purgation and purification. The intercession of the living faithful is effective in lessening this punishment, by the sacrifice of the Mass, prayer, almsgiving, and other pious works which the faithful are wont to do."[5]

From the earliest centuries until the Protestant Reformation in the sixteenth century, praying for the dead went unchallenged. The Reformers, however, denied the doctrine of purgatory and the accompanying teaching of praying for the dead, holding them to be Catholic inventions. Deliberately opposing these denials, the Fathers at Trent reasserted official teaching by solemnly defining both the existence of purgatory and the value of prayer for the deceased. The Catholic Church teaches, they said, that "there is a purgatory, and that the souls detained therein are aided by the suffrages of the faithful and chiefly by the acceptable sacrifice of the altar" (DS 1820).

The Fathers at Vatican II reaffirmed Catholic doctrine on the practice of praying for the departed: "In full consciousness of this communion of the whole Mystical Body of Jesus Christ, the Church in its pilgrim members, from the very earliest days of the Christian religion, has honored with great respect the memory of the dead; and, 'because it is a holy and a wholesome thought to pray for the dead that they may be loosed from their sins' (2 Maccabees 12:46) she offers her suffrages for them" (*Lumen Gentium*, No. 50).

The Church's Prayers for the Faithful Departed

According to Church tradition, how we pray tells us what we believe. In 1979, the Vatican's *Letter on Certain Questions Concerning Eschatology* resolutely recalled that the Church's prayer life is a point of departure for doctrine. In examining new theories dealing with what happens between the death of a Christian and the general resurrection, the Congregation for the Doctrine of the Faith stated: "The Church excludes every way of thinking or speaking that would render meaningless or unintelligible her prayers, her funeral rites and the religious acts offered for the dead" (*Recentiores episcoporum Synodi*, 1979, No. 4). Praying for the dead is anchored in the Church's profession of faith.[6]

Such prayer sheds light on what the Church believes about the "possibility of a purification of the elect before they see God, a purification altogether different from the punishment of the damned" (*Recentiores episcoporum Syndoti*, No. 7) No binding doctrine exists, however, regarding the "fire" of purgatory, its duration, or the kind and intrinsic nature of its punishment.[7]

How the Church worships puts her faith on the line. And nothing is clearer in the Church's current funeral liturgy than the fact that the community gathers to pray for the departed. This rich treasury of liturgical prayers tells us what she professes about what happens to those who die in the Lord. These prayers remind us that the pilgrimage to glory is not immediately over for those who have died in the state of grace.

Funeral Rites

The *Order of Christian Funerals* (No. 6) affirms the value of praying for the departed: "The Church through its funeral rites commends the dead to God's merciful love and pleads for the forgiveness of their sins. At the funeral rites, especially at the celebration of the Eucharistic Sacrifice, the Christian community affirms and expresses the union of the Church on earth with the Church in heaven in the one great communion of saints. Though separated from the living, the dead are still at one with the community of believers on earth and benefit from their prayers and intercession."

The Church's funeral rites direct our attention to praying *for* the dead: that they may be forgiven their sins, cleansed from human weakness, welcomed into the joys of heaven, and raised up on the last day. She repeatedly places petitions such as the following on the lips of those celebrating the funeral liturgy: "God of faithfulness, in your wisdom you have called you servant N. out of this world; release him/her from the bonds of sin, and welcome him/her into your presence."

Only the opening prayer for the funeral Mass of a baptized child declares that the deceased is now in God's kingdom. Every other official prayer stops short of affirming that the departed person has already been led safely home to heaven. Carefully phrased so as not to assert the certainty of glory already attained, the liturgical prayers repeatedly direct the mourners to implore God's mercy so that the faithful departed will be admitted to the joyful company of the saints.

Eucharistic Prayers

Among the most ancient pious practices surrounding Christian care for the dead is the custom of commemorating the faithful departed at the Eucharist. Even today we should not forget that at every Mass we pray for the deceased. In the ancient *Roman Canon*, we pray: "Remember, Lord, those who have died and have gone before us marked with the sign of faith, especially those for whom we now pray, N. and N. May these, and all who sleep in Christ, find in your presence light, happiness, and peace" (Eucharistic Prayer I).

Each of the other Eucharistic Prayers contains a similar commemoration. "Remember our brothers and sisters who have gone to their rest in the hope of rising again; bring them and all the departed into the light or your presence" (Eucharistic Prayer II). "Welcome into your kingdom our departed brothers and sisters, and all who have left this world in your friendship" (Eucharistic Prayer III). And lastly, "Remember those who have died in the peace of Christ and all the dead whose faith is known to you alone" (Eucharistic Prayer IV).

The meaning of these prayers is obvious. Catholics believe that the departed can derive great benefit from the spiritual fruits of the Mass. And what profit could this be if not that of being purified of the effects of whatever still prevents them from entering paradise (Vagaggini, 338)? The Eucharistic Sacrifice speeds them on their journey to the kingdom prepared for them from the foundation of the world (cf. Matthew 25:34).

Supernatural Solidarity: The Communion of Saints

"By the hidden and kindly mystery of God's will," wrote Paul VI, "a supernatural solidarity reigns among men and women" (*Indulgentiarum Doctrina*, 1967, No. 4). Just as we are interdependent during this life, so are we beyond death. Without this communion of saints, praying for the dead would be senseless.

The Church is the communion of the "holy ones" or "saints" who dwell on earth, in heaven, and in purgatory (*Catechism of the Catholic Church*, Nos. 946-962). As the Council Fathers at Vatican II wrote: "All, indeed, who are of Christ and who have his Spirit form one Church and in Christ cleave together (Ephesians 4:16). So it is that the union of the wayfarers with the brethren who sleep in the peace of Christ is in no way interrupted, but on the contrary, according to the constant faith of the Church, this union is reinforced by an exchange of spiritual goods" (*Lumen Gentium*, No. 49).

A link of grace and mutual concern ties together those who have reached their heavenly home, those who are being purified, and those who are still pilgrims on earth. All are branches engrafted onto the single vine that is Christ (cf. John 15:1-8).

For Christ, and those united in his Body, the dead are alive. Death does not dissolve the relational and social nature of humanity. The supernatural fellowship of charity that unites members of the one Body of Christ (cf. 1 Corinthians 12:27) includes those in the state of purgation. Human solidarity reaches even beyond the confines of death.[8]

Because in the communion of saints all share the profound fellowship of grace "with the Father and with his Son Jesus Christ" (1 John 1:3), they also experience a solidarity in the spiritual goods flowing through the whole Body of Christ — on earth, in heaven, and in purgatory. In the Church no one lives for himself alone, just as no one dies for himself alone (cf. Romans 14:7). Everyone suffers and rejoices together (cf. 1 Corinthians 12:26). Each act of love profits all those who are united in Christ, just as every sin harms them (Catechism, No. 953).

After death, therefore, those in purgatory do not stand alone before God. The Church's faith tells us that the saving power of love transcends the grave. The bonds forged during life are indestructible. Consequently, the prayers and the merits of the living can help the departed in obtaining salvation from "God, who is rich in mercy" (Ephesians 2:4).

Intercessory Prayers for the Dead

Our prayers for the dead are efficacious because we are "in Christ," in the Body of which he is the head (cf. Ephesians 1:22-23). Such petitions are often called *suffrages*; that is, they are intercessory prayers and good works. As intercessory, they make a request through Christ, imploring God to free those in purgatory so that they will be cleansed from whatever still needs purification.

These prayers are made with filial confidence. Catholics believe that the Father knows what we need before asking him (cf. Matthew 6:8) and that "the Spirit helps us in our weakness; for we do not know how to pray as we ought, but that very Spirit intercedes with sighs too deep for words" (Romans 8:26).

To intercede on behalf of others through prayer is a practice that goes back to Abraham's intercession for Sodom and Gomorrah (cf. Genesis 18:16-33). In the New Covenant, Christ himself is our intercessor before the Father: "he is able for all time to save those who approach God through him, since he always lives to make intercession for them" (Hebrews 7:25). Since Christians are united to Christ in "one body" (Ephesians 4:6), praying for the brethren was part and parcel of early Church life (cf. Acts 12:5). In the communion of saints, the pilgrims on earth look not only to their own interests, but to the interests of others (cf. Philippians 2:4), joining their prayers to those of Christ (*Catechism*, Nos. 2635-2636).

Unlike us, the souls in purgatory cannot pray for themselves. Death ends the time in which an individual can merit. To emphasize this inability to help themselves through prayer, Catholics frequently refer to those in purgatory as the "poor souls," a designation that enjoys no official church sanction.[9] Those being purified are totally dependent upon the charity of their fellow members in the Mystical Body.

As a testimony to their supernatural solidarity with those in purgatory, the living may request that God apply to the purgatorians the spiritual "fruits" of their own good works and prayers. The love undergirding such actions releases the infinite love of Christ for the beloved deceased.

Likewise, the more individuals have the mind "that was in Christ Jesus" (Philippians 2:5), the more their prayers will be efficacious for others.[10] Precisely how this is accomplished we do not know. Without dictating to God how their good works can be "applied" to the faithful departed, Catholics trust that his love and mercy will prompt him to speed the purification of the faithful departed.

Purgatorians at Prayer

In earlier centuries, whenever the question was raised whether the faithful could pray not only *for* the souls in purgatory but also *to* them, theologians answered negatively. Yet the spiritual solidarity of the Mystical Body raises the question whether those in purgatory can pray for us, as the saints in heaven do. Can these souls, unable to help themselves, help those on earth?

Although the Church has no official prayers to the poor souls and has not officially encouraged them, she has never condemned this practice.[11] Two theological arguments support the custom. First, the spiritual interchange within the communion of saints speaks in its favor. Second, though not yet in heaven, those in purgatory are truly friends of God. United as they are in the one body of Christ with many members (cf. Romans 12:4), it is reasonable to maintain that the departed can reciprocate the love shown to them by praying for those on earth.[12]

Why Do the Dead Need Our Prayers?

Temporal Punishment Due to Sin

Is it true that even after God has forgiven our sins the need for reparation still remains? Yes. Even remitted sins must be atoned for (*Indulgentiarum Doctrina*, Nos. 2, 3).

The Church teaches that "the punishment due to sin, whether mortal or venial, is not always and necessarily forgiven along with the guilt of sin; hence this punishment is to be paid by the sinner either in this life or in the next before he can enter the kingdom of heaven" (DS 1580, 1712).[13] As pilgrims of the earthly city we can now do penance or make satisfaction for our sins.

A difficulty presents itself. Society has conditioned us to think that once God has forgiven us, everything has been taken care of. But forgiveness does not mean pretending that the lasting effects of sin are negligible. Every sin entails consequences that are not removed simply with the act of forgiveness. Theologians call these repercussions the "temporal punishment due to sin." Although God forgives the guilt of sin (eternal punishment) at the time of reconciliation, he does not exempt sinners from the need of "making up" for their sin (temporal punishment). Taking place in time, this atonement is temporal. As a consequence of sin, it is called punishment.

Temporal punishment is a consequence of the sinful act itself. "In sinning," writes Peter Phan, "human beings violate and de-

stroy their own nature and experience an inner contradiction between what they sinfully choose to be and what God intends them
to be. And this radical contradiction produces pain, the punishment of sin (*Eternity in Time*, Cranbury, NJ: Associated University Press, 1988, p. 125). Purgatorial suffering is the gradual and
painful removal of this self-imposed contradiction which was not
completed on earth.

In the past, this theological idea of temporal punishment was sometimes misunderstood. People often thought that purgatory entailed
the soul's passive endurance of God's vindictive punishments. It was
almost as though a person's sins deserved some kind of sentence imposed by a vengeful divine judge. If this penalty of suffering had not
been paid off in this life, then it would be in the next one.

For many centuries much popular piety focused on the suffering,
even the torture, experienced by those in purgatory. In exhortative
preaching, its painful dimension was emphasized to discourage moral
laxity. The more terrifyingly purgatory was portrayed, the more
preachers wanted to incite their listeners to timely conversion. Sermons, holy cards, paintings, and devotional writings fed the vision
of purgatory as infernal — a veritable, even if provisional, hell.

In one hymn of St. Louis-Marie Grignion de Montfort (d. 1716),
the prisoners of purgatory cry out to the living: "Friends, this aveng-
ing God sets up our torture. We feel the rigors of all his justice."[14]
Purgatory was likened to a jail where captive souls clamored for
release from their torments.

These dreadful punishments were elaborations of St. Augustine's
assertion that "this purgatorial fire is harsher than any pain which
one can see, feel, or imagine here below" (*Sermon*, 104: PL39, 1947).
Pyromaniac phantasms were given free rein. Whether this fire was
physical or metaphorical was a theological question. Many people
assumed that those in purgatory suffered the rages of material fire.
This belief gave rise to the images and language of "burning" in
purgatory and of being held captive in its "flames."[15]

Preaching a purgatory of suffering also served to stimulate the
compassion of the living, provoking their prayers on behalf of the
deceased. Praying for the dead was like praying for the release of a
prisoner from jail. The faithful offered these prayers because they
hoped that their suffrages would be accepted as partial payment of
the debt owed by the sinner and that his prison sentence would be

lightened.[16] The ways to relieve the suffering of the dead were to have Mass celebrated, give alms, receive Communion, acquire indulgences, and perform good works on their behalf.

Joyful Purification

In her revolutionary *Treatise on Purgatory*, St. Catherine of Genoa (d. 1510) described purgatory less as a torture chamber and more as a place of happiness. She declared in one of her visions that "there is no joy save that in paradise to be compared to the joy of the souls in purgatory (*Purgation and Purgatory, the Spiritual Dialogue*, trans. Serge Hughes, New York: Paulist Press, 1979, p. 72). The source of this delight is the certain hope of possessing God, a hope which gives birth to joy. Those in this state of purification also know that they are not yet ready to "come and behold the face of God" (Psalm 42:2). Even though they experience this temporary deprivation of the beatific vision as a great suffering, "it is sweetened and consoled by the assured hope of possessing him," writes St. Robert Bellarmine (d. 1621). "From this hope there arises an incredible joy, which grows in measure as the soul approaches the end of its exile."[17]

Relying heavily on the writings of St. Catherine of Genoa, many contemporary theologians emphasize purgatory more as the forecourt of heaven rather than as the antechamber of hell. Purgatory is a bittersweet experience. There the souls of the just know that they are destined to see God "face to face" (1 Corinthians 13:12). Purgatory is a one-way street. Its only direction is upwards. The principal suffering of purgatorians is the purification of love that gradually matures by becoming more worthy to possess God (*Civilta Cattolica*, "Preaching About Purgatory Today," p. 15).

When this more joyful vision of purgatory takes hold, the value of suffrages for the dead is less immediately evident. The purpose of praying for the dead is no longer understood as begging God to shorten the time of a prison sentence. Instead, theologians point out that such prayers are a help in readying souls for being with Christ in paradise (cf. Luke 24:43).

Helping the Soul's Transformation

Think about purgatory less as a place of horrors and more as a gracious opportunity to be prepared for seeing God "as he is" (1

John 3:2). Although frequently misinterpreted in legalistic terms, Catholic teaching on the temporal punishment due to sin is doctrinally sound. Purgatory is for these who are not quite "dead" enough, for those who have not yet wholly died to themselves. Since most people die with attachments to sin and self, they need further purification. The souls in purgatory voluntarily accept their temporary separation from God. What they did not do during their life on earth in erasing self-seeking, they now undergo willingly because they are certain of their heavenly reward.

Sin always leaves some wound that needs healing. St. Thomas Aquinas (d. 1274) speaks of the "remnants of sin" remaining after divine forgiveness (*Summa Theologiae*, III, q. 86, q. 5). We are responsible for the disorder introduced into world through our sins. The hurt of our words and actions endures beyond the moment. A sin's effects exceeds the ability of individuals to discern them and leaves scars that penetrate below the level of consciousness into the marrow of a person's being.

What was impossible to achieve, for most people, in the time before death — the full integration of their lives with God and with others — must be brought to full maturity. Because the effects of sin linger after judgment, they must be purged away. Total conversion never occurs at a single blow. It involves an arduous process. We must be restored to that holiness and blamelessness for which we were destined "before the foundation of the world" (Ephesians 1:4).

In his mercy, God allows us to assume responsibility for righting what we did wrong. Through prayer and good works we can share in repairing the damage caused by our sins (*Catechism*, No. 1459). Even if the one offended offers us unconditional forgiveness, some chance to make amends guarantees human dignity, freedom, and responsibility. Those in purgatory can no longer do this for themselves. With their pilgrimage on earth ended, they cannot actively perform such deeds. Like infants, they depend totally on God and those persons through whom he chooses to show his mercy.

Purgatory brings all our earthly deficiencies under the searing gaze of Truth. Romano Guardini describes what happens to those undergoing this purification: "The pain that was refused must be accepted; the truth that has escaped cognition must be learned; the imperfect love must be made full and perfect (*The Last Things*, trans. Charlotte E. Forsyth and Grace B. Branham, New York: Pantheon Books, Inc.,

1954, p. 47). Experiencing this intense love of God burns up all remnants of self-love, ingratitude, and refusal. Purgatory is a process which removes every obstacle so that the holy souls can possess God, fully realizing their call as "children of God" (1 John 3:1).

Most contemporary theologians present purgatory as a spiritually transforming experience. According to them, purgatory completes our assimilation to the saving mystery of Christ into whose death and Resurrection we have been baptized (cf. Romans 6:3-11). As attachment to one's former self is purified, God draws the person closer and closer to himself. In fact, it is God himself who completes the work of perfection that people leave unfinished in this life.

Our prayers can be truly useful for those in the purgatorial state. We can help others become spiritually mature, to become perfect, according to each one's capacity, for heaven. Still self-centered and lonely, those in purgatory stretch out their hands through barred windows, hoping for contact from the outside. They need to experience God's love through other members of the Mystical Body. Speaking to those in purgatory. George Maloney says: "When they, who still walk this earth, lovingly remember you, you are called out of the tomb of isolation and loneliness into a new-founded state of self-identity. The healing power of love consists in the therapy of destroying isolation and building a community (a oneness, a togetherness in loving union) (*Everlasting Now*, p. 71).

This love, concertized through the prayer and good works of the living, awakens deeper love in the departed and prepares them for being with Christ in the plenitude of trinitarian love. The prayers of the pilgrim Church are intercessory. She implores that those in purgatory receive the grace needed so that their love will be perfected. Then, fully "pure in heart ... they will see God" (Matthew 5:8).

Ministry of Mercy

The brink of the third millennium is an opportune moment to reaffirm vigorously the Catholic custom of praying for those in purgatory. No doubt many neglect this practice because of the hideous images that purgatory evokes for them. Too often in earlier generations preachers described it as a mini-hell, a short-term experience of damnation. Quite rightly people today sense that when purgatory is presented as a prison of vindictive and cruel punishment, it calls into question the mercy of God.

In his masterful poem, *The Dream of Gerontius*, which tells of the death, judgment, and passage to glory of an old man, Cardinal Newman describes Gerontius's purgatory. His guardian angel takes the old man in his arms and dips him into the lake of purification, where the angels attend to him and the prayers of the Church on earth and in heaven support him:

> Angels, to whom the willing task is given,
> shall tend, and nurse, and lull thee,
> as thou liest;
> And Masses on earth, and prayers in heaven,
> shall aid thee at the throne of the
> Most Highest.

Purgatory is a forceful reminder that a Christian's death involves the community which prays for the departed.

Many of our practices surrounding death — waking the body, offering condolences, and grieving — give comfort only to the living. That is where we spend our money and invest our time. Yet, because of the holy bonds of the communion of saints, we can also help the departed. The ties of affection uniting members of the Body of Christ and knitting them together in life do not unravel with death. The Mass, prayers, and good works, with the grace that they obtain, can assist the departed's journey to the holy city.

Praying for the dead does more than retain their presence in our thoughts. It is also an act of mercy. The ministry of consolation falls to each of us when a fellow member of Christ's Body dies. We are called to comfort the bereaved, but also, and more importantly, to pray for the deceased. Our suffrages for the faithful departed help them to purify their love so that every trace of sin and its remnants will be erased. Sustained by this supernatural solidarity, those in purgatory will receive their citizenship in heaven, from where they await the resurrection of the body (cf. Philippians 3:20). Such generosity will surely be rewarded. "Blessed are the merciful, for they shall obtain mercy" (Matthew 5:7).

Endnotes

1. Jacques Le Goff, *The Birth of Purgatory*, trans. Arthur Goldhammer (Chicago: The University of Chicago Press, 1984), p. 45.

2. Cited in Cyprian Vagaggini, *Theological Dimensions of the Liturgy*, trans. Leonard J. Doyle and W.A. Jurgens (Collegeville, MN: The Liturgical Press, 1976), p. 337.
3. J.H. Wright, "Dead, Prayers for the," *New Catholic Encyclopedia*, vol. 4 (New York: McGraw-Hill Publishing Co., 1967), p. 672.
4. Editorial of *Civiltà Cattolica*, trans. Kenneth Baker, "Preaching about Purgatory Today," *Homiletic and Pastoral Review*, 93:5 (February 1993), p. 12.
5. Henricus Denzinger and Adolphus Schonmetzer, eds., *Enchiridion Symbolorum Definitionum et Declarationum de Rebus Fidei et Morum*, 32nd Edition (Freiburg: Herder, 1963) DS 1304.
6. International Theological Commission, *"De quibus quaestionibus actualibus circa eschatologiam"* (1990), No. 8, in *Gregorianum*, 73:3 (1992), p. 425.
7. Elmar Klinger, "Purgatory," in *Sacramentum Mundi*, ed. Karl Rahner, vol. 5 (New York: Herder and Herder, 1970), p. 167.
8. Zachary Hayes, *Visions of a Future: A Study of Christian Eschatology* (Wilmington: Michael Glazier, 1989), p. 117.
9. R.J. Bastian, "Poor Souls," in *New Catholic Encyclopedia*, vol. 11 (New York: McGraw-Hill Book Co., 1967), p. 569.
10. George A. Maloney, *The Everlasting Now* (Notre Dame: Ave Maria Press, 1980), p. 73.
11. Bastian, "Poor Souls," p. 569.
12. Maloney, *Everlasting Now*, p. 79.
13. R.J. Bastian, "Purgatory," in *New Catholic Encyclopedia*, vol. 11 (New York: McGraw-Hill Book Co., 1967), p. 1035.
14. Cited in Jean Delumeau, *Sin and Fear: The Emergence of a Western Guilt Culture in 13th-18th Centuries*, trans. Eric Nicholson (New York: St. Martin's Press, 1990), p. 389.
15. Delumeau, *Sin and Fear*, p. 392.
16. Fortman, *Everlasting Life*, p. 164.
17. Cited in Reginald Garrigou-Lagrange, *Life Everlasting*, trans. Patrick Cunnings (New York: Herder, 1952) p. 166.

Part One:

THE HISTORICAL PERSPECTIVE

The Vision of St. John Climacus

Chapter One

Early Funeral Customs

The history of funerals begins in antiquity. All ages and cultures have had some form of disposal of the dead, almost always with group sanction, honor, and ceremony. Countless generations have expressed the need to share bereavement and resolve grief.

Many hold a firm belief, rarely expressed, that every person has the right to a decent burial. In America, although funeral customs differ slightly from one end of the country to another, and different ethnic groups have customs particular to their own heritage, many of today's burial rituals stem from or were influenced by those of ancient times.

The Egyptian Influence

Today's funeral practices are probably most influenced by the civilization of ancient Egypt. The Egyptians attributed a divine origin to the soul and held that, after life, its final state was judged according to its owner's behavior on earth. Those justified before Osiris, the god of the underworld, passed into perpetual happiness; those condemned fell into perpetual misery.

Among the oldest customs in Egyptian funeral ceremonies are offerings of food and drink, which were entombed with the deceased for their use in the future. In the earlier periods it was not unusual to sacrifice servants, who were also entombed, and make presentations of food and money to aid the soul on its journey to the sun. Continued attention to the grave and the spirits of the dead by surviving relatives was considered necessary.

The need for protecting the body and its funeral treasures led to the building of the tombs. The pyramids, the most enduring monuments in the world, were both memorials and tombs for the rulers of Egypt.

After the burial, offerings were made at particular times of the year, and the main inscription on the tomb begged passersby to say a prayer for the deceased.

Like the ancient Chinese, the Egyptians were concerned with the proper disposal of their dead, for sanitary as well as religious reasons. Embalming was of major importance because of the belief that the deceased would resume his normal activities in the afterlife, but cavity embalming was too expensive for all but the most wealthy. For common people, "dry burials" were used to keep the products of putrefaction from seeping into the soil and generating plague. The bodies were shrouded in coarse cloth and laid upon beds of charcoal under six or eight feet of sand on the edge of the great plain, above the reach of the Nile. The dry air and chemicals in the soil provided for their slow decomposition and preservation. The desire to keep bodies from touching the earth was characteristic not only of the Egyptians but of most early African peoples as well.

The first coffins were made of mats, skins, reed, wood, or earthenware. These were rectangular and massive. Inscriptions covering the exterior were devoted to prayers, genealogies, religious, and magical texts. Later the shape changed to a manlike form, and a portrait of the face of the dead was reproduced on the top. About the eighteenth dynasty, the coffins began to be elaborate, and many contain beautiful hand-painting and rich inlays of lapis lazuli, glass, mother-of-pearl, and semiprecious stones. That of King Tutankhamen was made of gold and jewels. The coffins were placed in massive sarcophagi made of stone or granite.

The Egyptians preserved the bodies of their dead in order for the soul to reenter the body in the afterlife. Although this belief did not make its way into Christian theology, Christians in Egypt were embalmed and mummified as a matter of custom. The members of the Osiris cult believed that the soul's entry into the world beyond depended somewhat on magical procedures, but even more on the candidate's having lived a life free from evil. The implications of this belief were felt in the Hebrew and early Christian religions, and represented one of the earliest introductions of a sense of inner values, or conscience.

Egyptians used symbols as funerary devices. The many clay scarab beetles buried in Egyptian tombs symbolized resurrection. Likewise wheat, which lies dormant then grows from the germ, became a respected funerary symbol.

When wheat symbols were used on Christian tombs, a sacramental meaning was added. Grapes and wheat represent wine and bread, the appearances under which Christ offers himself and is received by the faithful on Christian altars (Habenstein, pp. 1-15).

The Influence of the Ancient Greeks

To the ancient Greeks, death was one of the harsher lots of mankind. Early Greek beliefs conceived of the dead as living a bodily existence under the earth. Later, about 700 B.C., this belief gave way to the concept of a shadowy afterlife peopled by disembodied souls. The general response of the Greeks to death was resignation; they did not look forward with joy to the anticipation of a glorious afterlife.

The belief that body and soul would be separated in the afterlife may account for the introduction of cremation to the Greeks, although the practice of burning the dead had been brought into the Grecian peninsula before this time. This type of fire burial had been practiced by the early Scandinavians for over two thousand years, beginning in the Middle Bronze Age, and lasting until about the tenth century. Cremation, it was believed, freed the spirit of the dead from the prison of its body, and kept it from harming the living. Cremation was infrequently practiced in Greece at first, but shortly before the historical period (700 B.C.) it took the place of earth burial.

Reverence for the dead permeated the burial customs of the Greeks through all the ages, and in classical times the law of Athens required the burial, or at least the covering with earth, of the corpses of strangers. Neglect of the dead was condemned and considered a disqualification for office. Lest the dead from battles remain unburied, the Athenians cremated them on immense pyres on the battlefields where they had fallen and gathered the bones to return them to Athens to be entombed with due honor and ceremony.

As soon as death occurred the eyes and mouth of the deceased were closed by relatives or friends. Since passage into the netherworld required crossing the river Styx, a small coin was placed in the dead man's mouth for Charon, the ferryman. Without such a fare the unlucky shade was doomed to wander a hundred years along the shores.

The body was prepared for burial by family members who began by washing the corpse with warm water in hopes those only apparently dead might revive. From earliest times, the Greeks buried their dead in clothes that at one point became so extravagant that laws were passed forbidding excessive finery. (These laws were echoed centuries later in the American colonial period when, again, excessive funerary display came into play.)

The dead were robed in white and wreaths of flowers were presented by friends and relatives. A honey cake was provided for Cerebus, the three-headed guardian of the lower region. Mourning was indicated by dark, subdued colors.

After preparation for death was made, the body was laid out in state. This practice in part served to guarantee friends and relatives who viewed the corpse that the death had truly occurred and the corpse had not been met by violence. After the viewing, the corpse was carried on a bier to the place of burial where, if it was not cremated, it was buried in a coffin of wood, stone, or painted baked clay.

The final step was a funeral feast, which broke the fast the bereaved had been keeping, and the offering of sacrifices at the sepulchre on specified days.

Like the Egyptians, the primitive Greeks sometimes slaughtered servants and horses to serve their masters in the afterlife. Later, small figures of clay were used to symbolize these servants and animals (Habenstein, pp. 15-21).

The Influence of the Ancient Romans

Many details of Roman funeral arrangements foreshadowed the funeral operations of today. Here began the role of a secular, versus a religious, undertaker. This was a precursor to the occupation of the modern funeral director.

Roman beliefs in the afterlife varied through the centuries. Early beliefs held that the soul, although separated at death from the body, hovered around the place of burial for its continued peace and happiness. Thus, it required constant attention in the form of offerings of food and drink. Early Romans believed that if they neglected these attentions, the soul would cease to be happy and turn into an evil spirit, which would bring harm on those who neglected it.

The Roman's contact with the civilization of Greece brought about change in the Roman conception of life after death. As Christianity emerged as the dominant religion of the Roman Empire, for the first time there was a theological orientation to death. Death customs for the most part became patterned after the mode of the sepulchre of Christ.

The Romans practiced both cremation and earth burial. Cremation was more popular until the first century after Christ. Then fire burial was replaced by inhumation. A major cause for this change stems from the Christian emphasis on the hallowed nature of the body.

Burial within the walls of the city was prohibited for sanitation reasons. The great roads outside the city walls were lined with the elaborate and costly tombs of the wealthy. The corpses of the poor, slaves, and aliens were laid in the *commune sepulchrum*, the common burial pit, outside the walls. Great tombs, *columbaria*, were built, filled with niches for the urns holding the ashes of the cremated dead. The builders rented urn space to those who could not afford an extravagant tomb of their own. Although burial of the poor eventually became a function of the state, burial societies were formed to assure appropriate burial for the poor.

In Rome, a person died in the presence of the immediate family. The body was washed and dressed in a white toga. It was then put on a funeral couch, feet to the door, to lie in state for at least three days. Flowers were strewn about the couch, incense was burned, and cypress or pine boughs were set outside the door as a warning of the possible pollution by death.

Libitina was the goddess of corpses and funerals. Deaths were registered at her temple. A *libitinarius* was the Roman equivalent of the head undertaker; he provided anointing or embalming, supplied hired mourners, and arranged clothing and other accessories for funeral pomp. He arranged services designed to ease the grief of the bereaved.

Roman funeral processions could be costly and elaborate. They included musicians, singers, buffoons, and jesters. Wax masks of the dead man's ancestors were worn by actors dressed in clothes from the proper time period. It must have seemed as if the ancient dead had returned to lead the newest member to his place among them. Finally, the body was placed on a lofty couch and carried with its face uncovered to the burial place. Next in line came the family and freed slaves.

Ordinary funerals were held at night; persons of higher status were buried by day. A funeral oration in the Forum was given for those of high rank. At the end of the ceremony came the *conclamation mortis*, or calling out of the dead. Tearing their hair, rending their clothes, and scratching their faces until they drew blood, the hired mourners circled the coffin three times shrieking out the name of the deceased.

By the time of Constantine (314 A.D.), laws had been enacted to provide for the funeral of any Roman who could not afford a proper burial. A group of workers was established to dig the grave and to prepare and carry out the procession. Sumptuary laws prohibited excessive spending, and overcharging for funeral items was declared illegal. An ancient manuscript records that every person was eligible to have a coffin without payment, and even the poorest were to be followed to the grave by a minimum of a cross-bearer, eight monks, and three acolytes. From this time through the Middle Ages, funerals became more and more the province of the Church (Habenstein, pp. 21-29).

The Swan Song

The last performance of an artist is called his swan song. Why? Swans do not normally sing, but a legend tells us that they sang a beautiful melody just before they died. Socrates said this was in happiness at their impending reunion with their god. Other ancient myths told that swans accompanied the dead to their final resting place, and that the souls of dead humans reside in swans.

Early Hebrew Funeral Rites

Early Hebrews believed man was composed of two elements: *basar*, or flesh; and *nefesh*, or breath. The *nefesh* was a spirit-like substance in the blood that persisted at death, when the *basar* returned to dust. Like other Semites, the Hebrews believed the soul led a shadowy afterlife in a netherworld called *Sheol*. Their death beliefs were influenced by Persian and Greek domination, and changed slightly from time to time. They believed that after death the souls of the righteous passed directly into a blessed existence, while the souls of the wicked were sent into a state of punishment, but that both would be raised from the netherworld at the day of the last judgment for their final rewards and punishments. To the early Hebrews, burial places were sacred and used for worship, the making of vows, and for sanctuary.

Immediately after death, the eyes and mouth of the corpse were closed, and the body was washed and anointed with spices. It was dressed in its best attire. In the early days it was bound up like a newborn child; by the time of Christ the body was wrapped in linen.

Burial commonly took place on the evening of the day of death. In the warm climate of Palestine, putrefaction began quickly, so this rapid burial was a hygienic necessity. Early Hebrews did not use coffins; these were first used after the Babylonian captivity in 547 B.C.

The body was borne on a bier to the grave. The poor were laid in a shallow trench and a mound of earth was shoveled over the body. The wealthy were buried in natural caves or artificial sepulchres hewn out of rock. Officials and kings were buried with gold and silver ornaments.

A fast was begun by family members at the moment of their loved one's death that lasted until after the burial. The nearest of kin "rent their garments" and stripped down to a loin cloth of goat or camel hair. Sandals were discarded. Although their clothes were removed, the Hebrews kept their heads covered with a drape or their hands. Although later forbidden, the earliest Hebrews practiced the cutting of their flesh as a sign of grief. A tuft of hair on the forelock was cut, or a beard was shaved as a sign of grief. In later times, small symbolic tufts were removed. The original custom of throwing oneself in the dust was replaced by symbolically sitting in the dust or placing dust upon the head. The family wailed lamentations and often hired mourners to join in.

In Jewish belief, family ties were not necessarily severed at death and family members who were buried together remained together in *Sheol*. Because of this belief, the earliest tombs were placed on family lands or near family dwellings. Early Hebrews attempted to live near their families and commonly placed offerings near family tombs. Abraham's tomb stood at the edge of his field; those of the Kings of Judah were in the royal gardens in Jerusalem; Samuel and

Joab were buried in their own houses. The burial place of Joseph of Arimathea was in a garden.

Although the Kings of Judah made tombs for their families in Jerusalem, even in early times these were placed beyond the walls of the city for sanitary reasons. The belief had gradually crystallized that graves were filled with uncleanness and would defile the living. By the time of Christ, the graves were whitened with lime so their ceremonial impurity could be recognized from a distance and avoided.

Because of their stern opposition to ancestor worship, the Hebrews preferred simple tombs that were unadorned and without description. There were four common varieties of Hebrew graves: a sunken grave with a stone cover; a bench grave; a trench grave; and the oldest and most common form, a single chamber containing recessed graves. The recessed graves were oblong excavations about a foot-and-a-half wide and six-feet long, hewn lengthwise into the chamber wall.

In all historical periods the Jews interred their dead. Both Jacob and Joseph were embalmed, although this was not a general practice. Cremation was considered an indignity to the corpse and was regarded as a means to intensify the disgrace of the death penalty. An age-old belief held that even after death there was a bond between the body and the soul, and the spirits of the unburied and the cremated wandered disconsolate about the earth, finding no peace in *Sheol*. It was a sacred duty, incumbent on all, to bury an unburied body. Violation of a grave was considered a great outrage. Interment was denied only as a punitive act to foreign enemies. A public place of burial was provided for the extremely poor, strangers, and criminals. Criminals who were stoned to death were considered buried beneath the mound of stones that had slain them.

After Jesus' death, the chief priests took the money used to bribe Judas and bought the potter's field to be used as a burying place for strangers (Habenstein, pp. 33-37).

Sacrifice to the dead continued in practice for a long time with offerings of treasures, incense, spices, and food. The firstborn son was given a double portion of inheritance because by law and custom he had the duty of bringing sacrifice to the dead. Part of the Hebrew desire for a son was because of a fear that without a male heir no one would bring the sacrifices that would allow his soul to enjoy rest.

The Burial of Christ

Christ was buried in a new tomb belonging to Joseph of Arimathea in a garden cemetery near Calvary, the place of his execution. This garden lay on a rocky hillside just outside the western wall of Jerusalem. Originally the area was a limestone quarry. One of the poorer quality rocks was left unquarried and eventually became a place for public execution. After the quarry was played out, it was planted as a garden, possibly with a grove of olive trees. Tombs were dug into the underlying rock or cut into the west wall of the old quarry.

Joseph of Arimathea showed boldness in asking Pilate for the body of Jesus, as those who were crucified were normally denied a decent burial. As we read in the Gospel of Mark, his request was granted and Christ was buried in the new tomb that Joseph had prepared, but not used, for his family.

As explained above, there were a number of Jewish burial customs. Sometimes, as in the case of Christ, the body was placed on a ledge or in a burial niche in the tomb.

Each tomb held several of these ledges or niches, because they were made to provide for an entire family, and a new death might occur before the previous corpse had decayed sufficiently. The intention was to have the body remain on the ledge until it decayed to bones that would then be put into a small pit or container in the tomb, along with the bones of ancestors. In Christ's time, small limestone boxes were used as bone repositories; they usually held the bones of more than one person.

After the crucifixion there was brought "… a mixture of myrrh and aloes, weighing about one hundred pounds. They took the body of Jesus and bound it with burial cloths along with the spices, according to the Jewish burial custom" (John 19:39-40).

Myrrh was one of the main ingredients in the spices used in the purification of the dead. The aloes referred to in the New Testament differed from that mentioned in the Old. New Testament aloes refers to the thick, fleshy leaves of a succulent plant that grows around the shores of the Indian Ocean. It was dissolved in water and added to the sweet-smelling incense used in purifying the bodies of the dead.

The linen used to wrap the body of Christ was made from flax, the oldest fiber known. The flax plant grows only about three feet high and appears very delicate, but Near Eastern people early recognized its value in making a strong fabric. The stalks were laid on the roofs of houses to dry in the sun, then the fibers were separated from the stalks and spun into linen of different grades. Fine linen was used in the clothes of the rich, for curtains and hangings in the Temple, and even for the sails of Phoenician trading ships. The poor people, however, wore only ordinary coarse linen. The Bible does not specify that Jesus was wound in fine linen, so we can assume the linen of the humble people was used (Farb, pp. 146-148).

In the year 135 A.D., Emperor Hadrian built a pagan shrine over the tomb of Jesus, attempting to efface the memory of this "false prophet." His effort failed, however, because the Christians remembered that Jesus' tomb lay beneath the temple. Two hundred years later, St. Helen, the holy mother of Constantine, had Hadrian's temple destroyed and dug beneath it to locate the tomb of Jesus.

Writings from the bishop Eusebius describe the discovery of the tomb. It had been dug into the wall of the old quarry. The first church at this sight was built around 335 A.D., when Constantine had the hillside around the tomb carved away and built a domed rotunda around it. He built a great basilica with the rock of Calvary in one corner so that Christians could visit and pray at the site of their redemption. This giant church, which was separated by a courtyard from the rotunda, was destroyed in 1009 by a Muslim ruler and the tomb of Christ was broken down almost to floor level. Later on this site, Christians built a replica of the tomb, which was modified through the centuries. Today, the Church of the Holy Sepulchre stands over one of the old tombs in the garden cemetery. It dates from 1809 and provides some idea of what the tomb was like. The rock of Calvary has been encased in marble and is hidden behind a balcony. A chapel is built over the place of Jesus' crucifixion (Martin, *Catholic Digest*, April 1993).

The Potter's Field

Why is a pauper's burial ground called a potter's field? After the betrayal of Christ, Judas was filled with remorse and threw away the thirty pieces of silver he had been paid. The elders used this money to buy the potter's field to bury strangers in. (The Jews were mandated to bury the dead.) The field became known as the field of blood and the thirty pieces of silver were henceforth known as blood money.

Early Christian Practices and Beliefs

Early Christian beliefs regarding the disposal of their dead were based on the ideas of the Hebrews as expanded by the teaching of Christ. An analysis of Semitic rites and ceremonies establishes the foundation of belief that death does not mark the absolute separation of the dead from the living (Morgenstern, p. 160).

Jesus preached the infinite and equal value of every human soul, which is both spiritual and immortal. The soul is not annihilated in death; there is a resurrection of a glorified body.

In spite of the assurances of St. Paul, the earliest Christians often held onto a superstitious dread that they could not have any part of the resurrection of the flesh if their bodies did not rest in the grave. But according to Paul, the disposition of the body after death is largely a matter of indifference; the resurrection is a miracle of God. Bodies buried, burned, or lost at sea share equally in the miraculous transformation.

The Church held it revolting that the human body, once the "temple of the Holy Spirit," should be burned, except in well-defined cases of need, such as when it was necessary to prevent the spread of disease. Therefore, Christians customarily buried their dead; during the reign of Constantine, cremation was prohibited.

In the old *Code of Canon Law*, cremation was forbidden. The new *Code* permits cremation as long as it is not done in contempt of Catholic doctrine. For example, under the new *Code*, Canon 1184 lists the only three types of people to whom funeral rites are to be denied: (1) notorious apostates, heretics, and schismatics; (2) persons who have chosen cremation *for reasons opposed to Catholic faith* (for example as a denial of the Resurrection); and (3) other manifest sinners for whom ecclesiastical funeral rites cannot be granted without public scandal to the faithful. When there is any doubt, the local bishop must be consulted (Sheedy, *Our Sunday Visitor*, March 14, 1993).

Central Christian death beliefs held that in death all men were equal and their earthly status, wealth, or rank was not a factor in assigning their eternal rewards. The word "cemetery" designates a sleeping place, and death came to be represented as sleep. Death to the early Christian became a kind of birth into eternity and a triumphal transition; therefore, unlike the non-Christians, the Christians did not consider death an event calling for hopeless and unconfined grief.

Primitive Christian burial customs were simple, like those of the early Hebrews. Burial of the dead was one of the seven listed corporal works of mercy enjoined on all Christians.

Early canon law set simple requirements for burial. The body was to be decently laid out with lights beside it. It should be asperged with holy water and incensed at stated times. A cross was to be placed on the breast; if no cross were available, the hands should be folded. The body was to be buried in consecrated ground, but there was no regulation that a coffin must be used.

The early Christian community provided burial services even to the poor as a corporal work of mercy, without hired assistants even in the time of the plagues. A great plague swept Rome in the third century. In the writings of Eusebius we read of the heroic conduct of the Christians, "Thus, they would take up the bodies of the saints in their open hands to their bosoms and close their eyes and mouth, and carry them on their shoulders and lay them out."

Among the early Christians, the family ministered to the dying and took charge of the dead. Because the body was considered holy and sacred, they made a major break from Hebrew tradition in that there was no taboo or legal defilement in touching the dead.

Somehow, the naive fancied that the soul would leave the body beginning from the feet, progressing up the body and exiting through the mouth. Thus, one task of administering to the dying was to stretch out their feet. They were also given Viaticum (Communion administered to the dying as a means of giving them strength for their journey into eternity). This word came from the Roman, meaning an allowance of money or supplies for transportation.

At death, the eyes and mouth of the body were closed, the body was washed, anointed with spices, and wrapped in a linen sheet. Aloes and myrrh were the common spices used to perfume the corpse. This was done in reverential imitation of Christ's burial and was a practice the pagans considered foolish. The pagans deemed it wasteful to use expensive spices on dead bodies when they could be put to better use on the living. Then the body was placed on a couch and relatives and friends were invited to view the face of the deceased. The body remained thus for at least eight hours before burial.

This "watching" or "waking" of the dead was rooted in an old Jewish practice that stemmed from a concern that the dead might inadvertently be buried alive. To further ensure against premature burial, the sepulchre was left unsealed for three days and the corpse was frequently scrutinized for signs of life. The early Christians used this occasion to gather and say prayers for the repose of the dead. The wake also gave consolation to the family, and often during the night psalms were sung. Christian practices regarding the wake came from a number of cultures. The element of time remained flexible, varying with the prestige of the dead person and the amount of money available to preserve the corpse.

In the burial rite, the Christians administered a final kiss, the Kiss of Peace. This custom continues today among the laity in the final kiss sometimes given to the corpse, although the practice has long since been discontinued by the clergy. The Council of Auxerre forbade the priest to bestow the ceremonial kiss upon the dead, as well as prohibiting dressing the corpse in rich raiment.

Although the Christians in Rome and the Holy Land generally anointed the corpse, in other countries where Christianity was becoming established the burial practices of the country were often adapted. Although the Christians did not accept the religious beliefs of the countries, they added new funerary practices to their own.

One practice the early Christians did not accept, however, was the use of the traditional pagan mourning colors of red, black, and purple. Instead, they used white. Later there was a return to the conventional dark colors. Today's priestly vestments at funerals are white, rather than the somber black formerly used, to symbolize the joy of the Resurrection. In modern times, in more and more American cities, participants at funerals are seen in bright colors.

If Christian burial took place in the forenoon, Requiem Mass was said and Holy Communion was distributed. Afternoon burials consisted of singing psalms, recitation of prayers, and a special service of the dead. The service contained hymns, prayers, and scriptures.

Early Christian funeral processions reflected the customs of the locality of the burial. In all cases, a subdued and reverent attitude, colored by a latent sense of triumph over death, marked the Christian processions. Instrumental music, actors, clowns or buffoons, and noisy display were excluded from Christian processions, and young men, as a corporal work of mercy and not for pay, served to carry the bier to the place of burial. Solemnly and quietly the procession of family and friends passed; although daylight burials were preferred, lighted torches were carried symbolically as befitted victory.

After the time of the persecutions, a funeral oration honoring those of merit was customarily included in the burial service for leaders or saints, although a funeral sermon as we know it today was not a part of the ceremony. Alms of food and money were distributed to the poor at the grave and public prayers were offered for the dead.

Until they were banned because of abuses, the Christian agape meals were often used as memorials to the dead. The agape meal took place in the small chambered family vault. This meal probably often preceded, or was followed by, the Eucharist. The original intent of the meal, sometimes called a "love feast," was to celebrate charity. St. Paul, in Corinthians 11:20, seems to disapprove of the meals, citing rumors of abuse. Eventually, the meals were prohibited and the custom disappeared by the eighth century (Ball, 1994, p. 167).

The third, seventh or ninth, thirtieth or fortieth days, and the anniversary of death, were designated as special memorial days for remembering the dead with Requiem Masses. Rites sometimes ended with the anointing with oil and flowers were occasionally strewn on the grave.

Perhaps the earliest clear case of Christian prayer for the dead is in the Passion of St. Perpetua, who saw in a vision her little brother Dinocrates. He had died of ulcers on the face, a very painful disease, and she saw him first as the same miserable little boy, trying to reach a fountain that was far too high for him. But in another vision, after she had prayed for him, she saw him drinking from the same fountain, which was now at the level of his waist, and running away safe and happy. It is obvious that the fountain is a symbol of Christian baptism. By his sister's prayers, Dinocrates was able to receive the benefits of this world in the other (Every, p. 108).

Early Cemeteries

The Church has always prescribed the designation of special places suitable for the burial of her dead. This ground containing the relics of saints and martyrs was considered sacred, and according to the customs of the times it was given a special religious significance and blessed by suitable religious rites.

It was not possible for the early, persecuted church to maintain cemeteries as we know them today, so the earliest Christian burials from apostolic times to the persecution by Domitian (Roman emperor from 81-96 A.D.) were in family vaults outside the walls and along the roads leading from great cities. St. Peter, St. Paul, and many other early martyrs and saints were originally given burial outside the city walls. The bodies of Sts. Peter and Paul were transferred about the year 258 into the catacombs to avoid their profanation during the persecutions. For the first three centuries, tomb burial was the norm for Christianity.

Out of this type of burial grew the catacombs. These were originally galleries, chambers, and passages openly hewn out of soft rock with public entrances. Later, they were extended enormously due to crypt enlargement for burial purposes. They originated in the tombs of the wealthy Christians who had them constructed in their gardens or villas and permitted their use to fellow Christians. At the time they were begun, the Roman government approved the construction of these excavated cemeteries and protected them against vandalism. Their secondary use, for shelter and as places of assembly where persecuted Christians held secret religious rites, resulted in their later destruction, culminating in 253 A.D., when a decree by the Emperor Valerian forbade Christians to hold assemblies or to enter their cemeteries.

The catacomb-type of burial was practiced not only at Rome but also in Naples, Palermo, Syracuse, Greece, Persia, Egypt, Syria, and in other places. For example, the catacombs of Paris are a series of charnel houses where the contents of cemeteries, thought to contain pestilence, were dumped.

In the Roman catacombs, the walls near places where martyrs' bodies rest are usually covered with inscriptions. All these writings belonged to the faithful, who wanted to leave a memorial of themselves close to the martyrs' remains or, more often, those of their deceased friends and relatives. Usually the graffiti consists of the names of persons, accompanied by a wish for salvation in the next world. The graffiti soon took on the form of cryptographic writing, whereby the early Christians could secretly express their feelings and the highest ideas of the faith in a brief and effective form during times of persecution. Many of the Christian symbols we are so familiar with today had special meaning for these early, persecuted members of the Church (Guarducci, pp. 96-100).

One sign of the new freedom of the Christian Church, when the great persecutions came to an end at the close of the fourth century, was the establishment of open-air cemeteries. Although early Roman law decreed burial must take place outside city walls, these open-air cemeteries were often located in the vicinity of churches within the walls.

About the fourth century, the Church established great religious feast days to commemorate the anniversary dates of the death of the martyrs. Also about that time, death of the faithful was linked to the church service, and the bodies began to be brought to the church before burial for a service there. A dead bishop was commonly borne into several churches before being taken to the grave. His body usually rested on a bed of ivy, laurel, or other evergreen.

After the fourth century, the church established a stylized, formal set of religious and social controls over funerals. The Reformation divided this traditional behavior but did not basically change the underlying Christian death beliefs, nor did it modify many of the funeral practices (Habenstein, pp. 37-53).

Today, although we dogmatically hold that the essential element of our loved one is elsewhere, the grave remains the spot where we took our leave of him and where we can appropriately honor his memory. Rather than a frightening place to be avoided, today's Christian should consider the cemetery a quiet, inviting place for reverential prayer and remembrance of our beloved dead.

Chapter Two

The Middle Ages

Roman power declined in the West, barbarians overran the Empire, and the world entered what is today referred to as the "Dark Ages." Even at the worst of this tumultuous period, however, the light did not entirely fail and the Church, in many cases, preserved civilization. By the thirteenth century, the descendants of the barbarians had been converted and built great cathedrals, created literature in new tongues, and adopted a different valuation of human life. Humanitarian ideas brought about the creation of a group of institutions designed to care for society's rejects and medicine had begun to develop.

In spite of the preaching of the early fathers against it, Christians lost the custom of burying their dead in simple, new, white linen garments and had adopted the practice of burying persons in the costumes that indicated their positions in life. Kings were arrayed in royal finery, knights were shrouded in military garments, the dead bishop wore his episcopal garb.

About the fifth century in England, the body of an Anglo-Saxon of importance who died was placed on a bier or in a hearse, and on it was laid the book of the Gospels and the cross. A pall of silk or linen was thrown over the corpse for the journey to the grave.

After the Norman Conquest in 1066, the funerals of rich Englishmen grew in pomp and length, and sometimes lasted a full week. Death was announced by the tolling of bells. The body was embalmed or anointed with fragrant herbs or spices. It was placed in the great hall of the manor and lay in state under black hangings and the bright gleam of many torches. Although wax was expensive, sometimes as many as four-hundred large candles were burned for a single burial. After a three-day vigil, the corpse was sealed in a leaden coffin and brought to the church for a solemn Requiem Mass. At this time, the clothes of the deceased were distributed to the poor. At last, after the body was laid to rest, the clergy and family and friends returned to the hall to eat the "funeral baked meats."

Church Burial and the Plague

Although by Roman law and by many church decrees the burial of Christians in or near their churches that were inside the city walls was forbidden, the Christians did not like to see their dead carried far from them. Ironically, just as the laws of nature began to be better understood, Christians pushed for church burial in defiance of the danger of disease. This type of intramural burial was contested for centuries.

Burial in consecrated soil was considered necessary. The fear of vampires and ghouls in some places during the Middle Ages made churchyard burial a much sought-after privilege, because it was believed that evil spirits were powerless in consecrated ground.

The Church, in its concern for the remains of the dead, produced regulations concerning burial. The concept of consecrated soil brought a break with the past. Communal, rather than individual, places of interment became the rule.

The Church also took measures to ensure that the consecrated ground was not profaned. For example, in England beginning in the mid-700s, there was a prohibition against burial of those who "lay violent hands upon themselves." The prohibition did not include those whose suicide came in a fit of madness. Those found guilty of murder of one's self were sometimes buried at a crossroads with a stake driven through the body, or, if buried in the churchyard, only by night.

Throughout Europe until the time of the Black Plague in the fourteenth century, it was common for each church or town to maintain a small churchyard burial ground for its parishioners. Because the dead were not buried in coffins and there was no attempt at preservation of the bodies, the land could be used over and over. Except for the times of the plagues the small plots sufficed. During the plagues, large extramural cemeteries were used, which later were turned over to monks and became monastery grounds.

In the middle of the 1500s, the state of these churchyards was denounced because of their horrid stench and the disease they caused. The belief that the dead infected the air was common, and funerary laws were enacted regarding the proper disposal of bodies. The theory that the plague was due to corruption of the dead was commonly held in the sixteenth century and for a long time thereafter (Habenstein, pp. 60-64).

The bubonic plague had first entered Europe in the sixth century, and again and again cycles of the plague swept across the continent. The cycle of epidemics known as the Black Death, which occurred in the fourteenth century, was the most severe. The epidemics continued through the seventeenth century, creating burial crises that are fascinating by their sheer magnitude. In 542 A.D., 10,000 people in Constantinople died in a single day. In 1665, nearly 70,000 of the total London population of 460,000 died.

In 1563, 5,000 people a week were dying in London alone. Christian burial of so many was impossible. Great pits were dug and bodies laid in layers, with small amounts of dirt between, until they were filled. It was difficult to find persons to carry the corpses to burial for fear of contagion. In spite of this there was no cremation (Habenstein, pp. 68-71).

Formation of Leagues of Prayer

The Catholic doctrine of purgatory was in part responsible for the formation during the Middle Ages of a number of confraternities, guilds, brotherhoods, and leagues of prayer devoted to burying the dead and praying for the souls of the faithful departed. For example, when a member of the Guild of All Souls in London died, the other guild members gave the poor a loaf of bread for the repose of his soul. This custom survived into the nineteenth century.

In England, the "Death Crier" or "Death Watch" dressed in black with a skull and crossbones painted on the front and back of his gown. With a bell in hand, he went 'round the city calling out, "Of a charity, good people, pray for the soul of our dear brother or sister [naming the dead] who departed this life at [the time of death]." Hearing his cries, the citizenry threw open their doors and windows and said an Our Father or a Hail Mary.

As the funeral procession passed by, bystanders uncovered their heads and stood by reverently, or joined in the procession for part of the trip to the cemetery. Remnants of the old processional dress still survived as late as the nineteenth century in the scarf and hood of black silk worn by ladies and the "weeper's bands" worn on the arms of the men in mourning.

The cost of burial in the early and late Middle Ages was partially defrayed by the guilds, which held in common such items as hearses, a pall, bier, and other funerary equipment. This equipment was used by the families of guild members when needed, and the families paid for use with a certain quantity of wax to be made into more candles. When these items were not furnished by the guilds, they were often provided by the Church (Habenstein, p. 64).

The Wake In the Middle Ages

The Vigil for the Dead, begun by the Hebrews to ensure against premature burial, was continued by the Christians of the Middle Ages as an act of piety. An English canon law of the tenth century enjoined the parish priest to "not allow any absurdity with the corpse but with the fear of God bury it wisely." An Irish canon set a penance for wailing after the death of a layperson.

The Welsh had a custom known as "sin eating." Poor people were hired to take upon themselves all the sins of the deceased party. At the wake, when the corpse was laid upon the bier, a loaf of bread was brought out and delivered to the *Sinne-eater* over the corpse. Also given was a *Mazar-bowle* (gossip's bowl) of maple, which was filled with beer he was to drink. The sin-eater was paid sixpence to take upon himself all the sins of the defunct, which freed the deceased from walking the earth after death. In North Wales, instead of a bowl of beer, the sin-eater was given a bowl of milk.

In Shropshire, and the villages adjoining Wales, notice of a death would be sent to an old sire, who then sat outside the door of the house where the death had occurred. The family would give him a *groat* (money), a crust of bread, and a full bowl of ale. Afterward, he stood up from the chair and pronounced the ease and rest of the soul departed, for which he had pawned his own soul (Frazer, pp. 155-156).

The learned monk Regino, an abbot in France in 892, wrote about proper comportment at wakes and warned against diabolical songs, jests, pagan dancing, and drunkenness. However, the custom of behaving riotously at wakes became widespread, and by the fourteenth century disorder at wakes had progressed beyond rioting and drunkenness. In this grim kind of horseplay, irreverent practical jokes were played on superstitious relatives to frighten them, and liberties were taken with the corpse.

The Council of York in 1367 condemned "those guilty games and follies and all those perverse customs which transform a house of tears and prayers into a house of laughing and excess." Yet everywhere the families of the dead plied the wakers with intoxicants and food (Habenstein, pp. 64-67).

The Funeral Feast

The wake filled a number of functions in addition to serving as a time of prayer. It ensured against premature burial, provided an opportunity to clear those who had been present at the death of any suspicion of foul play, provided witnesses for an equitable distribution of property among the heirs, and served as a banquet to welcome the principal heir.

The old name for the funeral feast was *averil* or *arvel*, which meant "heir ale." A common practice in medieval England was to place a cup of wine in the coffin next to the corpse. By drinking a taste from this cup, the living felt they had established a type of communion with the dead. There was no particular set menu for the funeral feast, although roasted meat and pancakes were favorites.

The Use of Effigies

The funeral of a well-known or wealthy person might last several days to a week. Wax death masks were often made of the nobility as soon as possible after death, and many times wax effigies were exhibited on the catafalque in church in place of the real body. Especially during the summer months, putrefaction would have caused problems if the real body had been on display. This custom persisted until the middle of the seventeenth century.

The elaborate funerary rites given to King Henry V of England illustrate the custom of bone burial. Henry died in France, and some method was needed to preserve the corpse. His body was boiled to obtain a perfect skeleton, which was then encased in boiled leather shaped to form an image of the king. This was taken to the church of Notre Dame and a fitting funeral service was conducted. Then the coffin was placed in a splendid hearse draped with a covering of red velvet sprinkled with gold leaf. The body was accompanied by the King of Scotland as chief mourner, and along with all the lords and knights, the funeral procession moved from town to town to the port of Calais. Next it was taken by boat to London, where it was finally laid to rest in Westminster Abbey. Henry's widow had a silver-plated effigy of her husband made with a solid silver-gilt head, which was mounted on the tomb. The effigy was destroyed during the Reformation (Habenstein, p. 67).

Monuments

The first monuments in England were the tops of tombs laid flat to form the floor of the church. A simple cross or other emblem was engraved on these. Later, the tops of the tombs were raised, which prevented walking on them. An effigy of the person was carved on them and later they were surmounted with a festoon or canopy. As these encumbered the church, they began to be placed at the east end. Some of these monuments were splendid and expensive, covered with semiprecious and precious stones and adorned with lifelike figures of brass. The first tomb effigies were made of wood plated over with bronze or copper. Later, brass was used; a few were covered in silver.

There was a stylistic method of indicating the person's status and occupation, and symbols, such as a lion for courage, displayed the person's virtues. Later medieval monumentary art consisted more of skull and crossbones, which was less in keeping with Christian tradition (Habenstein, p. 67).

During the French Revolution, almost all of the beautiful tomb monuments of France were destroyed. Family burial vaults were broken open and leaden coffins were removed, which were turned into bullets. The tombs were also searched for saltpeter. The copper sheeting and bronze statues were melted down. The beautiful statue of Blanche of Castille became a cannon. The dead rose from their tombs to fight side by side with the living (Male, p. 159).

In the seventeenth century, Roger de Gaigniees spent the greater part of his life devoted to the recording of funeral monuments and tombstones. Why he made the record we do not know. The eccentric himself probably could not have said. Nonetheless, his thirty volumes have preserved for posterity a portion of old France (Male, p. 156).

The Use of Coffins Rare in Middle Ages

Although the use of coffins is cross-cultural and ancient, today's practice of universal coffined burial is a development of recent centuries. The word itself comes from the Greek word *kofinos*, meaning basket, coffer, or chest. Basketry, clay, stone, and even glass were used in early pagan cultures, but in most instances only the wealthy were buried in coffins.

The only recorded Old Testament coffin burial was that of Joseph, the son of Jacob. The Romans used many types of coffins, including those of lead and glass, but they preferred a particular type of stone quarried in ancient Troy. They believed this stone had the property of consuming the body, except for the teeth, in a few weeks. From this supposed power came the Greek word *sarcophagus*, or "body-eating," which was given first to the stone and later to the principal object made from it.

The majority of burials throughout history, however, were made by simply laying the body wrapped in a cloth shroud into the earth. This practice continued through the middle of the seventeenth century when coffined burial began to come into vogue (Habenstein, pp. 71-76).

Embalming During the Middle Ages

Although embalming was not common during the Middle Ages, the art as derived from the Egyptians was not lost, and it had a limited vogue. As a rule, only royalty and the very wealthy were embalmed. Edward I of England, King Canute, William the Conqueror, Henry I, and Pope Alexander V are a few whose remains were found in a well-preserved state due to embalming by various means. Distressing experiences with unembalmed corpses pointed out the need for better methods of preservation. Surgeons and anatomists, who were familiar with the human body, were often the ones who inherited the task of embalming for funerary purposes.

Mourning Clothes

A curious medieval custom was the distribution of mourning robes. The mourning garment was called a "weed" or a "doole." This was a long, black, loose-fitting cloak similar to those worn by nuns. These robes were provided by close relatives of the dead and were worn by relatives, close friends, poor servants, and the clergyman conducting the service. For one sixteenth-century funeral in England over nine hundred of these robes were provided. Extravagance such as this led to the passage of sumptuary regulations (Habenstein, p. 76).

Other Funeral Customs

Special conventions governed the conduct and clothing of the widow during the Middle Ages. Unless she were a young woman, remarriage was frowned on. An older widow was expected to retire to a convent or to live in seclusion. A *barbe*, a long pleated arrangement of linen, was one of the unusual pieces of clothing worn by mourning widows. Its placement, determined by the status of its wearer, was either under the chin or, for the upper classes, above the forehead. The widow's bonnet was derived from the nuns' habit; the streamers were a suggestion of the nun's veil.

*****

Among the Irish, it was an old custom for the priest to bless a handful of earth and sprinkle it on the corpse before burial. This was construed by the pious to be an appeasement to the other occupants of the graveyard.

*****

At English funerals, a sprig of rosemary was handed to all who attended the burial rites. This was to disinfect against the plague. The sprig was thrown into the open grave at the end of the service. The custom continued until the middle of the nineteenth century. When the custom crossed the ocean to America, carnations or other flowers pulled from the funeral floral offerings were substituted for rosemary.

*****

In Wales, the east wind is called the "Wind of the Dead Man's Feet," from the custom of burying the clergy with their feet pointing east. An old belief held that Christ would appear in the East on judgment day, and the clergy would thus be fitted to be the first to arise and lead their flocks (Habenstein, pp. 80-81).

The Dance of Death — *Memento Mori*

Memento mori — Remember that thou wilt die. The poor heard this exhortation from the mendicant orders, while the rich heard it from the sermons of men like Denis the Carthusian, who reminded his audience that when a nobleman lay down in his bed at night he should consider that soon other hands would be laying his body in the tomb. The medieval Christian became fascinated with the physical properties of death and forgot to contemplate the happy Christian message of the Resurrection.

One of the greatest plays of the fifteenth century, *Everyman,* treated death allegorically, reminding its audience that at the last all things forsake Everyman save good deeds.

This popular morbid preoccupation brought forth the dance of death. The theme of the *danse macabre* planted itself in the popular imagination. It was shown in the woodcuts of Guyot Marchant, the poetry of Jean LeFevre, in the murals and frescoes of the church of LaChaise-Dieu, and the churchyard of the Innocents at Paris. Holbein illustrated it with his dancing skeleton. Fourteenth-century painters pictured the dead as rising from their graves to join the *danse macabre* to search for new members for their fellowship. Even tombs were decorated with images of decaying corpses (Habenstein, pp. 81-82).

Cardinal Lagrange died at Avignon in 1402. He had two tombs: one for his flesh at Amiens and another for his bones at Avignon. Although most of the Avignon tomb is destroyed, one of the remaining fragments is a bas-relief representing his corpse, dried up and mummified. On a banderole above the corpse we can read the harsh words in Latin that the Cardinal ordered written: "Wretch, what reason hast thou to be proud? Ashes thou art and soon thou wilt be like me, a fetid corpse, feeding-ground for worms."

At one time the slightest rain on the sixteenth century cemetery in Rouen, the Aitre Saint-Maclou, uncovered thousands of little white "pebbles" — teeth. All around the cemetery ran a cloister surmounted by a charnel house, which once held the bones of the dead who were dispossessed of their graves by new corpses. Carved wooden friezes decorated each story of the cloister. Bones, coffins, the grave-diggers' shovel, and the acolyte's bell are woven into a funeral garland. The columns of the cloister are ornamented with a group in relief, couples in a dance of death. A cadaver issuing from a tomb reaches out to snatch by hand the pope, the king, the countryman, and drags them briskly off. This moribund art reminds its viewer of the shortness of life and the vanity of earthly power and riches.

In 1425, the Dance of Death was painted at the Cemetery of the Innocents in Paris. This burial place was venerated as sacred. A bishop of Paris who could not be buried there requested that a bit of earth from this cemetery be placed in his grave. Twenty parishes had burial rights in the narrow enclosure, but the dead did not rest there for long. Rich and poor alike, after a certain time their tombstones were sold and their bones thrown into the charnel house on top of the cloister. Countless skulls showed through the openings.

Most impressive of all was the dance of death on the cloister walls. The figure of death has *la main qui tout agrape* — the hand that seizes all. Unfortunately the fresco was destroyed in the sixteenth century with no known artistic copy. Manuscript descriptions of the fresco remain, however, and some scholars consider that the wood engravings of Guyot Marchant, the Parisian printer, which were published in 1485, may be a reproduction of the fresco.

Unlike Posado's nineteenth century Dance of Death, the figures in the fifteenth century were not skeletons but desiccated corpses. Excavations near Bordeaux turned up hideous mummies, which were displayed in several places toward the end of the Middle Ages, and served the artists as models. Marchant's laughing cadavers leap gaily as they lead hesitant living men along the way. The verses stun us with their ironic harshness and cruelty. The abbot is grossly insulted: "Recommend the abbey to God," his companion tells him, "It made you big and fat, the better to rot." The cadavers poke fun at the physician who cannot heal himself, at the astrologer who looked for his destiny in the stars and found it in the grave, at the judge who will now himself be judged. Only for the poor countryman does the specter show a trace of compassion:

Glebesman, thou thy life hast spent

Always in toil and poverty.

Death to thee should welcome be,

From thy woes to set thee free.

Yet even the farm laborer is in no hurry to follow his companions:

Often have I death besought;

Now he comes, I want him not.

Let it rain or let it blow,

Rather I'll the vineyard hoe.

The desire to live and the impossibility of escaping death has never been more forcibly presented. The Dance of Death may shock us, but there is no denying that it is a great artistic expression that has rendered visible fundamental realities of the soul (Male, pp. 142-150).

The Vanities

In the sixteenth century, people began to surround themselves with pictures and objects that evoked the swift passage of time, the illusions of this world, and even the tedium of life. These objects were referred to by a moralistic term that clearly expresses the flavor of renunciation — vanities. The practice became rarer, but continued into the eighteenth and early nineteenth century. In our own times, the practice finds remnants in the folk art and celebrations of a number of countries.

Symbols of the end of life were not relegated to paintings and sculpture, but spilled over to furniture and clothing. Girolamo Savonarola, an Italian reformer, recommended that everyone carry with him a small death's head made of bone and look at it often. Death head rings were popular and were later distributed, along with mourning gloves, to those who attended burial services in New England. Watches and brooches were made in the shape of death's heads or coffins. Furniture was marked with skulls and skeletons.

As late as the mid-nineteenth century, the skeleton was still a favorite subject for earthenware dishes. Engravings recalling the uncertainty and brevity of life were commonly found over fireplaces.

The Sexton

With the growth of the custom of churchyard burial, a new occupation came into being. Peoples' desire to be laid in consecrated ground caused burial practices to become less domestic and more in the domain of the church. Communal burial called for a person to care for the property. The sexton, originally an under-officer of the church, filled this need. To him was delegated the care of church property, the ringing of bells, the care of the graveyard, and often the digging of graves. Thus the church, in the person of the sexton, began to perform the tasks which were earlier performed by secular officials.

The one exception to this was the function of the embalmer for mortuary purposes. At the beginning of the Middle Ages embalming was infrequent, but was much more common by the close of the Renaissance (and is almost universal now).

Early Christians considered the body the temple of the Holy Spirit and looked with disfavor on the Egyptian practice of embalming as involving mutilation. Christians *looked on embalming* from a different perspective when fragments of the bodies of saints and martyrs began to be preserved and regarded as holy relics.

For example, the heart of St. Ignatius (d. 107) has been preserved as a relic. The heart of St. George (d. 303) was reputedly brought to England by the Emperor Sigismund in 1416. The heart of St. Catherine of Sienna is said to be interred behind the high altar of the Church of St. Mary Supra Minerva in Rome (Habenstein, p. 82).

Separate Organ Burial

In the Middle Ages, the custom of independent heart and organ burial began to attain popularity. Not even a papal decree was able to stamp out this practice of dividing the body for burial, with separate graves and funeral rites for the several portions. Divided burial was not rare in the seventeenth century and there were many instances of it in the eighteenth and nineteenth centuries.

Royal prestige was lent to the custom by Jeanne, Queen of Navarre, who kept the heart of her husband, King Philip, apart from his body until her death, when by her orders it was enshrined in the same urn as her own. The English King Edward I had parts of Queen Eleanore's body deposited in three tombs erected in her honor (Habenstein, p. 84).

In France, members of the great families frequently had several monuments. Often their wills directed that their remains be divided into three parts and each part sent to a different church for interment. For example, the body of King Charles V lay at Saint-Denis, his entrails at Maubuisson, and his heart at the Cathedral of Rouen.

Because of this type of burial, France had an abundance of tombs. Often the figures on the tombs gave an indication of the burial. The statues were sometimes shown with a heart in their hands or a sculptured leathern pouch of the kind used to contain the entrails (Male, pp. 157-159).

Bone Burial

It has always seemed important to be buried in one's native land. Without embalming and refrigeration, and with the slow methods of transport of early days, it was virtually impossible to transport the bodies of those who died in foreign lands home for burial. The Macedonians preserved the body of Alexander the Great in honey to return it home; the Spartans used the same medium when transporting the corpse of King Agesipoles.

During the Middle Ages, another practice came into vogue. As we've seen, although the bodies of the poor were disposed of near the place of their death, the bodies (or parts thereof) of the rich and important were often returned home for burial using this method: the bodies were cut up and boiled to remove the bones, which were placed in a chest to be taken home and buried. The juices and the soft portions were buried with a form of ceremony near the place of death.

This custom was particularly prevalent during the Crusades, and many knights' bones were taken home for Christian burial. However, Pope Boniface III pronounced this an "abuse of abominable savagery," and outlawed the practice. Still, many Englishmen who died in the Hundred Years' War were buried this way, some after obtaining papal dispensation from Boniface's successor (Habenstein, pp. 84-85).

The *Artes Moriendi*

One of the most curious monuments of art and thought of the fifteenth century was the *Artes Moriendi*. With its dramatic text and dreadful engravings, this book had a profound effect upon the men and women of the fifteenth century, who were continually possessed by thoughts of death (Male, p. 150).

These books were treatises on the technique of dying well. Each page of text was illustrated with a woodcut picture, so that not only the *literati* but also the *laici* (those who could not read) could catch the meaning (Aries, p. 107). The rising printing trade multiplied the book by the thousands, and illustrations from it were commonly hung on the walls of homes.

The book tells of the anguish of a dying man who feels that everything is abandoning him. It is this tormented hour that the demon has been waiting for. The dogs of hell, which prowl around the dying man's bed, attack the Christian more furiously than he has ever been attacked before. If at the last moment he despairs or blasphemes, his soul goes to the enemy.

St. Bernard prays, "O Virgin, protect him. A single soul is more precious than the whole universe. May the Christian learn, while there is still time, to die well and to save his soul."

The dying man is exposed to five temptations. God, however, does not abandon the Christian and five times sends His angel to console him. The artist has conveyed the violence of the struggle by which a soul is born to eternal life, and the last pages of the book bring the sense of deliverance and relief. A soul is saved and the demons howl futilely (Male, pp. 150-155).

Tenebrae Services

During the Middle Ages, *Tenebrae* services were recited in total darkness. The name comes from the Latin: darkness, lower world, death. A candle-stand holding fifteen candles, known as a hearse, stood before the altar. At the end of each of fifteen psalms read daily, one candle was extinguished until only a single candle at the top remained lighted. At last this lighted candle was hidden behind the altar, until the end of the service when it was brought forward again. The symbolism of the service involved the desertion of Christ by the apostles and emphasized his suffering and descent to the dead. The reappearance of the last candle symbolized the Resurrection. A din at the end of the service was originally the sound of chant books being closed, but later symbolism attached to the noise the chaos following the crucifixion at the "sixth hour." These services, in a modified form, were carried out on Holy Thursday, Good Friday, and Holy Saturday until the reforms of Pope Pius XII in 1955.

The Social Functions of the Cemetery

In medieval times, the cemetery, together with the church, was the center of social life. Until the middle of the seventeenth century, it took the place of the Roman forum and corresponded with a public square or mall. Cemeteries offered the privilege of sanctuary or asylum, and were protected from abuses by civil authorities by the patron saint. Here the people conducted spiritual and temporal business, played games, and carried on love affairs.

Medieval writers remarked on the differences between Christian public cemeteries and solitary pagan tombs. Some people even lived in the cemetery. Pious female hermits, dedicated to a life of prayer, sometimes confined themselves there, while civil authorities sometimes sentenced prostitutes or female criminals to imprisonment there in perpetuity. In the Carolingian period (*circa* 843-987), judicial assemblies of both church and civil authorities were held in the cemetery, and as late as the fifteenth century, Joan of Arc was tried by a church court in the cemetery in Rouen.

During the twelfth and thirteenth centuries, the cemetery was the scene of a ceremony inspired by the funeral service that celebrated the civil death of lepers. Also, widows could free themselves from debt by a ceremony during which they laid their belts, keys, and purses on the graves of their husbands. Communal equipment, such as ovens, were sometimes set up in cemeteries.

The right of sanctuary caused the cemeteries to become not only public forums and meeting places but also marketplaces and fairgrounds. The synods of the time — at Nantes in 1405 and Angers in

1423 — established prohibitions to curb the secular activities at the cemeteries and the council of Rouen had forbidden "dancing in the cemetery or in the church under pain of excommunication." The disapproval of the synods was reiterated for centuries as the people continued to use the cemeteries as town meeting places. Gradually, the commerce moved just outside the cemetery walls, but remained close, as if the separation was against its will (Arias, pp. 62-70).

A picture from the *Artes Moriendi*. The book is a treatise on how to die well.

Chapter Three

The Reformation and Beyond

Although the Reformation did not change the fundamental Christian doctrine of the value of the human body, it did bring about many changes in funeral beliefs and customs. For example, the questions concerning indulgences (the remission of temporal punishment for sins) was tied to the doctrine of purgatory, one of the major points at issue in the dispute between Martin Luther (1483-1546) and the Church.

The new service of the Church of England, compiled in 1546-1547, consisted of scriptural passages in conformity with a new religion that rejected belief in purgatory, and therefore denied the validity of prayers for the dead. Slowly, other old practices disappeared. Until the reign of Queen Mary Tudor (d. 1558) a period of lying-in-state was common for everyone, including the poor, as an opportunity for friends and relatives to gather and pray for the departed soul. This custom ended in England at the time of the Reformation, except for those of high rank. Monastic orders and burial, and purgatorial groups, were abolished. Funeral services and processions were less solemn. Pageantry yielded to plainness. (Although during the Counter-Reformation in the mid-sixteenth century, the practices of the Church went in the other direction, and church decorations and ceremonies became lavishly splendid.)

Reformers had kept the belief in the resurrection of the dead, so fitting burials and burial places remained necessary. Burial, as a concern of the church, meant the congregation had a large part in the ceremony. Whenever the congregation gathered, there was a desire to provide pious instruction, and a funeral was no exception. In a Protestant funeral, the singing and scripture readings were supplemented by a discourse on death and resurrection, and for a fee the minister prepared and delivered a special sermon making reference to the life and death of the deceased. Out of this early practice came today's Protestant funeral sermon. And although Luther and the Augsberg Confession permitted the blessing of the dead, the reformed church unconditionally rejected prayers for the dead (Habenstein, p. 92).

Undertakers and Coffins

Before the seventeenth century, funeral undertaking was not a distinctive secular occupation. Beginning around 1698, the clear-cut role of the undertaker began to emerge in England. The first appearance in American newspapers of the title "undertaker" — one who undertakes to supply funerary paraphernalia and services — was in 1768, although the word may have been in common verbal usage for sometime before this.

Originally, the trappings for a feudal funeral were family-owned. This included yards of black drapery, an elaborate black mourning bed, funeral carriages, a velvet pall, a hearse, mourning clothes, and gifts. The purchase of these items was very expensive, and often a big drain on a dead man's estate. One major reason, then, to have an occupational group to "undertake" the funeral arrangements was to conserve costs.

The handbills of undertakers of this period were filled with decorative details such as grinning skulls, thigh bones, hearses, etc. Wooden shop signs featured quaint drawings, or were made in the shape of a coffin. Some undertakers made a sideline of upholstery, and some drapers made a sideline of furnishing funerary goods.

Although, as we've seen, using coffins to bury important persons extended from antiquity, the popular practice of coffined burial had developed only in the last few hundred years. The majority of persons were simply placed in the earth wrapped in a shroud. But because of the increased popularity of coffin burial, carpenters and joiners were added to the list of tradesmen in the undertakers stable. Often cabinetmakers crafted coffins as a sideline to their lines of furniture.

Slowly added to the undertaker's embalming function was his dramatic role in the funeral, in which he became a sort of stage manager, creating an appropriate atmosphere and moving the funeral party through a drama where emotional release was provided through ceremony (Habenstein, p. 112).

The advent of the funeral home as we know it today was a slow one, emerging for numerous reasons. The increase in apartment living in the cities and towns made funeral homes an attractive alternative to the previously-used home setting for funerals.

At the end of the eighteenth century in Germany there was a movement to establish "repositories," where bodies could be kept under observation until the onset of decomposition, in order to be absolutely certain of death. This was due to an excessive, and world-wide, preoccupation with premature burial. These first "funeral homes" were called "shelters for doubtful life."

One such home provided the setting for a novel by Mark Twain, who was fond of macabre tales. In it, the arms of the bodies were attached to small bells, which rang at any unexpected movement!

Burial and Sanitary Reforms

From the Reformation to the present, representatives of various denominations have sometimes criticized funeral customs, expenses, and the behavior of undertakers, alleging that some of the pomp and majesty of the traditional feudal funeral represented a reversion to pagan worldliness and was unbefitting Christians (Habenstein, p. 112). The post-feudal funerals were bound to increase this criticism because of their mummers, hired-by-the-job retainers, plumes, and lavish paraphernalia. This was especially true when even the poor made lavish expenditures for elaborate funerals. At worst, however, the undertakers of the seventeenth, eighteenth, and nineteenth centuries gave the people what they demanded.

Not only were reforms called for in the name of religion; an equally loud demand came in the name of better sanitation.

For centuries in England, the use of intramural burial resulted in the accumulation of the dead on small plats of ground, until finally the resulting sanitation problem could no longer be ignored. During the cholera years of 1831-1833, 51,000 deaths in England and Ireland led to the establishment of a public health agency.

Edwin Chadwick began to investigate the conditions in which the urban English worker lived, worked, and died. After his investigations, his recommendations were far in advance of his time. He called for all cemeteries to be "municipalized," and for religious rites to be simplified and standardized. In order to prevent child murder for insurance — all too common at the time — he recommended that a medical officer be required to certify before burial the fact and cause of death. Many of Chadwick's recommendations were incorporated in the Public Health Bill in 1848, but they did not go unchallenged.

At this time, because of the high expense of funerals, Friendly Societies became popular. These were the forerunners of today's burial insurance companies. Through them the poor could contribute weekly to a fund that would eventually help them meet the burdensome cost of family funerals.

The sanitation movement influenced reform to existing burial grounds and the prohibition of new cemeteries within cities. In both England and America, the movement was partially responsible for the increased practice of cremation (Habenstein, pp. 112-115).

Coffins and Caskets

The earliest American colonists simply buried their dead in the bare earth, but with increasing prosperity, the practice of using wooden coffins became popular.

Then, beginning around the first half of the nineteenth century, coffins of materials other than wood began to appear. Since that time, coffins have undergone a number of style and composition vogues.

The changes in style and composition of the burial receptacle were based on five things: utility, indication of status of the deceased, preservation of the body, protection, and aesthetic representation. American coffins have been made from stone, metal, cement, clay, vulcanized rubber, papier-mâché, cloth, and celluloid. Metal coffins were particularly popular during the Civil War when bodies were returned to their homes for burial.

The idea of beauty in burial cases led to the introduction in the mid-nineteenth century of a distinctively American type known as the casket. To the European mind, this word conjures the vision of jewels and suggests a container for something valuable. Today, Americans no longer use the European wedge-shaped octagonal coffin, but the American casket has not yet been popularly accepted in Europe.

During the nineteenth century, many Americans experienced a fear of being buried alive. Due to this fear, a number of caskets were patented that made provisions for some type of signal in case the buried person awoke. Historically, many societies made provisions to test if the soon-to-be-interred were really dead and not simply in a coma. It was American inventiveness, however, that came up with inventions designed to test if life still existed in the grave. This century also saw the invention of several types of caskets designed to protect the body from ghouls and grave robbers.

At the same time the first outer boxes, or vaults, came into popular use. Today many cemeteries demand the use of such vaults of concrete or metal because of the problem of maintaining the grave sites.

Embalming

Almost every society has had to decide whether or not to preserve the corpses of their dead. It was in nineteenth-century America, however, that the need was first felt to preserve the body of the deceased as a necessary preliminary to a proper interment.

The custom of nobility and persons of high rank lying in state for a period of about a week reaches back into classical antiquity. As we saw, it reappeared in Christian care of the dead during the Middle Ages, reinforced by the preservation and distribution of parts of the bodies of religious leaders and saints, which were later distributed as relics.

In Colonial America, a number of crude methods of preservation were used to delay the putrefaction of the corpse. This was necessary because the mourners at the funeral often traveled a long distance to attend.

In 1773 Benjamin Franklin speculated on the possibility of embalming bodies in wine. Lord Nelson was returned to England in a barrel of rum. Samuel Sewall, a noted Colonial American jurist, reported observing the body of a friend "long dead but well preserved in his coffin packed full of tansy" (Barnett, p. 20). In America, most efforts at preservation of the body used simple refrigeration, or airtight seals on the caskets.

About the time of the Civil War, the contemporary use of chemical embalming by injection was introduced into American funeral practice. It gained popularity for two reasons: First, families wanted the bodies of their sons and brothers shipped home, and injection embalming provided the preservation necessary to do so. Second, America was becoming more sanitation-minded, and chemical embalming was seen as a way to reduce epidemics and plagues.

In 1862, a general order of the Army instructed regiments to mark off plots near every battlefield to use as burial places. Because of a lack of means of identification, however, about half of all the federal dead are in graves marked "unknown." A number of undertakers began to contract to attempt to locate a family's dead, and some even passed among the troops issuing handbills advertising their services.

Eventually, abuse crept in, and in 1865 the War Department issued an order which established a system and required examinations to determine the qualifications of persons who sought to embalm the military dead, providing licensing and bonding. It established uniform fees for services and prices for merchandise. This became the prototype for many of today's sumptuary laws.

American Colonial Funeral Practices

In early America, secularization and Puritanism caused a disassociation of religious belief from the phenomenon of death. Several Protestant sects decreed that funerals were a civil — not a religious — responsibility, and directed that they be performed without ceremony. Just as with every other facet of colonial life, the anti-Catholic bias was felt in the matter of funerals. Nonetheless, funeral sermons eventually were preached in church, beginning about 1700, and later prayers were said in graveside ceremonies (Habenstein, p. 120). Early American burial, however, was in the churchyard.

In the colonies, death was simply a fact of life and not ignored. The graveyards were familiar to the living and gravestones became a medium of popular expression, with epitaphs that did more than merely identify the bodily remains. One of the most persistent symbols was the skull and crossbones.

In the seventeenth century, New England funerals were models of simplicity. In order to avoid the "popish error" of saying prayers over the dead, the minister and mourners simply followed the coffin and stood by silently as the grave was filled. Later, mourning took on a social character and the custom of giving away mourning gloves, scarfs, and rings came into vogue. This practice got so out-of-hand and caused such an expense for the family of the deceased that eventually laws were passed to regulate this type of expense.

By the mid-eighteenth century, when someone died the neighbors would wash and lay out the body. A local carpenter would build a coffin. Relatives and friends who lived within a few day's travel would be notified immediately, because it was not customary for the body to lie in state. In warm weather, the body was emboweled and put in a cerecloth made of sheeting soaked in alum, pitch, or wax. Rings, scarfs, or gloves would be given to all who were invited to the funeral. The service would begin in the church with prayers and a sermon. Sometimes these sermons were printed, decorated with a skull and crossbones and black borders, and circulated among the public. A slow procession to the cemetery was made on foot. Underbearers carried the coffin on a bier. A number of men of dignity known as pallbearers held the corners of the pall, or cloth covering. If the town had no grave-digger, the local sexton or neighbors of the deceased supplied this labor. After the body was committed to the ground, all those who had traveled some distance to attend were feted with a funeral feast. These feasts mixed festivity with gloom. A great deal of strong liquor and copious quantities of food were served. The cost of one funeral feast in 1797 was equivalent to between five and ten thousand dollars in today's purchasing power (Habenstein, p. 129).

The pattern of funerals in New York and Virginia was somewhat different. The Dutch buried their loved ones three or four days after death. The best parlor was used for the funeral and prayers were said. The pall-covered coffin and bier were carried to the churchyard by twelve pallbearers. At the feast afterward, food, tobacco, and drink were distributed, as the occasion became a festive time. Special utensils known as monkey spoons were presented to the pallbearers. Usually only adult males attended the main funeral services. In Virginia, a funeral was equivalent in festive air to a horse race or a wedding. Excess in drink and food was often accompanied with gunfire.

The Embargo Acts in 1807 limited the number of imported items, so the custom of the distribution of gloves, rings, scarfs, and other funeral favors gradually began to die out. Also, black ribbons for the ladies and mourning bands for the men began to replace the full suits of mourning clothes.

In America, it was in the first part of the nineteenth century that a distinct occupation for funeral undertaking began to be recognized. Until that time, family and neighbors handled the major portion of the arrangements for funerals. The rapid expanse of America and the absence of clear-cut church regulations allowed craftsmen to begin to add special funeral skills to their regular occupations.

As cities grew and cemeteries were created away from the church, the task of carrying the coffin to the place of burial became more difficult and the practice of using carriages and wagons came into vogue.

Although it was not universal, churchyard and church cemetery burial was the major mode of sepulchre in America until the nineteenth century. The church caretaker or sexton was charged with many of the duties of the funeral and with maintaining the cemetery. Later, his function grew to include many of the duties of today's undertaker.

Transportation

From antiquity, the funeral procession is the oldest of all processions. The word "funeral" is derived from *funeralis*, Latin for torchlight procession. One of the standard pieces of equipment has been the hearse, used to transport the body to the point of sepulchre.

The first hearse was a framework of wood, which held lighted candles and decorations and was placed on a bier or coffin. It later developed into an elaborate pagoda-shaped object of wood or metal for the funerals of royalty and the wealthy. It held banners, candles, and other heraldic devices. Written verses or epitaphs were often attached to the hearse (Habenstein, p. 234).

The forerunner of the hearse as we know it today was a bier in the form of a hand-carried stretcher, on which the uncoffined body was carried to the grave. As coffined burial became more common, arrangement began to be made to allow for longer carries. One solution was to have two sets of bearers. As long as bodies were buried near churches, the hand-carried bier was functional. Once this became restricted and burial in cemeteries outside the city came in vogue, some form of horse-drawn vehicle became necessary.

In early America, the first hearses were simply horse-drawn wagons. Later, lavishly decorated coaches were imported from England, and these were copied by American craftsmen. Because the expense of a family hearse was high, livery stables began to keep a hearse and black horses to rent out for funeral services. By the mid-1800s, styles in hearses began to change with cyclical regularity at intervals of about every fifteen years.

The hearse of the mid-1850s was basically a long, rectangular box with curtained glass windows along the side. Shafts were usually for one horse and the driver's seat was on top. Plumes and urns were added as decoration.

By the time of the Civil War, the hearse had become higher and longer with full glass sides, fancy scrollwork, and more horses. Shortly after the war, hearses for children came into use. Unlike adult hearses that were always black, those for children were painted white and beautifully decorated with religious sculpture.

At the Chicago World's Fair in 1893, a company exhibited the most elaborate and outstanding funeral car of the nineteenth century. Of extraordinary size, it featured a church-like design with massive carvings in bold relief, heavy gold fringes and tassels, and lamps of gold. Angels, cherubs, crucifixes, and statues covered the hearse, which weighed a total of 2,400 pounds. This awe-inspiring vehicle, drawn by eight horses, was used immediately after the close of the fair for the funeral of the assassinated mayor of Chicago (Habenstein, p. 241).

In 1889, the street railway company of Atchison, Kansas, began operation of a trolley funeral car to nearby Mt. Vernon cemetery. It was fitted with a table in the center to hold the casket and had seats along the glass sides of the car for the undertaker and bearers. Additional cars for mourners were of the conventional trolley-car variety. The use of funeral trolleys lasted through the 1920s in most of the major cities.

In the decade from 1910-1920, the automobile began to dominate the field of funeral transportation. Today's modern hearse evolved from a number of stylistic changes in hearse design.

Funerals in the Late Nineteenth Century

America has traditionally showed wide variations in funeral thoughts and customs, especially between rural and urban areas. Any attempt to describe completely such customs can at best show only basic patterns, thanks to American individuality and the fact that various states enacted contrasting laws. For example, in Catholic funerals in some cities in Ohio, it has long been customary to seat mourners on the right or "epistle" side of the church. In other cities, they are customarily directed to the left or "Gospel" side.

In an American home of 1880, death brought a funeral mood of stiff formality overlaid with gloom. The pompous, elaborate, rigidly-prescribed, prolonged, morbid, feudal-type of funeral had been transplanted to America from England (Habenstein, p. 258).

During the first decade of the nineteenth century, immediately after a death a boy went on horseback to notify friends and neighbors within about a ten-mile radius of the sad tidings. On the day of the funeral, everyone stopped work and attended, riding on horseback or in rough wagons. The funerals were filled with simple sincerity.

In late nineteenth-century America, most deaths occurred in the home; but if not, the body was immediately returned there and the home was the central point of mourning. Silence and sadness reigned. The women closed the eyes and straightened the limbs of the deceased. In cities, the undertaker or funeral director was called and relieved the family of many of the duties that were performed by the relatives in the rural areas. In rural areas, the news spread rapidly and relatives, neighbors, and friends all assisted in one way or another. The vast majority of funerals were held in the home, although as early as 1880 undertaking parlor services were available in some places. These were generally used for people who had no home of their own or who had no relatives or friends to offer the facilities of their quarters.

The funeral director became an important advisor to the family, discussing with them the decisions to make regarding the funeral, such as the length of time before burial and the purchase of the coffin or casket.

The body was laid out either by the family or by persons in the neighborhood who had experience in this. Washed, dressed in their best or favorite clothes, the body was moved from the bedroom to the parlor to be viewed, even before a casket was obtained. Friends began pouring into the home and the family, seated in the living room, accepted their condolences. All tiptoed into the parlor to view the corpse and commented on how peaceful and natural it looked. Food, the gifts of friends and neighbors, began to appear in the kitchen.

Naturally, since the funerals were conducted from the home, the undertaker was required to bring with him all items necessary to prepare the body and conduct the services. The family had a choice between ice preservation or chemical embalming. An undertaker who was trained in embalming stressed the use of this method and, to allay fears of desecration, often invited a close friend or adult male member of the family to watch the process. Many people had the erroneous idea that embalming necessitated the removal of the internal organs, but when the observer saw the tiny incision necessary to raise an artery, they generally were satisfied and did not remain to watch the entire process.

On his first visit, the undertaker would bring the appropriate door crepe or badge and attach it to cover the door bell or knocker. Black was the color for the old, white for the young, and black with white for young adults. By 1890, combinations of purple, lavender, and grey were added. Still later, floral wreaths replaced door crepes.

Also on this visit the undertaker consulted with the family about many of the same decisions made for today's funerals: notifications, choice of clergy and pallbearers, choice of casket, biography of the deceased, etc.

By 1895, with the establishment of the Bureaus or Departments of Vital Statistics, undertakers began to be required to meet certain legal requirements regarding burials. Tasks such as having the physician sign the death certificate and securing the burial permit were handled by him as a service to the family. The family often sent a representative with him to the cemetery to discuss the burial place and the construction of walls in the grave. Sprigs of evergreen might be used to trim the grave and soften the harshness of the freshly turned clay. For a child's burial, fresh flowers would be used instead.

The news of death traveled fast in small cities, and in keeping with Christian tradition most of the people were involved with the services and shared the sorrows of the bereaved. In cities, people received news of the death by special couriers who delivered funeral notices, invitations, and mourning cards. By 1900, mourning cards had changed into a letter edged in black, and newspaper notices served for those not closely touched by the event.

In turn-of-the-century funerals, solemnity and gloom were made obvious in the home by using crepe draperies, which were placed on the door and in the room in which the dead lay. Often the entire downstairs portion of the house was draped with black or deep shades of grey.

On the day of the funeral, the undertaker arrived well in advance of the event. Catholic funerals required that he bring a portable altar, candles, and other items not necessary for Protestant funerals. Services at the home were long and drawn out. After the service, an assistant gathered the flowers for transportation to the grave site, while the undertaker directed the loading of the casket and the seating during transportation of the mourners. After the procession left the home, an assistant immediately began to restore order there, removing folding chairs, pedestals, and other funeral items so that on return the family found nothing to remind them that a funeral ceremony had taken place.

Gradually, home funerals gave way to funerals in church. They began in the home — and later in the funeral parlor — with the viewing of the body. Then a procession was made to the church for the main ceremony, and the funeral was completed by the conventional trip to the cemetery and the committal service.

In the typical Catholic church ceremony, the undertaker was met in the vestibule by the priest, who preceded him up the aisle. The body was placed at the head of the center aisle and flowers were arranged about it in stands or on tables. Three candles were placed at each side of the bier.

In spite of strong objections by both undertakers and clergy, the custom of opening the casket in church for a final view of the body persisted during the nineteenth century. Fraternal escorts were given a special position so that in leaving they would occupy the same place as on entering. After the Mass, the casket was carried to the hearse and the procession moved slowly toward the cemetery.

At the cemetery, the pallbearers deposited the casket over the grave and the priest began the committal ceremony. At the words, "earth to earth," either the priest or the undertaker sprinkled a handful of fine dirt over the casket. The casket was then lowered into the grave. Rarely was the grave filled before the departure of the family.

Although the funeral process was similar in rural areas, there were variations and a much greater emotional atmosphere. More people were involved and the bereaved remained as the grave was filled by masculine friends who often vied for the honor of shoveling dirt.

Special colors and customs attended the period of mourning after a death. Servants as well as family dressed in black. Widows were expected to wear black for two years; widowers for at least a year. During the first six months, known as the period of deep mourning, social and recreational contacts were forbidden. Even in the matter of correspondence, mourning customs dictated the color and type of stationary and writing. Slowly, mourning colors lightened. By the time mourning garb was dispensed with, so also were all social restrictions. Because of the prescribed dull black fashions for women, the jet buttons so highly prized by collectors today crept into vogue as a way to add ornamentations in lieu of jewelry.

Flowers

Around the middle of the nineteenth century, a demand for more aesthetically-pleasing funeral decorations began to be felt. This was implemented by changes in casket linings and the use of by floral backdrops. Beginning with the placing of a small bouquet on a table beside the casket, there was a slowly-increasing sentiment in favor of complementing the color, beauty, and aesthetic appeal of the casket with the natural beauty and color of flowers. Church officials in particular criticized excesses in display as a departure from Christian custom. In 1878, the Bishop of Rochester, New York, wrote in a letter to the *Catholic Times:*

Whatever of sentiment may have been in the use of flowers on and around a corpse when, at first, loving hands placed a few near it was killed by usage demanding that such tributes should be repaid on the first occasion available. Thus, in time, floral tributes for the house of mourning became a question of give and expect: a compliment to a friend with a marketable value attached. No wonder that some families deprecate the invasions of their homes with such tributes and cry out, 'Omit the flowers' (Habenstein, p. 274).

Flowers were opposed on the grounds they were pagan, that their extensive use was wasteful, and that their reciprocal use was worldly. Nonetheless, their lavish use continued in vogue.

In 1886, the main floral offering at the funeral of a fire chief was a large floral fire engine, nine-feet-high and six-feet-long, covered with smilax, carnations, and roses. Lettered in violets on the border were the words, "Our Chief." During this same year, the custom of writing with white ink on the leaves of natural flowers became popular. Inscriptions became the trend in funeral flowers and the funeral directors' association advised their members to use flowers instead of crepe. Artificial flowers were widely sold and a number of elaborate arrangements were available through a catalog featuring *immortelles* — nonperishable, artificial, prepared, or dried natural flowers. Perhaps the most elaborate floral funeral was that of the antislavery clergyman Henry Ward Beecher. For his service, the entire church was decorated with flowers rather than the previously-customary crepe.

Sepulchre and Memorialization

Throughout the nineteenth century, changes gradually occurred in the placing of cemeteries. At first, bodies were buried by the families on their own land. Space was set aside for "God's acre." This created a problem when land was sold, because the new owners did not want custody of the previous family's dead, nor did the previous family wish to desert the remains of their beloved.

Gradually, it became more common to inter the remains in plots near churches or in small intercity plots. Because of the number of dead interred, this too created problems, especially from the odors arising from the plots. As early as the 1820s, it became necessary to spread quicklime in some of these cemeteries to hold down the noxious odors.

There was a movement at the turn of the century to establish larger cemeteries outside the corporate limits of the cities. Although many of these were in the custody of religious groups, it became more and more common for them to be managed by corporations established specifically for this purpose. The remains from many of the previously-used small cemeteries were transferred here.

Two major factors contributed to the style of modern cemeteries. The great epidemics of cholera and other communicable diseases caused health concerns and many laws were passed in this regard. Additionally, the American wish for beauty caused the cemeteries to become similar to large parks.

These efforts at beauty gained further expression in the memorialization of the dead. The original plain marble or limestone slabs began as safeguards to protect the graves from wild beasts. Names and dates were added for identification. Sculptors now began industriously adding cornices, scrolls, imitation tree trunks, and statuary.

Epitaphs represented pious sentiments consistent with the person's life, or cautions for the instruction of the living. Bible quotations have always seemed appropriate. The inscriptions and decorations on the tombstones provide a clue as to the prevailing ideas and attitudes about death among the American public. The earliest memorials minced no words and did not sugarcoat the harsh reality of death. Before and during the eighteenth century, and well into the next, the tombstones spelled out the reality of death. They called sinners, sinners, and saints, saints. Skulls and crossbones were familiar symbols and crude jests or merry puns were common (Habenstein, pp. 276-281).

Here are some examples of cemetery verse of this time period:

THIS ROSE WAS SWEET A WHILE

BUT NOW IS ODOUR VILE.

SOON RIPE

SOON ROTTEN

SOON GONE

BUT NOT FORGOTTEN.

A young woman who died in childbirth was immortalized thus:

> EIGHTEEN YEARS A MAIDEN
>
> ONE YEAR A WIFE
>
> ONE DAY A MOTHER
>
> THEN I LOST MY LIFE.

The lines for a child dead of burns from an overturned coffee pot were:

> THE BOILING COFFEE ON ME DID FALL,
>
> AND BY IT I WAS SLAIN.
>
> BUT CHRIST HAS BROUGHT MY LIBERTY
>
> AND IN HIM I'LL RISE AGAIN (Habenstein, pp. 280-281).

Some of the epitaphs found on early American gravestones are extremely funny and often even seem inappropriate to today's readers. But in their day, these were accepted and not considered uncommon. One example of this graveyard humor comes from Vermont:

> IN MEMORY OF ANNA HOPEWELL
>
> HERE LIES THE BODY OF OUR ANNA,
>
> DONE TO DEATH BY A BANANA;
>
> IT WASN'T THE FRUIT THAT LAID HER LOW,
>
> BUT THE SKIN OF THE THING THAT MADE HER GO.

Another, from Maine, reads:

> HERE LIES OUR WIFE SAMANTHA PROCTER,
>
> SHE KETCHED A COLD AND WOULD NOT DOCTOR.
>
> SHE COULD NOT STAY, SHE HAD TO GO.
>
> PRAISE GOD FROM WHOM ALL BLESSINGS FLOW (Pellowe, p. 34).

A tombstone in an Arizona cemetery carries the following epitaph, terse and humorous:

> HERE
>
> LIES
>
> LESTER MOORE
>
> FOUR SLUGS
>
> FROM A .44
>
> NO LES,
>
> NO MOORE.

Another, from Rockford, Illinois, was the headstone of a famous criminal lawyer. It reads:

> THE DEFENSE RESTS (Pellowe, p. 44).

Cautions and instructions given to the living have a rough humor of their own. For example:

REMEMBER MAN, AS YOU PASS BY,
AS YOU ARE NOW, SO ONCE WAS I;
AS I AM NOW, SO YOU WILL BE:
PREPARE FOR DEATH AND FOLLOW ME.

Another reads:

WHEN I AM DEAD AND GONE
AND ALL MY BONES ARE ROTTEN,
COME ALL YE FRIENDS AND KINFOLK DEAR
AND SEE THAT I AM NOT FORGOTTEN (Pellowe, p. 46).

Unexpectedly, tombstones, which seem most unlikely places, were sometimes used in advertising things commercial, as seen in the following:

HERE LIES JANE SMITH, WIFE OF THOS. SMITH, MARBLE CUTTER. THIS MONUMENT ERECTED BY HER HUSBAND.... MONUMENTS OF THIS SAME STYLE ARE $250.

This one from New England bears a different form of advertisement:

SACRED TO THE MEMORY OF JOS. H. RANDOM. HIS WIDOW MOURNS AS ONE WHO CAN BE COMFORTED. AGE 24 AND POSSESSING EVERY QUALIFICATION FOR A GOOD WIFE. LIVES AT NO. 4 CHURCH ST. IN THIS VILLAGE (Pellowe, p. 53).

After 1850, monument prose, verse, and art more and more softened the hard facts. The winged cherub and other symbols of faith and hope replaced the skull and crossbones. By 1880, a wife would inscribe:

STRANGER CALL THIS NOT A PLACE
OF FEAR AND GLOOM,
TO ME IT IS A PLEASANT SPOT
IT IS MY HUSBAND'S TOMB.

Another sweet sentiment was:

SHED NOT FOR HER THE BITTER TEAR
NOR GIVE THE HEART TO VAIN REGRET
'TIS BUT THE CASKET THAT LIES HERE
THE GEM THAT FILLS IT SPARKLES YET (Pellowe, p. 39).

By the 1880s, sentiments on tombstones reflected in verse and mood those that were also printed on small mourning cards that were distributed to friends and relatives of the deceased. One example reads:

THERE IS NO DEATH. WHAT SEEMS SO IS TRANSITION;
THIS LIFE OF MORTAL BREATH

Is but the suburb of the life elysian
Whose portal we call Death.

A poem written for the card and grave of a young child reads:

Sleep on in thy beauty,
Thou sweet angel child.
By sorrow unslighted,
By sin undefiled.

The impulse to memorialize our dead in verse and the willingness to provide copy for such memorials have both persisted to our day. Although mourning cards are no longer fashionable, poetic memorializations still occasionally appear in daily newspapers at the time of the funeral and sometimes on anniversaries of deaths. Also, although the previously-used mourning cards that were inscribed with fancy lettering and verse on four-by-six-inch cards are no longer popular, Catholics in many places have continued to issue small "holy card" memorials containing a picture of the deceased, or of the Blessed Mother, or a saint, along with a bible verse and the name and dates of the deceased (Habenstein, pp. 276-281).

Mementoes of the Dead

In addition to memorial cards, mementoes of the dead have been kept throughout the centuries. Entire bodies of saints have been enshrined and displayed in the churches of Europe. Relics are preserved in beautiful reliquaries in churches and monasteries, and second- and third-class relics have been given to the laity. This practice continues today.

Other remembrances of our beloved dead have been kept by friends and families. In much earlier times, entire mummies were kept in the home. More recently, objects belonging to the dead have been popular reminders of the missing loved one. In the nineteenth century, objects made from the hair of the deceased were particularly popular. At the Victoria and Albert Museum in London, there is an entire series of jewelry that are either designed to contain hair or are partly made of hair. Bracelets made of hair were particularly popular in the nineteenth century (Aries, p. 388). In the American South, pictures embroidered with hair from deceased members of the family were popular in the early part of this century.

Blessings for the Cemetery

The Church considers the cemetery to be a holy place and strongly suggests that new cemeteries be blessed and a cross erected as a sign of Christian hope in the Resurrection. Visiting cemeteries is also a practice encouraged by the Church. The new *Book of Blessings* has special blessings for both these occasions.

Catholics have always preferred that their dead lie in consecrated ground. Before the recent lifting of the Iron Curtain, many people from communist-controlled countries took dirt from their loved ones' graves and had it blessed by a priest. Since the priest could not come to the grave, the grave went to the priest.

Papa's Funeral, 1941

The following is excerpted from the letter of a young wife to her parents in 1941. In it, she gives a vivid description of the funeral of her father-in-law. The funeral was a typical one for a small Southern town of this time period. Although this was a Protestant funeral, a Catholic funeral would have been the same, other than the prescribed ritual of the funeral Mass at the church and the service at the grave site.

As you will read, after Papa's death, his family tended the body before it was turned over to the funeral director. It was moved to the funeral home, then back to the home. It was taken to the church for the funeral before being taken to the cemetery.

Family, friends, and servants all had a part to play. While everyone felt a sense of loss, some also felt a sense of gain. Then, as today, food and flowers were an integral part of the ceremony.

Monday evening

Dearest Mother and Daddy,

Mother, I feel different. I don't think I can explain it — how I feel, I mean — I just do. In a way, I feel more capable — more sure of myself. I feel now that when I have something to do I can do it. My love for Julian seems so much deeper and greater. He was so wonderful thru all of it. He is so kind, sweet and dependable — that is papa in him.

Papa told Julian — one of the last things he told him — that he would have to take his place — the tie to keep the family together. If anyone can do it in this family, Julian can. Bless him — he feels this responsibility so and I hope and pray that they will all unite. Papa wanted that so much and if it can happen it will be the greatest tribute they can give him.

Mary has been sick today, and Margie told me she wanted to go up to the cemetery to see all the flowers again and that "Miss Mary" wanted some of them. So I told Margie that I would be glad to drive her out and get the flowers for Mary. We did this morning. Mother, you have never seen so many flowers. Oh they were beautiful ! The house was overflowing. We had them in every room downstairs — Papa's room was almost a solid blanket of flowers — we even had them on the banister on the stairway. At the church, they had to put some down the aisles and today at the cemetery the whole lot was covered. They were rather wilted and wind blown, but we got a few for Mary. I also took one carnation from your offering and one from the children's. When we were leaving the cemetery yesterday, Julian stopped and picked one flower from someone's offering. He said he wanted to keep something. I thought this morning he would rather have one from their spray and I wanted one of yours. He seemed to [have] appreciated my thinking of it. Mother, your offering was beautiful. And the loveliest thing happened.

Wednesday

Julian came in while I was writing the other night so I stopped to talk to him. He is so sweet. We talked a long time about what had happened and then he asked if I would like to hear the will.

Mother, I can't help but wander about in this letter — there is so much to tell. Back to the flowers. Mrs. Bone was so thoughtful in doing what she did. She got your wire and called Julian and told him that if it was agreeable with them, she wanted to fix your offering especially lovely and for the casket Saturday. I know that you and daddy — and me — appreciate the thoughtfulness — the honor that was ours to have your flowers placed there. It was a beautiful spray — pink carnations and *calla* lilies. The children's offering was placed there Sunday.

When did I write you last — last Tuesday or Wednesday? Papa was conscious after Wednesday. I stayed down at Louise's — hoping I could be of some service. I could answer the phone, go to the door, see about their meals, and little things like that. Julian wouldn't let me go in Papa's room after Tuesday. He said he wanted me to remember him as he was before he was so sick. But I stayed there all the time — I mean, at the house. Julian stayed with Papa constantly — didn't even go to bed for two nights and we couldn't get him to rest during the day. Louise was with him too, most all of the time — even tho' they had a day and night nurse. Margaret, Robertha and I made a list Thursday of the wires and calls that would have to be made. The children looked it over Thursday night. I was sitting in the living room when it happened.

I heard people running. Louise ran upstairs — and, mother, I was amazed that from the minute Papa passed away everyone had something to do — and seemed to know just what to do. Gus ran to the phone — I grabbed the list we had made — and he started calling as I gave names and numbers (out of town calls). Everything happened so fast. Julian helped the nurse get Papa ready to be moved. Again — Julian was wonderful. He wanted to do those last things for Papa himself — he held on to himself so beautifully — he just kept busy. Williamson's was there immediately and Margie, Nora and Floyd were in his room the minute he left — cleaning and straightening it. I had never been around a death before — and I am still amazed at the comparative calmness, the speed, and of the fact of everyone having a duty to perform. Aunt Ora was there — she was in the dining room at the time and rushed upstairs with Louise — to help her. Gus, Philip and I stayed at the phone — and before we could realize it — everything was over and done — all we could do then. They kept Papa at Williamson's Friday night. Gus asked me to go with them — the children —

to select the casket. We went there after all the family had dinner in Florine and Marion's apartment. Wasn't that nice of them to have us all there? They brought Papa home to his room Saturday morning. We all stayed there at the Big House. Louise's Sunday school class sent dinner that day and the missionary society sent it Sunday. I took charge of all the food being sent in — marked plates, etc. Margaret took charge of the flowers coming in. Oh — those beautiful flowers! The house was full of people — friends and relatives. We didn't sit down for two days — I don't believe. Sister held up wonderfully, too. We were all afraid that in her nervous condition she would go to pieces again — but she held on to herself bravely. She came to the house Sunday for the family prayer in Papa's room before the funeral, but she didn't go to the church or the cemetery.

Brother Treadwell gave a prayer at the church and Brother Strother gave the talk. It was a beautiful talk — so comforting. The

In Loving Memory

LOUIS MUMFORD ADAMS

born January 11, 1920 - Pelican, Louisiana
died July 10, 1992 - Houston, Texas
at rest - Rambin, Louisiana

Example of a contemporary memorial card distributed at funerals.

church was overflowing with people. Papa had so many, many friends — old and young — rich and poor. The service at the cemetery was comforting too — a short prayer — then it was all over. Bless Papa, in his going he has given some of his wonderful being to all of us. Julian feels it greatly — and even I feel like he passed something good and strong on to me.

Dell was certainly wonderful to us thru all of it — she did so many thoughtful little things.

My hand is tired and I imagine your eyes are from all this writing. But I wanted to tell you so much.

Love to all,

Ora Louise

Part Two:

We Celebrate Our Dead

Statue of Our Lady of Fatima, known as the "Weeping Madonna."

Chapter Four

Our Lady's Part

The Gospel records that Mary was present at Calvary (John 19:25). Here she cooperated with her Son as Coredemptrix. Because of love, every suffering of the Son was anguish for the Mother. She loved Jesus and the greatness of her love measures the greatness of her sorrow. "Just as there was never a love like hers, so also there was never a sorrow like hers" (Richard of St. Victor).

And from the cross, Jesus gave His mother to us — "Behold, thy mother" (John 19:27).

*****

God our Father, by the precious blood of your Son, you reconciled the world to yourself and, as she stood beside his cross, made his Mother the Reconciler of sinners. By her kind intercession, may we obtain the forgiveness of our sins. We ask this through Jesus Christ, Our Lord. Amen (from the Mass of Our Lady of LaSalette).

*****

Virgin Mother of God, thou art the help of the helpless, the joy of the sick, the consoler of the afflicted (St. Ephrem).

The Seven Sorrows of Mary

A medieval canticle recalls the seven sorrows of Mary. As we meditate on her sorrows, we pray for the help of her sorrowful and immaculate heart.

1. Remember, O Virgin Mary, the sword of sorrow that pierced your heart with the prophecy of Simeon who foretold to you the death of Jesus; pierce our hearts with the sword of contrition.

2. Remember, O Virgin Mary, the sorrow you felt when obliged to

flee into Egypt; bring us, your exiled children, back from the darkness to the light, and lead us to the splendors of our eternal home.

3. Remember, O Virgin Mary, your sorrow when you sought Jesus for three days before finding him in the temple; grant that we may thirst for Christ, that we may seek Him always and everywhere, and that our search may be crowned with success.

4. Remember, O Virgin Mary, the sorrow you felt when Jesus was seized and bound, then scourged and crowned with thorns; heed your children's cries and break the bonds of our sins.

5. Remember, O Virgin Mary, your sorrow when Jesus was raised on the cross and, amid unspeakable spasms, gave up His spirit to the Father; grant that we, too, may benefit from the sacrifice of the cross.

6. Remember, O Virgin Mary, your sorrow when the sacred body of Jesus was placed in your arms with sentiments of profound devotion; embrace us, too, O Mother, so that we may enjoy your love.

7. Remember your sorrow, O Virgin Mary, when Jesus was wrapped in a sheet and laid in the sepulchre; cleanse our souls with his Most Precious Blood, and at the end of our lives fill us with deep compunction, so that the gates of heaven may be opened to us (Alberione, p. 193).

Mother of Mercy, Refuge of Sinners

St. Francis de Sales reminds us that God wishes all to be saved, even sinners. In speaking of Mary, he says, "She knows that Jesus, when dying, made her the Mother of all. She knows that mothers take special care of their weakest, sickest and neediest children."

In spite of our sins, Mary does not cease to be our Mother. She desires to lead us back to Christ, and offers refuge to sinners.

*****

"Omnipotent and merciful God, Who didst make of the Blessed Virgin a refuge and a help for sinners, grant that, through her protection, freed from every sin, we may enjoy the happy effects of Thy mercy" (from the Collect, Mass of Mary, Refuge of Sinners).

Our Lady of Pity (La Salette)

The sorrowful and merciful mother looks on her sinful children with love and with pity. Not only does she intercede for us continuously, in her pity she also issues warnings to encourage sinful mankind to turn again to God.

High in the French Alps, Our Lady appeared to two young cattle herders, Melanie Mathieu and Maximin Giraud, in the fall of 1846. In a twenty-minute apparition, she gave the children a message for the world. This message, echoed later at Lourdes and still later at Fatima, was a call to prayer and penance. In her pity, Our Lady came to warn and to plead with sinful mankind to avert his descent to calamity.

At La Salette, the children first noticed a brilliant light in the field where they had accompanied their herds. In the middle of the light, a beautiful woman sat on a rock, weeping. The children noticed her costume — a golden crown, a dress strewn with bursts of light, a shawl and slippers edged with roses, a heavy chain on her shoulders, and a luminous golden crucifix. On one side of the crossbar of the crucifix was a hammer; on the other rested a pincers.

Slowly and with an unearthly grace, Our Lady arose and spoke to the children. Although she was speaking directly to the two children, she addressed a world where the sacraments were neglected, where there was more cursing than praying, and where Christian attitudes and observance had given way to self-indulgence, greed, and a worldly spirit. Her message was a call for spiritual renewal.

After delivering her message, she stood still for a moment, then rose through the air. The children saw her look toward heaven and smile, ending the fall of crystalline tears she had shed during the entire time she was speaking with them. The pulsating light surrounding the vision became even more resplendent, then slowly the apparition disappeared.

The children, as good messengers, repeated the warning and message of Our Lady of Pity. After a lengthy investigation, and with a call for "obedience and submission to Heaven's warning," the church authorized the cult of Our Lady of LaSalette. Through it, many have been brought back to a realization of the importance of their Catholic faith for time and eternity.

Within five years, a new religious congregation, the Missionaries of LaSalette, began to work in the church. Their work is reconciliation, bringing God and His people closer together.

The unique crucifix — the silent message of La Salette — has become their characteristic emblem. A little thought makes its significance apparent. The hammer indicates the sins of men which were the cause of Christ's crucifixion — the hammer which drove the nails into His hands and feet. The open pincers recall how these cruel nails were finally and mercifully extracted and remind us of our obligation to expiate the sins of the world through penance and prayer.

*****

Our Lady of LaSalette, Reconciler of sinners, pray without ceasing for us who have recourse to thee (S.P. Ap., Dec. 12, 1933).

Our Lady of Hope (Pontmain)

Devotion to Our Lady of Hope is an ancient Marian devotion. A shrine bearing that title was erected at Mezieres in the year 930. Closer to our own times, Our Lady of Hope appeared to six children in the French village of Pontmain in 1871. Here she revealed herself as the "Madonna of the Crucifix," and gave the world a message of hope through prayer and the cross.

The children who saw the apparition ranged in age from twenty-five months to twelve years. Although about sixty adults gathered, they were unable to see anything. The demeanor of the children made it plain that they did, indeed, see something. The Virgin appeared in a blue robe seeded with golden stars. Her hair was covered with a black veil and she wore a golden crown with a red line around the middle.

The adults spontaneously joined in hymns and prayers. During the several phases of the three-and-a-half-hour apparition, writing appeared that the oldest children spelled out to the adults.

The first sentence was, "But pray, my children." The next writing spelled out, "God will hear you in a short time." Then an invisible hand spelled out, "My Son permits Himself to be moved."

At the next phase of the apparition, the beautiful Lady appeared sad and recollected, and a large bloody cross with the words "Jesus Christ" appeared in front of her. She took it in her hands and seemed to pass it to the children. The red crucifix disappeared and small white crosses appeared on each of her shoulders. Again, the Lady lowered her hands and smiled at the children. In fullness of joy, the children cried out, "Look, she is smiling — she is smiling." Slowly, the apparition dissolved.

Today, where once stood the rude barn that was the site of the apparition, there is a beautiful church as a monument to Our Lady of Hope. The church, consecrated in 1900, was raised to the status of a minor basilica by Pope St. Pius X. In America, the devotion was given into the custody of the Oblates of Mary Immaculate, who spread Our Lady's simple message of hope through the cross of Jesus Christ.

*****

O Mary, my Mother, I kneel before thee with heavy heart. The burden of my sins oppresses me and the knowledge of my weakness discourages me. I am beset by fears and temptations of every sort. Yet I am so attached to the things of this world that instead of longing for Heaven I am filled with dread at the thought of death.

Obtain for me, O Mother of Hope, the grace of true sorrow for my sins, the gift of perfect resignation to God's Holy Will, and the courage to take up my cross and follow Jesus.

Above all I pray, O dearest Mother, that through thy most powerful intercession my heart may be filled with Holy Hope so that in life's darkest hour I may never fail to trust in God my Saviour; but by walking in the way of His commandments I may merit to be united with Him and with thee, in the eternal joys of Heaven (from the novena prayers to Our Lady of Hope).

*****

Our Lady of Consolation

"Comforter of the Afflicted" is one of Mary's sweetest titles. Our Lady of Consolation stands ready to console us with the tenderness of a mother. Mary sees our hurts and feels them in her sensitive heart. St. Anselm reminds us, "she is the solace of the afflicted."

Devotion to Mary as Consoler of the Afflicted was first expressed by St. Ignatius of Antioch in the second century when he wrote, "Mary, knowing what it is to suffer, is ever ready to administer consolation." Thus, Consoler of the Afflicted is one of the earliest Marian titles, and the tradition of asking the Mother of God for the gift of consolation dates back to the earliest Christian centuries.

One early source for the devotion to Mary under the title Mother of Consolation has been treasured for centuries by the Order of St. Augustine. In the fourth century, distraught with grief and anxiety for her wayward son Augustine, St. Monica confided her trouble to the Mother of God, who appeared to her dressed in mourning clothes and wearing a shining cincture (cord worn around the waist). Our Lady gave the cincture to St. Monica as a sign of her support and compassion, directing Monica to encourage others to wear it. Monica gave the cincture to Augustine, who later gave it to his community, thus instituting the order's wearing of the cincture as a token of fidelity to Our Mother of Consolation.

A second tradition, seemingly separate, dates from the fourteenth century and tells of a Roman nobleman in the Capitoline prison awaiting death. Reflecting on his approaching last moments, he dictated in his will that his son was to have a Madonna and Child painted and placed near the gallows for the consolation of all who would die in that place in the future. The son followed his father's wishes, and when in 1470 a youth who had been unjustly convicted was miraculously saved from the hangman's noose as his mother prayed before the picture, the place became a popular shrine. More miracles followed and a church was built. The painting was given the title Mother of Consolation. Because of the large number of pilgrims, the devotion spread rapidly over Europe.

Later, confraternities were established, but they ended in the nineteenth century because of political stress in Italy. The painting and the church remain under the care of the Capuchin Fathers.

The Corona of Our Mother of Consolation, also known as the Augustinian rosary, expresses our faith as we find it written in the Apostles' Creed. This chaplet consists of thirteen pairs of beads. Two additional beads and a medal of Our Lady of Consolation are attached to the body of the corona. The corona begins by calling to mind the scene in the Cenacle when the apostles devoted themselves to constant prayer. There were some women in their company, as well as Mary the mother of Jesus and his brothers (Acts 1:14). The corona begins with the sign of the cross. When said in a group, after the announcement of each of the twelve articles of the Apostles' Creed, a brief reading is taken from the writings of St. Augustine or other writings of the Augustinian tradition. Then a single Lord's Prayer and a Hail Mary are prayed. When praying the corona in private, the readings may be omitted. The final Our Father and Hail Mary are said for the intentions of the pope. The chaplet is ended by a recitation of the Hail, Holy Queen.

Comforter of the Afflicted (Luxembourg)

In the seventeenth century, when the bubonic plague ravaged the population of Luxembourg, the people formed a spiritual union to pray to Mary, Consoler of the Afflicted, for relief in their anguish and their fear of death. An image of her was enshrined in a small chapel and in 1652 the pope established a confraternity there. Because of the many favors and authenticated cures claimed by the throngs of pilgrims from many lands, the image was raised in the Cathedral of Luxembourg and she became patroness of the Duchy.

The devotion flourished in Europe for two hundred years and spread to North America. The first American shrine in her honor was established by Father Joseph P. Gloden at the mission in Carey, Ohio. A replica of the original image was brought to Ohio, where it is today honored at the Minor Basilica and National Shrine of Our Lady of Consolation. Relics of wood and cloth from the original image hang around the neck of the Carey image. The shrine is administered by the Conventual Franciscan Friars.

Another European center of devotion to Mary as Comforter of the Afflicted is at Kevalaer, Germany. Here there is a miraculous image, a faded paper print, three-by-five-inches, of the miraculous statue revered in Luxembourg. A miraculous icon of the Madonna of Consolation, believed to have been painted in the middle of the fifth century, is enshrined and honored at the Sanctuary of Consolation in Turin, Italy. Stemming from the devotion at Turin, a religious order dedicated to her was founded in 1901. Called the Consolata Missionaries, these priests, brothers, and sisters labor to bring the Gospel to the poor and the order has spread worldwide.

In our own times, we may turn in hope to our luminous "sign of comfort," Our Mother of Consolation, Consoler of the Afflicted, whose joy is to bring to broken human hearts the fruit of the Resurrection, God's own consolation.

Our Lady of Mt. Carmel

Devotion to Our Lady of Mt. Carmel is one of the most ancient, and strongest, of the Marian devotions. Although Carmel is a place, it is more — a spirituality and an entire manner of living that can properly extend to any Christian in any walk of life. The Carmelite charisma reminds us that the true spirit of devotion to Mary lies in our working with and through her to attain Christian perfection ... to God, through Mary, for love.

Traditionally, a special grace of the Virgin toward the Carmelites was her promise attached to the brown scapular of the order. The prior general, St. Simon Stock, appealed to Our Lady for assistance at a crucial time, begging her for a special privilege for the Brothers who bore her name. In 1251, while Simon was at prayer, Our Lady appeared to him at Ayelsford, England, holding a scapular and promising, "This shall be a sign for you and for all Carmelites. Whosoever dies in this shall not suffer eternal fire."

Even though there are historical difficulties, a case can be made for the story of the vision. The understanding of the scapular devotion is, however, the most important part. The scapular is a miniature habit, a highly indulgenced sacramental, and a privileged sign of affiliation with the Carmelite Order, which commits the wearer to follow Our Lady's way of life.

The wearing of the scapular is not a pious superstition and the scapular itself should not be considered some type of holy "good luck charm." It is a sacramental for constantly inspiring the wearer to trust totally in God, as Mary did. The scapular devotion was extended to the laity and spread rapidly in the late 1400s.

Seventy-one years after Mary gave the brown scapular to St. Simon Stock, she came to the supreme pontiff, Pope John XXII. He published the message she gave him in the papal bull of March 3, 1322: "So that with hastened step they shall pass over Purgatory, I, the Mother of Grace, shall descend into Purgatory on the Saturday after their death, and whomsoever I shall find I shall free, so that I may lead them unto the holy mountain of life everlasting."

It would be foolish indeed to expect that the mere wearing of a piece of cloth would gain for the wearer the guarantee of eternal life. Mary's promises to St. Simon and to Pope John appear so startling that they have often been misconstrued or made the basis for a superstitious belief in the efficacy of the sacramental itself. Unlike the sacraments instituted by Christ, the sacramentals were instituted and approved by the Church and are productive of grace *ex opere operantis*, by virtue of their ecclesiastical approval and the dispositions with which they are used.

The first scapular promise has been interpreted to mean that anyone wearing the scapular at the hour of death will receive from her the favor of dying in the state of grace. Popes and saints have warned against the folly of abusing Mary's promise. Pope Pius XI warned, "Those who wish to have the Blessed Mother as a helper at the hour of death must in life merit such a signal favor by abstaining from sin and laboring in her honor." The wearing of the scapular, therefore, is a sign that the wearer is in the livery of Our Lady and dedicated in a special way to her.

The Sabbatine Privilege, based on the bull said to have been issued by Pope John XXII, is frequently understood to mean that those who wear the scapular and fulfill the other conditions made by the Blessed Virgin (in an apparition to John before he became pope) will be freed from purgatory on the first Saturday after death. However, all that the Church has ever said officially in explanation of this is that those who fulfill the conditions will be released from purgatory through the intercession of Our Lady soon after death, and especially on Saturday.

The conditions for gaining the Sabbatine Privilege are that the wearer should (1) wear the brown scapular faithfully, (2) observe chastity according to one's state in life, and (3) recite the Little Office of the Blessed Virgin or, when permission to do so has been obtained, to pray five decades of the rosary daily.

Isidore Bakanja, Martyr for the Scapular

"The White man did not like Christians ... he did not want me to wear the scapular.... He yelled at me when I said my prayers."

The Zairois catechist, Isidore Bakanja, groaned as he answered the questions of the Trappist missionary priest, Father Gregoire. The youthful catechist lay on his stomach, because his back was one large, festering sore and his hipbones protruded from his skin. He promised the priest not to harbor hatred in his heart against the man who had caused him to be so cruelly beaten with an elephant-hide strap studded with nails. He went further than forgiveness: "Certainly I shall pray for him. When I am in heaven, I shall pray for him very much."

The death of the young black man was not an isolated incident. In the Belgian Congo in the early 1900s, white colonizers often treated the native Africans in an inhumane and cruel manner. King

Leopold II had requested that Pope Leo XIII send missionaries to the colony, but the priests were often met with hateful opposition.

Isidore Bakanja was born a member of the Boangi tribe. As a youth, he worked as an assistant mason in Mbandaka, where he heard the Good News of Christianity. He became one of the missionaries' most fervent catechumens and was baptized in 1906. Isidore, who later died for refusing to discard his scapular, had been trained to see in this devotion the external emblem of the unsurpassed gift of faith (Valabek, p. 147). For Isidore, the brown scapular and the rosary were the badges that identified him as a Christian.

When his contract for work in Mbandaka was finished, Isidore eventually went to work as a servant-boy to a Belgian colonizer, and followed his employer into the bush near the equator to work on a large rubber plantation. On this plantation there was an avowed anti-Christian and freethinker named Van Cauter, also called Longange. He avowed that religion was a farce and that priests were "stupid," "ignorant," and "zeros."

Isidore used his free time to teach the other natives about prayer and the Christian religion. He told his cousin that Longange had told him not to teach his people how to pray. His own master, Reynders, told Isidore that if he wanted to pray he should pray in his heart but not to let anyone see him praying with his rosary in public.

In such a tense, hate-filled and antireligious atmosphere, things were bound to come to a head. One evening when Isidore and his friend Iyongo were serving their masters at supper, Longange spied the scapular around Isidore's neck and commanded him to remove it. Isidore, however, was too fervent a Catholic to discontinue wearing his scapular. A few days later, on noticing that Isidore still had his scapular, Longange flew into a rage and had Isidore beaten with twenty-five strokes. The other blacks, all non-Catholics, did not understand Longange's raging at the "animal of stupid priests."

On February 2, 1909, Longange and two other Europeans were relaxing on the veranda, having afternoon coffee. Longange sent his boy after Isidore, who was walking toward the marshlands nearby to say his prayers.

When Isidore asked Longange why he had been summoned, the Belgian accused him of teaching the workers about Christianity. Longange ripped the scapular off Isidore's neck and tossed it to his dog. He then grabbed Isidore by the neck and threw him to the ground, ordering one of his domestics to beat Isidore. This man, Bongele, was terrified of the Belgian and began whipping Isidore as hard as he could. Two other servant boys assisted, holding Isidore's hands and feet while Longange kicked the fallen catechist. Although Isidore begged for mercy, the beating continued until Bongele's arms could not take it any more. More than two hundred blows had ripped Isidore's back apart.

Fearing that Isidore would report him to a superior, Longange imprisoned him for several days in the rubber processing room, chained by his feet and with his wounds unattended. At the threat of a visit by the company director, Longange ordered Isidore to go to a different town with one of the other Europeans. Isidore escaped and hid in the woods. A servant of the inspector found him and listened to his story before presenting him to the inspector.

After hearing Isidore's story, the inspector called for Longange, who then attempted to kill the young catechist. The inspector restrained him and took charge of Isidore, personally dressing his wounds. The inspector took the invalid first to a different plantation, then to the central office of the company in Busira. The company provided medicine on a regular basis, but his wounds were too infected to hope for recovery.

In July, the missionaries came and administered the last sacraments to him. Father Gregoire heard his confession and gave him the anointing of the sick. The next day, the missionary brought him the Eucharist in the form of Viaticum.

The now-invalid Isidore was moved to the porch of the town catechist, Loleka. Here, throughout his final days, which were filled with pain and suffering, Isidore was never without his rosary. Toward the end, because of the intense pain, he was often in delirium. One Sunday morning at the first of August, Isidore threw up blood and those around him recognized the smell of imminent death. All of a sudden, the prayerful African stood up and walked into the banana patch beside the catechist's house, holding his rosary in his hand. Shortly, he returned and lay down.

The people did not know how to explain this brief walk by one who for months had been unable to stand alone, sit, or even lie on his back. Isidore took part in the Sunday prayer session held by the local Christians in the catechist's home. He requested something to eat and soon afterwards died quietly. The Christians buried him simply, still holding his rosary in his hand.

The life of Isidore Bakanja shows the heroic degree to which a solid scapular devotion can lead even a recently baptized convert. In him, the scapular devotion has its martyr. Through the life and Christian attitude of this modern-day servant of God, the Universal Church has a new hero to emulate. Isidore Bakanja was beatified by Pope John Paul II on April 24, 1994.

The Dormition and Assumption of Our Lady

It would be unthinkable that Mary, after being set apart by God to be the sinless mother of Jesus Christ, and as one who enjoyed a special union with God by her love and fidelity, would at death receive no special privilege. God's wonderful dealings with Mary did not cease with the end of her earthly life (De Leonardis, p. 3).

The first annual feast day of the Virgin was probably celebrated in Palestine. In 529, Bishop Theodore of Petra wrote that the monks of Palestine annually celebrated a memorial feast of the Blessed Virgin. There is little doubt that the feast was celebrated on the anniversary of her "falling asleep," which according to ancient tradition was on August 15 (Weiser, 1958, p. 286).

Originally all Christians spoke of death as "falling asleep" until the general resurrection, when all would be reunited, soul and body, to enjoy eternal happiness (Stravinskas, p. 324). The annual commemoration of Mary spread throughout the Eastern church. Emperor Mauritius, in 602, confirmed the date and established the feast as a public holiday. The official title was the "Falling Asleep of the Mother of God." Almost immediately the feast was accepted by the Roman Church, which celebrated it under the same title as early as the seventh century. With the memory of her "falling asleep" was connected the ancient traditional belief that her body did not decay and that soon after the burial was united again with her soul and taken to heaven. This belief brought about a change in the title of the feast in the Latin Church, where it began to be called *Assumption*, or "Taking Up" (Weiser, 1958, p. 287). It is her assumption into heaven that has been celebrated from the beginning of the Middle Ages.

From the fifth century on, many legends told of the death of the

Virgin. Although none are historically provable, they confirm the ancient belief.

Tradition holds that the death of our Blessed Mother occurred about fifteen years after the death of Christ. She was in her sixty-third year and had come to Jerusalem with St. John after they left Ephesus. The apostles came and gathered around her as she lay on her deathbed. She gave them her blessing and promised she would always watch over them. She passed away in a rapture of divine love.

The disciples placed her sacred body in the tomb to the accompaniment of angel's voices singing. After three days, when they opened her tomb, to their surprise they found that the body was no longer there.

There is no direct biblical evidence for the Assumption, but the Church has long held this belief based on theological reasoning and tradition. The dogma of the Assumption states that Mary was taken up body and soul into heaven after the completion of her earthly life, since by reason of her Immaculate Conception she should not suffer the consequences of original sin. Pope Pius XII, after consultation with all the bishops of the Catholic church, proclaimed the Assumption of the Blessed Virgin Mary a doctrine of the faith on November 1, 1950. This is the only declared exercise of papal infallibility (Stravinskas, p. 101). The definition of the Assumption leaves open the question as to whether she died or was taken bodily into heaven alive.

In Hungary, there is a tradition that the first Hungarian king, St. Stephen (d. 1038), offered his royal crown to Mary and made her the patroness of the country. Pageants, parades, and rejoicing marked their annual celebration of the Assumption. Delegates from all parts of the country brought gifts from their harvest to Budapest. In Poland, a similar presentation included bringing *wieniec*, or harvest wreaths, to the president in Warsaw. In France, a traditional play was performed, in which a flowery platform with figures of angels was lowered within the church to a flower-covered sepulchre and was raised with a statue of the Virgin, while boys dressed as angels played and the people sang Marian hymns. In Austria on this day, the people processed through the fields led by the priest, who asked God's blessing on the harvest. Processions in honor of the day were held in most of central Europe, France, Spain, Italy, and in South America.

In the Italian procession, a statue of Mary was carried through the streets of the town until it was met by a statue of Christ. Three times, the images were inclined toward each other as if bowing, then the Christ statue conducted his mother back to the parish church for benediction. The procession is called *Candelieri* in Sardinia, because huge wax candles are carried through the streets to her shrine fulfilling a promise made in 1580, when a deadly plague was stopped on August 15 after prayers to the Virgin.

Herbs picked in August were said to have particular healing power. In Central Europe during the Middle Ages, the Church elevated a popular belief of pre-Christian times and made it a Christian rite with deep meaning by holding the "Blessing of Herbs" on Assumption Day. This practice remained in effect until recent reforms. The Eastern Rites had similar blessings. The Syrians even celebrated a special feast of Our Lady of Herbs on May 15.

The Armenians brought the first grapes to church on Assumption Day to have them blessed. The Sicilians kept a partial abstinence from fruit during the first two weeks of August, then on the feast day had all kinds of fruit blessed in church to be served at dinner. Baskets of fruit were a customary gift for the feast of the Assumption. In the German sections of Europe, the time from August 15 to September 15 was called "Our Lady's Thirty Days," and many of the medieval shrines show the statue of Mary clad in a robe covered with grain.

Annunciation of the Death of the Virgin — *Fra Filippo Lippi*

Another old and inspiring custom on the Assumption was the blessing of the elements of nature as the source of human food. In many parts of Europe, the priests blessed the fields, orchards, and farms on that day. In the French Alps, the priest rode from pasture to pasture with an acolyte sitting behind him holding the holy water. At each meadow, the priest blessed the animals, which were gathered around a large cross decorated with flowers. In the Latin countries, especially Portugal, the ocean and the boats of the fishermen were blessed. This custom is popular today in the United States in a number of coastal towns (Weiser, 1958, pp. 290-292).

*****

God, almighty and eternal, you took the Immaculate Virgin Mary body and soul to be with you in glory. Through her intercession, grant that we may always strive for heavenly things so that one day we, too, may merit a share in her glory.

The Perpetual Rosary for the Dead

The perpetual rosary for the dead was initiated by the Dominicans Petronis Martini (Bologna) and Timothy Ricci (Florence) in the seventeenth century. The records of the Perpetual Rosary at the Dominican Basilica in Krakow, Poland, date from 1902. The members of this rosary community pray the entire Rosary at a specifically set hour of the day or night, once a month or once a year.

The joyful mysteries of the rosary are prayed for the conversion of sinners. The sorrowful mysteries are prayed asking succor for the dying. The glorious mysteries are prayed in aid of the souls in purgatory.

Membership in this rosary fraternity is worldwide. Members are asked to attempt to receive the sacrament of reconciliation and the Eucharist on their chosen day of prayer.

Chapter Five

Reflections on Our Sister Death

Death Be Not Proud
(Holy Sonnets, Sonnet #10)

Death be not proud, though some have called thee
Mighty and dreadful, for thou art not so;
For those whom thou think'st thou dost overthrow
Die not, poor Death, nor yet canst though kill me.
From rest and sleep, which but thy pictures be,
Much pleasure; then from thee much more must flow.
And soonest our best men with thee do go,
Rest of their bones, and soul's delivery.
Thou art slave to fate, chance, kings, and desperate men.
And dost with poison, war, and sickness dwell,
And poppy or charms can make us sleep as well
And better than thy stroke; why swell'st thou then?
One short sleep past, we wake eternally,
And death shall be no more; Death, thou shalt die.

John Donne, 1572-1631

A member of a prosperous Catholic family, as an adult the English poet Donne converted to the established Anglican Church and became Dean of St. Paul's Cathedral. He was in line for a bishopric when he died. During his later years, Donne became obsessed with thoughts of death. It is said that he preached his own funeral oration several weeks before his death. He posed, wrapped in a shroud, for the effigy on his own tomb.

On the Death of the Nun Bernadette

October 31, in preparation for the great feast
That celebrates all the saints,
The soul of Bernadette flew home.
I can imagine it now —
In great expectation
Of the grand celebration
She smiles as she greets
With great joy, the crowd.
Home, and just in time.
A joyful daughter
Of a Church that preaches joy,
And love, and
Foreverness.
Home, and yet still here,
In accord with the promises of Christ.
For dying, He destroyed our death.
Her presence remains forever
In God and in us.
     — A.B.

If You Love Me, Do Not Weep

"Thou hast made us, O Lord, for Thee, and our heart is unquiet until it rests in Thee." With these words, Aurelius Augustinus began his *Confessions*, the most honest and impressive autobiography in the literature of the world. Born in 354 in what is modern-day Algeria, Augustine had an ambitious, unbridled youth. He had no peace of soul and vainly sought it in the heretical sect of the Manicheans. He traveled to Italy, where he taught rhetoric. In 386, by the grace of God, the tearful prayers of his holy mother St. Monica, and the influence of saintly friends, he was converted. He was baptized, along with his son, by St. Ambrose. He devoted himself entirely to God. In 391 he was consecrated priest and in 394 bishop in Hippo. Today, St. Augustine is known as one of the greatest of the Doctors of the Church.

After his baptism, Augustine and his mother set out to return to Africa. In his writings, he records that at the port city of Ostia on the Tiber, he and his mother joined in a moving conversation on the everlasting life of the blessed. Five days later she fell ill and died there.

These words from the soul of St. Monica to her son are among the most beautiful passages in all literature:

> If you love me, do not weep. If you only knew the gift of God and what Heaven is! If only you could hear the angels' song from where you are, and see me among them! If you could only see before your eyes the eternal fields with their horizons, and the new paths in which I walk! If only you could contemplate for one moment the Beauty that I see, Beauty before which all others fail and fade!
>
> Why do you who saw me and loved me in the land of shadows, why do you think you will not see me and love me again in the land of unchanging realities?
>
> Believe me, when death breaks your chains as it has broken mine, when, on the day chosen by God, your soul reaches Heaven where I have preceded you, then you will see her who loved and still loves you. You will find her heart the same, her tenderness even purer than before.
>
> God forbid that on entering a happier life, I should become less loving, unfaithful to the memories and real joys of my other life. You will see me again transfigured in ecstasy and happiness, no longer waiting for death, but ever hand in hand with you, walking in the new paths of light and life, slaking my thirst to the full at the feet of God from a fount of which one never tires, and which you will come to share with me.
>
> Wipe away your tears, and if you love me truly, weep no more.

The Colors of Death

> Strange and lovely are the colors
> that death sometimes wears —
> the maple's flaming leaves —
> the gold of straw
> that bore the grain —
> all gossamer the silkworm's tomb
> and fiery red the coal
> the ashes claim —

> this is life reaching out to life
> through death —
> this is life's final
> and most joyful — yes.
>> — courtesy of Sister Julia Hurley, R.S.C.J.

The Death of St. Francis

Francesco Bernardone (c. 1181-1226) was the son of a wealthy merchant draper, who as a young man led a frivolous and carefree life. One day in the church of San Damiano, when he was about twenty years of age, he seemed to hear an image of Christ say to him, "Francis, repair my falling house."

Francis became a man of tremendous spiritual insight and power, and his consuming love for Jesus Christ and redeemed creation found expression in all he said and did. In 1210, Francis and eleven companions were authorized by Pope Innocent III to be roving preachers of Christ, in simplicity, lowliness, and poverty. This was the beginning of the Friars Minor, the first of the large Franciscan family of religious. In 1212, with St. Clare, he established the first community of Poor Ladies. He wanted his friars to be identified by their following of Christ in poverty. To all Christians he gave the vision of a life lived wholly in the power and spirit of the cross. With the courage and simplicity to take the words of Jesus literally, Francis and his followers displayed an all-embracing love and a joyful enthusiasm for God and for all creation.

Two years before his death, the *Poverello*, as he was called, received the sacred stigmata, the marks of the wounds of Christ. From that time, his health failed and he suffered intensely from a number of ailments, including dropsy and partial blindness. Undoubtedly, the remedies practiced by the medieval doctors added to his suffering. In an attempt to cure his blindness, the doctors took an iron rod, heated it red hot in the fire, and drew it across his forehead. By making a wound near the eyes, they thought the fever might be drawn away from them. At last, the physicians ruled his illnesses incurable.

Blessed Francis talked with the doctor, who admitted that there was nothing further to be done, and gave his opinion that Francis had very little time to live. Then Francis, lying on his bed, spread his hands out to the Lord with very great devotion and reverence, and said with great joy of mind and body, "Welcome, my Sister Death." Then he asked his brothers to sing to him the song he had made in praise of all things. Before the last verse of the Canticle, he added some verses of Sister Death.

At the time of his illness, Francis was visiting with the old bishop in Assisi. Francis seemed to hear a little silver voice within that confirmed the physician's words, so he begged his brothers to carry him to the Portiuncula, the house he loved where his work on earth had begun. As he left the city, he paused to bless it, asking Christ to allow Assisi to forever be a beacon and an example to all Christians as a city where Christ is known and glorified.

Keeping faith with Lady Poverty, even unto death, Francis died in a habit loaned to him by one of the brethren. As he lay on his bed, the brothers gathered 'round and he took each one by the hand and said goodbye, blessing them tenderly. When they asked what they could do for him, he asked them to sing again and again the song he loved best. All day he lay smiling and listening; when evening came he begged for a few bites of food.

After he had eaten, Francis asked the brothers to read to him from the Bible. As the brothers read, Francis lay gazing upward, still smiling happily. Suddenly he rose up on his bed, stretched his thin hands out and in a voice quivering with joy he cried, "Welcome, welcome, Sister Death."

Weeping, the brothers gathered about the bed in the little room. Suddenly one of the brothers saw a soft light hovering over the bed, shining like the sun glistening on water. It lingered awhile, then faded slowly away. At the hour of his passing, the larks — birds that love the light and dread the shades of twilight — flocked in great numbers onto the roof of the house, even though night was descending, and wheeling about it for a long while, sang even more joyously than customarily, to offer their witness to the saint who so often called them unto the divine praises.

The brothers carried Francis to the house of Clare and the sisters so they could see their loved friend again and touch the marks on his hands and feet. Although they wept, they knew he was happy and would not have asked him to return.

So ended the earthly life of one whose whole heart was full of love. Even though he had passed from their sight, the brothers and sisters often felt he was near them. When life was hard, they seemed to hear his voice exhorting them to bravery.

The Song of Brother Sun
(In praise of created things)

Most High, Omnipotent, Good Lord.
Thine be the praise, the glory, the honour, and all benediction.
To Thee alone, Most High, they are due,
and no many is worthy to mention Thee.
Be Thou praised, my Lord, with all Thy creatures, above all
    Brother sun,
who gives the day and lightens us therewith.
And he is beautiful and radiant with great splendour,
of Thee, Most High, he bears similitude.
Be Thou praised, my Lord, of Sister Moon and the stars,
in the heaven hast Thou formed them, clear and precious and
    comely.
Be Thou praised, my Lord, of Brother Wind,
and of the air, and the cloud, and of fair and of all weather,
by the which Thou givest to Thy creatures sustenance.
Be Thou praised, my Lord, of Sister Water,
which is much useful and humble and precious and pure.
Be Thou praised, my Lord, of Brother Fire,
by which Thou hast lightened the night,
and he is beautiful and joyful and robust and strong.
Be Thou praised, my Lord, of our Sister Mother Earth,
which sustains and hath us in rule.
and produces divers fruits with coloured flowers and herbs.
Be Thou praised, my Lord, of those who pardon for Thy love
    and endure sickness and tribulations.
Blessed are they who will endure it in peace,
for by Thee, Most High, they shall be crowned.
Be Thou praised, my Lord, of our Sister Bodily Death,
from whom no man living may escape.
woe to those who die in mortal sin:
Blessed are they who are found in Thy most holy will,
for the second death shall not work them ill.
Praise ye and bless my Lord, and give Him thanks,
and serve Him with great humility.
    — St. Francis of Assisi

Customs of the Religious Orders

Most of the religious orders in the church have their own special customs regarding death and dying that are celebrated by its members. There are many beautiful, traditional services and prayers. Only a few examples are mentioned here.

Sisters of Providence, St. Mary-of-the-Woods

The Sisters of Providence of St. Mary-of-the-Woods, Indiana, trace the origins of their community to France. In 1840, Mother Theodore Guerin and a sturdy group of five Sisters of Providence came, at the request of the Bishop of Vincennes, to begin a new congregation in Indiana. In spite of the hardships of frontier life, the order grew and prospered. The archives of the community contain many beautiful prayers and customs surrounding the death of their members.

The rule of the sisters sets certain suffrages for each of the members and for their parents. Guidelines were given as to how to prepare the dying sister to face her final struggle. After death, sisters stayed with the body, replacing one another at hourly intervals during the entire night, and reciting the rosary for the deceased.

In the early days of the order, when a sister died her body was placed in an armchair with her feet resting on a high stool. Flowers were placed at her feet. When the body was placed in the coffin, the formula of the dead sister's vows and her crucifix or rosary was put in her hands. At the funeral and burial, the coffin was preceded by a group of sisters carrying lighted candles.

From the beginning of the founding of the community in America, on the eve of the Feast of the Holy Souls, the sisters held a beautiful candlelight procession on the grounds of the motherhouse. Singing hymns, the sisters processed from the chapel to the community cemetery. After 1972, the outdoor procession was discontinued, but the service continued to be held on that day in the Church of the Immaculate Conception, with private visits to the cemetery encouraged.

The Passionists

Under the original constitutions of the Passionists, the brethren and nuns of the order, at their death, were placed on a plain board on the floor. The head was sprinkled with blessed ashes and a crucifix was placed in the hands. Burial was within the monastery. Today the order follows the civil laws and customs of the area of the monastery, usually with embalming, a casket, and the concrete box. Deceased members are still buried in their habit with the Passionist sign or emblem and with a crucifix in their hands.

Brothers of the Christian Schools

The Brothers of the Christian Schools have the custom of writing down the life of each Brother after his death. Originally, these short biographies were sent to the motherhouse in Europe, where they were translated into the official language of the Institute — French — and published four times a year in a series of books entitled *Notices Necrologiques*. Today, the biographies are retained by the province where the Brother lived and kept with the provincial archives.

The Christian Brothers and the Order of St. Dominic

The Rule of the Christian Brothers reads, "The Brothers remember faithfully their deceased Brothers, especially those whom they have known and loved. The prayers and suffrages they offer for them show that there is a communion between those still on their journey and those already resting in the peace of Christ."

The Order of St. Dominic, following the example of their saintly founder, professes and practices a special devotion to the souls in purgatory. Many people were attracted to join the Dominican Third Order, in part because of the order's many suffrages and prayers for the dead. Among other suffrages, the *De Profundis* (Psalm 129) is recited daily. The cloistered Dominican nuns of Lufkin, Texas, recite the psalm after Compline, the night prayer that prepares one for sleep and the ultimate sleep of death. The melodious chant is accompanied by the tolling of the bell of the monastery.

Mystical Death

Mystical death was part of the core charism of the great mystic and founder of the Passionist Order, St. Paul of the Cross. For him, the mystical death was a death more precious than life, which demanded a great response in the soul. He felt the life of the true servant of God is to die every day; to die to self in order to live for God. He charged the members of his community to desire to die to all else for the love of God only. In the soul which is mystically dead, the divine nativity operates at every moment and the person can bear within one's self a new life of love — a deified life in the bosom of God. He urged them to be crucified with Christ for the sake of a holy union with Jesus, to die with Jesus crucified only to rise with Jesus triumphant.

Sisters for the Dying

Rose Hawthorne Lathrop, the daughter of author Nathaniel Hawthorne, founded a community of nuns, the Hawthorne Dominicans, who dedicate their lives to the care of dying cancer patients. A convert to Catholicism, Rose first encountered the suffering of death by cancer when she visited her friend, the poet Emma Lazarus. A wealthy young woman, Emma died painfully but in good care.

Rose began to wonder what happened to the poor who were afflicted with the dreadful disease. She found that less-fortunate cancer patients were often shunned, as cancer was then widely believed to be contagious. She wrote, "I set my whole being to endeavor to bring consolation to the cancerous poor." Her sisters in religion follow her footsteps even today at seven facilities around the United States.

Prayer, Mass, and Purgatorial Societies

Many orders, especially the cloistered ones, have prayer, Mass, or purgatorial societies. Persons enrolled are remembered in the prayers and at the Masses of the community. Donations received for enrollments are used to support the monastery or, sometimes, mission priests or other works of the order.

Chapter Six

The Angels of Death

Alleluia, Alleluia. Holy Archangel Michael, defend us in battle, that we may not perish in the dreadful judgment. Alleluia (from the gradual of the Mass of the Dedication of St. Michael the Archangel).

St. Michael the Archangel

Michael ("like unto God") is one of the three archangels liturgically venerated by the church. From earliest centuries, tradition has assigned to him the role of protector of Christians against the devil, especially at the hour of death, when he conducts the soul to God.

From the beginning of Christian history, there is evidence for the honor in which Michael the Archangel was held. He was venerated by the Jews. The Hebrews believed that he was one of the angels that sustained the throne of God. He was also worshiped by the Chaldeans.

Michael repeatedly appears in the apocryphal literature, and was considered by the early church as the captain of the heavenly host. For this reason, he is generally represented in art in knight's armor, holding a sword or lance, and fighting with, or stepping on, a conquered dragon or devil.

The cult of St. Michael apparently originated in Phrygia, but it soon spread to the West. In the East, Michael was looked on as a special guardian of the sick. A church bearing his name stands outside Constantinople, dating from the time of Constantine.

A legend of the fifth century holds that during the pontificate of Pope Gelasius, St. Michael appeared to indicate the spot on Mt.

Garganus where a shrine was to be built in his honor. A spring uncovered at this site became famous for miraculous cures and lent credence to his cult. All over Christendom, chapels in Michael's honor were built on the tops of hills and mountains.

During the twelfth and thirteenth centuries, Christian thought turned more and more to the Last Judgment. In the iconography of this time, Michael was charged with weighing the souls of the dead, and he is often depicted carrying a balance scales. The standard-bearing archangel became the patron saint of the dead. People prayed to him that he might usher them "into the light" (Aries, p. 103). Images of St. Michael enclosed in small protective icons meant to be worn on the breast were popular in the Slavic countries.

A number of ancient artistic representations of St. Michael show him as Lord of Souls. In some votive pictures he appears as the protector of those who have struggled with evil and gained a victory. In these pictures, he has his foot upon the dragon, or holds a dragon's head in his hand, and bears the banner of victory.

Represented with his scales, Michael is engaged in weighing the souls of the dead. In these pictures, he is usually unarmed and bears a scepter ending in a cross. The souls are shown as little, naked, human figures. The good souls generally kneel in the scales with hands clasped in prayer, while the rejected souls express horror and agony. Sometimes a figure of a demon, impatient for his prey, reaches out his talons or his devil's fork to seize the doomed spirits.

Leonardo da Vinci painted the angel presenting his balance to the Infant Jesus, who seems to be blessing the pious souls in the upper scale. The artist Signorelli painted this subject about 1500, in which the archangel in a suit of mail stands with the balance held above a fierce dragon. The archangel's lance has pierced the under-jaw of the beast and a hideous little demon resting on the tiny black wings of the dragon is clutching the condemned spirits in the lower scale.

St. Michael is often charged with the task of carrying the spirits of the just to heaven. The legend of St. Catherine of Alexandria tells that her body was borne by angels over the desert to the top of Mount Sinai, where it was buried. St. Michael is usually shown as one of the four celestial bearers of the martyr saint (Clement, pp. 68-73).

St. Michael is sometimes pictured in paintings of the Assumption or Glorification of the Virgin. This is from the legends of the

Madonna that teach that Michael received her spirit and guarded it until it was again united with her sinless form.

One of the legends of the Virgin Mary tells that it was St. Michael who announced to her the time of her death. The pictures of this announcement bear a strong resemblance to those of the Annunciation, except that these have the symbols of a palm on a lighted taper in the hand of the angel, instead of the lily of the Archangel Gabriel.

The legend tells that on a certain day the heart of Mary was filled with a great longing to see her Son and she was weeping sorely, when an angel clothed in light appeared before her, saying, "Hail, O Mary, blessed by Him who has given salvation to Israel. I bring thee here a branch of palm gathered in paradise; command that it be carried before they bier in the day of thy death; for in three days thy soul shall leave thy body, and thou shalt enter into paradise where thy Son awaits thy coming." Mary then asked his name and requested that he reunite the apostles with her so that she could give up her soul to God in their presence. She also asked that after death her soul might not be frightened by any spirit of darkness and that no evil angel be given power over her. In Michael's reply, he assured her that she should not fear the evil spirit because "thou hast bruised his head and destroyed his kingdom" (Clement, pp. 81-83).

Michaelmas day, September 29, was celebrated as a feast in his honor from the sixth century. In 1970, the feast was combined with feasts of St. Raphael and St. Gabriel and is still celebrated on that day.

The great archangel is not only protector of the Christians on earth, but of those in purgatory as well. After assisting the dying, he accompanies the souls to purgatory and afterward presents them to God at their entrance into heaven. Thus, he is the actual patron of the holy souls. This patronage was expressed in the offertory prayer of the former Requiem Masses.

Michael's patronage of the holy souls is also the reason that many cemetery chapels are dedicated to him. In past centuries, a Mass was offered weekly in honor of St. Michael and in favor of the departed ones in these mortuary chapels (Weiser, 1956, p. 190).

A contemporary song, "Michael Row the Boat Ashore," is possibly of American Negro folk origin. The song seems to incorporate a reminiscence of the old tradition of Michael as the receiver of the souls of the dead (Attwater, p. 245).

Just as Michael received and escorts the souls of the dead, tradition assigns St. Gabriel the Archangel the task of announcing the arrival of the souls in heaven.

Mourning Angels

Mourning angels appear more frequently in sculpture than in painting, and are much used as monuments to the dead. There are, however, pictures in which angels show their sympathy with sorrow and suffering. Angels cannot, by their nature, be unhappy, but they are not represented as joyful in pictures of the crucifixion and other sorrowful scenes in the lives of Christ, the Virgin, or saintly martyrs. They are shown hiding their faces, wringing their hands, and manifesting their grief in various ways. One famous representation shows a mourning angel kneeling before a crown of thorns with tears upon his face (Clement, pp. 151-152).

In cemetery art, angels are traditionally among the most popular motifs.

The cherubim represented as chubby infants without bodies and with two wings date from the Renaissance. This conception differs radically from the Bible's description in the vision of Ezekiel of having four wings and being "full of eyes." The cherubim are commonly found on the gravestones of babies and children.

Other than the representations of St. Michael, in cemetery art the angels are most often represented as women. These messengers and attendants of God serve as watch wardens of the sleeping bodies and are found in many poses as they grace gravestones and tombs (Bowen).

Dona Sebastiana

Carved images of a death angel known as Dona Sebastiana or *Nuestra Comadre Sebastiana* (Our Godmother Sebastiana) are still commonly seen in the folk art of the southwestern United States. Often seated in her death cart, a rude representation of a New Mexican ox cart, she serves as a vivid *memento mori*, a startling reminder of the mortality of man.

The figures of *La Muerte* (Death) were used in some of the rituals of the brotherhood known as *Los Hermanos Penitentes* (The

Penitent Brothers), a lay religious organization in the southwestern United States, primarily northern New Mexico and southern Colorado. The brotherhoods were originally organized for pious observances involving the expiation of sin through prayer and bodily penance, and for mutual aid. They became a conservative cultural force, preserving language, lore, customs and faith, especially in poorer rural and urban areas of predominantly Hispanic population. In some places, they acquired much political influence. Most of the fraternities evolved into a secretive religious society of restricted membership (Weigle, 1970, p. 3).

In the harsh frontier areas, which often had a scarcity of priests, the lay Brothers of Our Father Jesus organized public worship and provided an opportunity for the devout to practice a salutary asceticism. In this way, faithful Roman Catholics could better prepare for, and confront, death. Death was in no sense sought or worshiped, but a good death, a "*buena muerte* — one in the state of grace leading to entrance into heaven," was profoundly desired. In Hispanic eschatology, to pass away is to go on to a better life and fulfill one's destiny. There is a strong communion between the departed and the living. Philosophical about death, they do not invite it but are not afraid of it. *¡Sea por Dios!* (God's will be done) is the expression used to comment upon the passing of a loved one (Weigle, 1977, pp. 144-145).

Today's Dona Sebastiana is possibly the New World remnant of the Renaissance theme of the Triumph of Death. In the fourteenth century, Petrarch wrote the epic poem "*Trionfi*," in which the Death Angel was female. The influence of his poem on the arts was enormous. The "Triumph of Death" during the darkest moments of the work of salvation even served as a theme for processions.

In 1511 in Florence, one such pageant took place. The painter Piero was often called on to assist in arranging the carnival procession. He prepared the spectacle — the "Triumph of Death" — in the Hall of the Pope, with so much secrecy that his complete work was only made known at the time it was shown. The Triumphal Car was covered with black cloth and was vast in size. It had skeletons and white crosses painted on its surface and was pulled by black buffaloes. In the car stood the colossal figure of Death, bearing the scythe in his hand, while around him were covered tombs which opened at all the places where the procession halted. As the members of the procession sang lugubrious songs, certain figures clothed in black cloth, on which had been painted the gleaming white bones of a skeleton, stole forth. A wailing summons sent forth with a hollow moan from muffled trumpets called the figures of the dead from the tombs. Accompanied by plaintive and melancholy music, these skeletal figures sang "*Dolor, pianto, e penetenzia*" (suffering, tears and penance).

The medieval outlook upon the vanity of earthly things as expressed in Petrarch's "*Trionfi*" exerted great influence on the Spanish writers from the fifteenth century on. Many new triumphs in both literature and pageantry were created, based on the great Italian models. In the sixteenth century, it even served as a motif for a play in which the triumphant Death appears on the stage riding in a cart drawn by Abraham, Absalom, Alexander, and Hercules. In the play, the lines Death has to speak recall strongly the medieval dance macabre. Eventually, the Triumph of Death became detached from the rest of the "*Trionfi*" and passed through stages to become, in a greatly simplified form, part of the Easter ritual in the American Southwest (Wilder, plates 30-31).

As early as 1582, the Death Cart was an integral part of the procession of the Descent and Burial of Christ, signifying His victory over death. These Holy Week processions included the figure of Death in her cart. The processions were popular for centuries in Spain and traveled to the New World where they were practiced all over colonial Mexico before traveling north into the American Southwest. A 1767 inventory of the altar of the confraternity of Blessed Souls in the parish church at *Real de Rosario* (Sinaloa) mentioned a figure of Death stored with the other items used in the Holy Week processions.

Later descriptions of the use of the Death Cart in the United States are from the late nineteenth century, and indicate that its use by the *Penitentes* was as a reminder of the evanescence of life and as a penitential devotion (Wroth, p. 47). As a penitential devotion, one of the brotherhood would drag the *Carreta de la Muerte* (Death Cart) in a literal enactment of man's struggle against death. In addition to the figure of Dona Sebastiana, the cart also contained heavy stones to intensify the penance of dragging the cart (Weigle, 1970, p. 42).

Smaller death figures, or death angels, were also used in *Penitente* rituals. These figures have an iconic quality and seem closely related to the *memento mori,* such as the human skulls traditionally used by ascetics and formerly used by the *Penitente* brotherhoods. These smaller figures were carried by women and children in the Holy Week processions.

The carved wooden skeletons known as Dona Sebastiana are often dressed in black shawls and clothes to resemble an aged woman. They generally carry a bow and arrow or a wooden hatchet. The bow and arrow and the name Sebastiana apparently refer to St. Sebastian, who was martyred by being shot with arrows. Her name is possibly a case of New World iconographic confusion, wherein the arrows of St. Sebastian and the arrow of the Death Angel have become associated.

During *Penitente* rituals, *alabados* were sung. Most of these *alabados* are considered Spanish folk poetry, and they can be found in variant forms throughout the Spanish-speaking world. A number of these *alabados* honor the dead and are often sung at wakes. They are usually sung without accompaniment by a *cantador* or recognized singer of the town. The sight of Dona Sebastiana being pulled along in her ox cart and accompanied by an *alabado* is sometimes upsetting to Anglo-Americans who are unused to the Spanish penitential nature.

A tradition in the family of *santero* Jose Dolores Lopez holds that Lopez' father made the first New Mexican Dona Sebastiana around 1860, and no previous examples have been located to date (Steele, p. 130). Even today, New Mexican *santeros* (religious wood carvers) find much inspiration in the personification of Lady Death.

One contemporary Hispanic artist and *santero* is Louis Tapia of Santa Fe, New Mexico. His artwork blends tradition with contemporary culture, and through it the tradition continues to grow and flourish. His carvings display a gentle sense of humor that set a traditional *bulto* apart from the typical forms of Spanish Colonial art of New Mexico. Experienced art patrons and novices alike find a subtle draw to the soul expressed through Tapia's art.

"*Carreta de La Muerte*," one of Tapia's 1991 pieces, displays Dona Sebastiana being pulled in her cart by a skeletal ox across a painted vision of purgatory. Her posture indicates a hearty sense of laughter. Instead of her traditional weapon, she carries a skeletal parasol. Normally a defense against weather, this parasol, like its owner, has lost its skin. Even death has no protection and ultimately, having lost its sting, death waits for death, and life, through the Resurrection, triumphs.

Both in European and New World usage, the personifications of death have two distinct but related aspects. Since the Middle Ages, they have served as a reminder of the mortality of man, an inspiration to the faithful not to attach themselves to the things of this world but to prepare for the inevitability of death by a pious, prayerful, repentant life. The other aspect emphasizes the final superiority of Jesus Christ over death. Christ's victory over death is the triumph of his eternal and all-powerful divine nature.

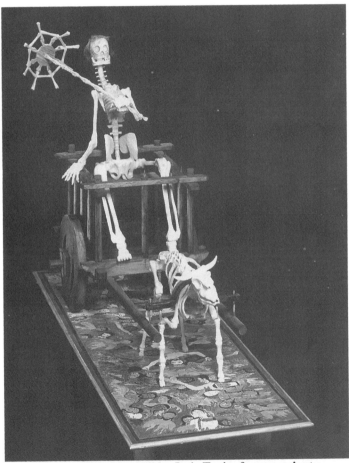

"*Carreta de la Muerte*" by Luis Tapia, from a private collection, Owings Dewey Fine Art, Santa Fe, NM.

Chapter Seven

The Church Suffering

T he Catholic Church believes that the faithful on earth are in communion both with the saints in heaven and with the souls in purgatory through prayer. The prayers and good works of the faithful help the souls in purgatory to gain their release.

The *Dies Irae* — The Day of Wrath

The *Dies Irae* is a famous poem written by a thirteenth-century Franciscan. It has often been ascribed to Thomas of Celano (1260), the friend and biographer of St. Francis of Assisi, although the authorship is not certain (Weiser, 1956, p. 126).

Formerly, the *Dies Irae* was used as the sequence of the Requiem Mass. The poem has been translated into many languages and has been set to music by some of the greatest composers of all times.

Dies Irae

That day of wrath, that dreadful day,
Shall heaven and earth in ashes lay,
As David and the Sybil say.
What horror must invade the mind
When the approaching Judge shall find
And sift the deeds of all mankind!
The mighty trumpet's wondrous tone
Shall rend each tomb's sepulchral stone
And summon all before the Throne.
Now death and nature with surprise
Behold the trembling sinners rise
To meet the Judge's searching eyes.

Then shall with universal dread
The Book of Consciences be read
To judge the lives of all the dead.
For now before the Judge severe
All hidden things must plain appear;
No crime can pass unpunished here.
Oh what shall I, so guilty, plead?
And who for me will intercede?
When even Saints shall comfort need?
O King of dreadful majesty!
Grace and mercy You grant free;
As Fount of Kindness, save me!
Recall, dear Jesus, for my sake
You did our suffering nature take.
Then do not now my soul forsake!
In weariness You sought for me,
And suffering upon the tree!
Let not in vain such labor be.
O Judge of justice, hear, I pray,
For pity take my sins away
Before the dreadful reckoning day.
Your gracious face, O Lord, I seek;
Deep shame and grief are on my cheek;
In sighs and tears my sorrows speak.
You Who did Mary's guilt unbind,
And mercy for the robber find,
Have filled with hope my anxious mind.
How worthless are my prayers, I know.
Yet, Lord, forbid that I should go
Into the fires of endless woe.
Divorced from the accursed band,
O make me with Your sheep to stand,
A child of grace, at Your right Hand.
When the doomed no more can flee
From the flames of misery
With the chosen call me.
Before You, humbled, Lord, I lie,
My heart like ashes, crushed and dry,
Assist me when I die.

Full of tears and full of dread
Is that day that wakes the dead.
Calling all, with solemn blast
To be judged for all their past.
Lord have mercy, Jesus blest,
Grant them all Your Light and Rest.
Amen.

All Souls' Day

All Souls' Day, a memorial feast commemorating all the souls of the faithful departed in a common celebration, was first begun by St. Odilo, Abbot of Cluny, in 998. He ordered that all the monasteries of the congregation of Cluny were to annually celebrate November 2 as a "day of all the departed ones" (*Omnium Defunctorum*). After vespers on November 1, the bell was tolled and the Office of the Dead was recited; on the next day, all priests of the monasteries were to say Mass for the repose of the souls in purgatory.

What was begun by the Benedictines of Cluny was soon followed by other Benedictines and the Carthusians. In 1003, Pope Sylvester II approved the practice and recommended it. It was some time, however, before the secular clergy introduced it as a common practice. From the eleventh to the fourteenth centuries, the feast gradually spread throughout Europe. Finally, in the fourteenth century, it was officially placed on the books for the Western Church.

The date was selected in order that the memory of all the souls, both of the saints in heaven and of those souls in purgatory, could be celebrated on two successive days. This would more clearly express the Christian belief in the communion of saints.

In the Greek Rite, the commemoration of all the faithful departed was called *Psychosabbaton*, or Saturday of the Souls, and it was held on the Saturday before *Sexagesima* Sunday. The Armenian celebration was on Easter Monday with the solemn Office of the Dead, although the Mass was that of the Resurrection. The Syrian-Antiochene Rite celebrated on three separate Fridays. The first celebration commemorated all departed priests; the second commemorated all the faithful departed; and the third was in honor of all those who died in strange places, away from their parents and friends.

In 1915, Pope Benedict XV allowed all priests to say three Masses on All Souls' Day in order to give increased help to the suffering souls in purgatory. Even today in many places the graves in the cemeteries are blessed on All Souls' Day, and solemn services are often held in parish churches (Weiser, 1958, pp. 124-125).

Customs of All Souls' Day

Numerous ancient customs have been associated both with All Saints' and with All Souls' Days.

A practice common to all Catholic countries is that of visiting the cemeteries, praying there, and decorating the graves. Sometimes the priest may lead his congregation in procession to the cemetery. Prayers for all the holy souls are recited and the priest blesses the graves with holy water.

In many places, candles are placed around the graves or at the foot of the markers, lighted on All Saints' eve, and left burning through the night. These are called "lights of the holy souls."

In central Europe, church bells are rung at the approach of dusk on All Saints' Day to remindthe people to pray for the souls in purgatory. When the bells are heard, the families gather and extinguish all lights except the blessed candle saved from Candlemas. They pray the rosary for the holy souls (Weiser, 1956, p. 127).

In the rural countryside of Brittany, eight men had appointed tasks for the evening of All Souls' Day. Four took turns tolling the church bell for an hour after dark fell. Four others traveled from farm to farm during the night, ringing hand hells, and chanting, "Christians awake, pray to God for the souls of the dead, and say the *Pater* and *Ave* for them." From the farmhouses, the people replied "Amen" as they awoke and rose for prayer (Weiser, 1956, p. 128).

All Souls' Day was traditionally kept as a public holiday in most of the South American countries. In Brazil, the cemeteries were full of silent, kneeling people, praying. In Puerto Rico, people dressed in their best clohes and carried vases of flowers to the cemetery. The priest visited each grave, saying the prayers for the dead, accompanied by all his parishioners.

In the Philippines, a novena is held before November 2. Each night, the people go to the cemetery to pray by candlelight. During these nine days, the people also clean the cemetery, plant flowers, remove weeds, trim the hedges, and repaint the tomb niches and crosses. On the evening of All Saints' Day, young men go from door to door, asking for gifts of cookies, candy, or pastry. They sing a traditional verse in which they represent holy souls liberated from purgatory which are on their way to heaven:

> If you will give us friendly alms,
> Please do not make us wait;
> We want to enter Heaven's door
> Before it is too late.

In Poland, and sometimes in the Polish churches of the United States, the faithful bring paper sheets with black borders called *Wypominki*, or "Naming," to the priest on All Souls' Day. The names of their beloved dead are written on the sheets. During the evening devotions in November and on Sundays, the names are read from the pulpit and prayers are offered for the repose of the souls.

Our pagan forefathers kept a number of "cult of the dead" rites at various times of the year. Some of their pre-Christian traditions became part of our Christian feast and associated with Christian ideas. For example, the pre-Christian practice of putting food at the graves or in homes during times when the spirits of the dead were believed to roam the earth. By offering token food to the spirits, the people hoped to please them and avert any harm they might do. From this practice came the custom of baking special breads in honor of the holy souls, and giving them to the children and to the poor. This custom remains widespread in Europe even today. All Souls' Bread (*Seelenbrot*) is made and distributed in most of the European and the Slavic countries.

In western Europe, people prepare a meal of cooked beans, peas, or lentils called "soul food," which is served to the poor, together with meat and other dishes. Polish farmers hold a meal with empty seats and plates ready for the "souls" of departed relatives. Portions are put on each of the plates and are not eaten by the family but afterward are given to beggars or poor neighbors. In the Alpine provinces of Austria, the poor went from house to house reciting a prayer or singing a hymn for the holy souls and receiving small loaves of "soul bread" in reward. The people also set aside a portion of all that is cooked on All Souls' Day and distribute these meals to the poor.

In northern Spain and in the Madrid area, the people distributed a special pastry called *Huesos de Santo*, "bones of the holy." In Catalonia All Souls' pastry was called *Panellets*, or "little breads."

Halottak Napja, the Day of the Dead, was kept in Hungary with the traditional customs common to all of central Europe. In addition, they invited orphan children into the family for All Saints' and All Souls' days, serving them generous meals and giving them new clothes and toys. Additionally, the Hungarian villagers take special care on the "forgotten" graves that otherwise would stay neglected and unadorned.

Day of the Dead is called *Jour des Morts* in Brittany. Here, the farmers visit the graves of their departed relatives, kneeling bare-headed, in long and fervent prayer. They sprinkle the grave with holy water and before leaving pour milk over the grave as a libation for the "holy souls." A large portion of the day's dinner is served before an empty seat and later given to the poor.

Many other customs of our pre-Christian ancestors have survived as superstitions today. In rural Poland, the people leave their doors and windows open on All Souls' Day to welcome the souls of their family dead. In Austria, there is a superstition that the holy souls wander the forests on All Souls' Day, sighing and praying for their release but unable to reach the living or indicate their presence. For this reason, children are told to pray aloud while going through the open spaces so the poor souls will have the great consolation of seeing that their invisible presence is known and that their pitiful cries for help are understood and answered (Weiser, 1956, pp. 126-134).

The town of Perugia, Italy, celebrates a festival that began in the Middle Ages, the Fair of the Dead. Vendors come from all over Italy to set up booths and sell everything from rolling pins and pasta machines to winter underwear. Food stands are everywhere selling confections known as *fave dei morti* (beans of the dead) or *ossi dei morti* (bones of the dead.) Vividly decorated sugar confections shaped like skulls are also sold. In Venice, this is a traditional day for couples to announce their engagement and an old custom has the suitor send his fiancee a box of *fave* cookies containing the engagement ring (Ball, 1993, p. 130).

At Naples, it was the custom on All Souls' Day to throw open the charnel-houses, which were lighted up with torches and decked with flowers, while crowds thronged through the vaults to visit the bodies of their friends and relatives. The fleshless skeletons were dressed in robes and arranged in niches along the walls (Knowles, 1993).

Although the Church has not established any season or octave for the feast, the faithful in Central Europe customarily devote the eight days after All Souls' to special prayer, penance, and acts of charity. This is called *Seelennachte*, or Soul Nights. Although Halloween's name is taken from a great Christian feast, Allhallows' Eve, it has nothing in common with the feast of All Saints' and is a tradition of pre-Christian times that has retained its original character in form and meaning (Weiser, 1956, p. 134).

In Mexico, and throughout Central America, the people celebrate *El Dia de los Muertos*, the Day of the Dead. This is a family feast to commemorate the dead and at the same time to celebrate life. On the morning of October 31, the souls of *los angelitos*, the little innocent ones, return. Their parents make altars in their homes for them and there the children will find their favorite sweets, toys, flowers, and candles. By noon on November 1, the souls of the children have left and the souls of the adults begin to arrive to find altars in their honor.

Chapter Eight tells about this custom in more detail.

Devotion to the Souls in Purgatory

From the time of the Council of Florence (1439), a great many churches in Catholic Europe held a side chapel consecrated to the souls in purgatory. In the New World, many churches followed this European custom and also included a side chapel for the holy souls (Lange, p. 67).

During the early Middle Ages, the common people and many theologians held the opinion that the souls in purgatory enjoyed a relief from their painful punishment every week from Saturday night until Monday morning in honor of the Lord's Day. It was not until St. Thomas Aquinas (1274) treated the problem in his masterful way, and disproved such opinions, that this claim was finally abandoned. While it lasted, however, popular piety inclined to help the holy souls in a special manner on Monday, since they were thought to return then from joy to suffering, and therefore, to need consolation and assistance more than at any other time. Without approving the popular belief, the Church facilitated this practice of prayer for the holy souls; hence the ancient rule that priests had to add a liturgical oration for the departed ones in their Masses on all "vacant" Mondays. This regulation was observed for many centuries until the provisional reform of the rubrics (1955) under Pius XII discontinued it. The same reform, however, made it possible for priests to say Requiem Masses more often than before (Weiser, 1958, p. 27).

The practice of spiritual and temporal works of charity and mercy, which had always been stressed by the Church in connection with Embertide fasting, produced the custom of devoting the Ember Days to special prayer for the suffering souls in purgatory and of having Masses said for them during the Embertides. Alms and food were given to the poor on Ember Days, and warm baths provided for them (Weiser, 1958, p. 36).

An ancient legend provided that many poor souls are allowed to leave purgatory for a few moments every Embertide to appear in visible shape to those relatives and friends who fervently pray for their departed ones, in order to thank them and to beg for continued prayerful help for themselves and for those holy souls who have nobody on earth to remember them. Today's laudable custom of praying for the "forgotten" souls in purgatory seems to be a happy relic of this medieval popular legend (Weiser, 1958, p. 37).

Graphic evidence for the depth and breadth of the devotion to the poor souls in the New World is found in Mexican tin painting. In *retablo* art, four main representations of Mary show her in hr role as intercessor for the Poor Souls. These are Our Lady of Mount Carmel, Our Lady of the Rosary, Our Lady of Light, and Our Lady, Refuge of Sinners (Lange, p. 67).

Early Franciscan missionaries brought their devotion to the *Arma Christi*, a dpiction of Christ Crucified surrounded by the instruments of the Passion. In Mexico, this takes on the name of *Cruz de Animas* (Cross of Souls), because half-figures of young females and bearded males with naked torsos have been lined up at the foot of the Cross to represent souls amidst the flames of purgatory. Often the painters of the *retablo* images added the name of the family and the names of all the deceased members of the family (Lange, p. 67).

The Augustinian St. Nicholas of Tolentino, patron of the dying and of the souls in purgatory, is also often depicted in the tin paintings.

Another popular devotion is that of the *Anima Sola*, or the Most Neglected Soul in Purgatory, who is depicted as a beautiful young woman with manacled hands, incarcerated in a grilled cell engulfed in flames (Lange, p. 67).

Novena for the Blessed Souls in Purgatory

A novena is a prayer extended over a period of nine days (or once a week for nine weeks) and is said for some special petition or occasion. Originally the novena was made for the repose of a deceased person. This meaning is still used for the novena of Masses said after the death of a pope. A novena may be carried on in church, but is usually a private devotion.

Novenas generally contain both prayers and reflections for meditation. Sometimes songs are included. A beautiful Spanish novena for the blessed souls in purgatory has, in addition to the pryers and reflections, *ejemplos*, or examples. These are historical vignettes from the lives of the saints and holy persons regarding the subject matter of the novena, in this case the suffering souls.

In this novena, the petitioner asks Christ's aid through the Precious Blood and the sorrows of Our Lady. He petitions for the grace to avoid sin and to persevere until death. He calls on the infinite kindness and mercy of God to console and to release suffering souls from purgatory.

Prayers and meditations in this devotion are directed to: Jesus sweating blood in the garden of Gethsemani, Jesus prisoner for our love, Jesus taken before the tribunal, Jesus mistreated and detained while Barabbas is released, Jesus whipped at the column, Jesus crowned with thorns, Jesus carrying the cross, and Jesus nailed to the cross. The final day, he prayers and meditations are in favor of the blessed souls liberated from purgatory by the prayers and suffrages offered during the novena.

The *ejemplos* for this novena include:

(1) A compassionate virgin named Christiana had a vision in which she was taken before God to contemplate the pains of purgatory. After she was shown the terrible sufferings of the souls, God gave her the choice to enter immediately into paradise or to return to earth to help the poor, suffering souls with her prayers. She ws so moved by the vision that without hesitation she opted to return to

earth in order to intercede for the souls of purgatory. She began a type of life so austere and strict that people began to criticize her. She responded that they only spoke that way because they ignored what happens in purgatory and that if they had shared her vision they, too, would do penance.

(2) Blessed John of Alvernia (1259-1322), of the Order of Minors, was accustomed to celebrating Holy Mass for the faithful departed on November 2 with so much fervor that he would appear to be completely consumed by continual grief. Once, at precisely the instant of the elevation, he directed to the Etenal Father a fervent prayer that through the merits of His Only Son, He would deign to free the holy souls from their pains. Blessed John then saw a vision where a great multitude of poor souls, like brilliant sparks that fly from a forge, were directed joyously to paradise.

(3) A father, being close to death, commissioned his son to remember to offer prayers and Masses for his soul. This the son faithfully did. Thirty-two years later, the son had a vision in which his father appeared to him completely surrounded by flames and lamenting bitterly about the lack of prayers for him. "How could you say such a thing," the son demanded. "I have commissioned Masses and prayers and I have personally fasted, prayed, and performed every type of good work on your behalf." Sadly the father replied, "My son, all the good you have done and are doing doesn't help me or you because you have done these things without love of God because you are constantly in a state of mortal sin. Your confessions were in vain because they were lacking in true sorrow and repentance. The goodness of God has sent me to you today to warn you, for your good and for mine." Having said this, the father disappeared. The son recognized his error, made a good confession, and began prayers and good works that eventually aided his father's soul and saved his own.

(4) Blessed Catherine Mattei (1486-1547), a virgin of the Third Order of St. Dominic, was sick in bed with a very high fever. She began to meditate on the flames of purgatory and the Lord took her in spirit to view them. Wishing to feel what the fire was really like, the Lord allowed a spark to touch her neck, which was contorted for some time afterward. Later, she testified that there is no suffering in the world that will compare with the pain of purgatory.

(5) A Dominican religious in the last days of his life begged a

priest friend of his to offer Mass upon his death. This the friend did without delay. After the Mass, while the priest was disrobing, the dead religious appeared to him in a vision, scolding him for leaving him in purgatory for thirty years. Startled, the priest pointed out that the religious had only died an hour before, and that his corpse was still warm. The deceased then said, "Learn from this how fierce is the fire of purgatory when only one hour seems to me like thirty years. Move yourself to pity and have mery on all the souls in purgatory."

(6) St. Malachy, Bishop of Ireland and the first canonized Irish saint (1095-1148), had a dream in which he saw his sister who was lamenting that, although on various occasions the Mass had been offered for her, she was still not at rest. The saint understood perfectly and began anew to offer Mass for the repose of her soul. Again she returned in his dreams, dressed in black at the door of the church. He continued to offer prayers and Masses for her and a later dream showed her in a lighter-colored dress inside the churc, but away from the altar. At last, in his dreams, he saw his sister in the company of other souls all dressed in brilliant white and near the altar. From this he understood that prayers and sacrifices had helped his sister complete what she owed God in purgatory.

(7) One reads in the life of the Venerable Mary d'Antigna that a deceased nun of her monastery appeared to her and requested that the nuns pray the devotion of the Stations of the Cross for her and for the other souls. Maria then heard the voice of Jesus in her heart saying that the prayer of the Way of the Cross is very helpful to the poor souls and requesting her to tell her sisters how much good they do with this devotion and the treasures they store up when they offer it for the holy souls of purgatory.

(8) A certain devotee of the Mother of God was accustomed to saying the litany of the Most Holy Virgin daily for the souls in purgatory. This man had enemies who swore to kill him. One day as he was resting, the enemies entered his house. Although they saw his clothes laying on the bed, God caused the pious man to become invisible to the eyes of his enemies. When the man awoke, he discovered the disorder in his house and guessed what had happened. Immediately he gave thanks to the Queen of Heaven for her intercession and for that of the poor souls.

(9) In the book of Tobit, one reads that this pious man often bur-

ied the dead, even the enemies of the Hebrews. Once he even got up from his dinner in order to do so. The Archangel Raphael was so grateful for this mercy of Tobias that he assisted his son and restored the old man's sight. Further, he gave Tobias to understand that his tearful prayers and his mercy in burying the dead pleased him so much that Raphael himself would present Tobias' prayers to God. This final *ejemplo* reminds Christians that all service in favor of the dead is most pleasing to the angels of God.

The novena ends with an *alabanza* (a chanted song/poem of praise) that extols the efficacy of the rosary said in favor of the Poor Souls.

Our Lady of Mt. Carmel with the Souls in Purgatory

An *Alabanza*

Leave, they leave, they leave
Souls of woe
Whose chains have been
  broken
By the Holy Rosary.
Look at them,
Consider
Those who will also come
To suffer these sad miseries!
Don't forget them there.
They are yearning
To allay their woe.
Be loving and tender.
With an Our Father
And a Hail Mary
They are given rest
In their agony.
Son, dear relatives
And Friends,
Father and Mother,
Have they forgotten us?
Hear their voices
Requesting
For love of God
That they be heard.
With sad laments
They are asking us
Relief from the miseries
Which they are suffering.
They ask us, brothers,
From the flames,
To aid them

By our sorrows.
Ask God, then,
To take us to Heaven,
That united together
We may sing to The Word.
Hear their cry.
See their agony.
The Holy Rosary
Pray to Mary.
With profound contentment
In their breasts
Today they ascend as friends
Of Mary in her heavenly
  reign.
They want to enjoy the vision
Of the True God
And sing His mercies there
Forever.
The souls cry out
That they are given rest by our
  prayers
Only on the Day of the Dead
  (All Souls' Day)
And for the rest of the year we
  forget them.
Leave, they leave, they leave
Souls of woe
Whose chains have been
  broken
By the Holy Rosary.
life, through the resurrection,
  triumphs.

Other Devotions

Many other devotions and customs connected with the Poor Souls, and with those in their last agony, are extant in the Church today. Many of the major devotions touch these subjects in some way. Only two are mentioned here.

Adoration of the Divine Face

Part of the Devotion to the Holy Face was brought to the world through a series of private revelations to Sister Marie of St. Peter, a discalced Carmelite nun of Tours, France. The devotion is one of reparation, and in one of her visions, Christ told Sister Marie that he would purify the souls at their death of those who defended His cause in this work of reparation.

Novena to the Divine Mercy

The Devotion to the Divine Mercy was strengthened in our own century through the private revelations to Blessed Sister Faustina Kowalska. Jesus instructed Sister Faustina to write down the novena and to bring souls to the fount of His mercy. He told her He would tell her which souls to bring each day into His Heart. On the eighth day, Jesus requested Sister Faustina to bring him the souls who are detained in purgatory.

Chapter Eight

The Church Triumphant

God, as we venerate all your saints in one celebration, we beg Thee to see them as our intercessors and grant to us an abundance of Thy mercy through their merits.

All Saints' Day

A commemoration in honor of all the martyrs was kept from earliest times at Antioch on the first Sunday after Pentecost. It was introduced to the West by Pope Boniface and by the end of the seventh century was celebrated everywhere as a public holiday. The pope was given the old Roman Pantheon and on May 13, 615, he dedicated it as a church in honor of the Virgin and all the martyrs. From that time the feast was celebrated on that date in Rome. In 844, Pope Gregory IV transferred the celebration to November 1. Some scholars argue that the reason for the transfer of dates was to Christianize a day that had been kept as a pagan feast; others argue that it was easier to feed the many pilgrims after the harvest than it was in the spring. Meanwhile the practice had spread to include all the saints, not just the martyrs, in this celebration. Pope Gregory III dedicated a chapel in St. Peter's in honor of Christ, Mary, and "all the apostles, martyrs, confessors, and all the just and perfect servants of God whose bodies rest throughout the whole world." The feast spread throughout Europe and in 1484 it was established as a holy day of obligation for the entire Latin Church. At this great feast, the merits of all the saints are venerated in common; because of the large number of martyrs and saints there were simply not enough days on the calendar to honor them individually. In addition, any negligence, omission, and irreverence committed in the celebration of the saints' feasts throughout the year is to be atoned for by the faithful, and thus due honor may still be offered to these saints.

Our Saintly Patrons

As members of the communion of saints, a link of grace and mutual concern ties us together with those who have reached their heavenly home and those who are being purified. For Christ and those united in his Body, the dead are still alive. A close bond of communication and love unites the members of the body of Christ. Those of the Church Triumphant stand ready to assist us with their prayers.

Through the centuries, certain saints have come to be associated with those persons in their final hours on earth or those in purification. Some of this association is due to incidents or legends in the saint's life. By the same token, a number of customs and practices of today stem from the actions or words of our saintly predecessors. Only a few of these saints and their traditions are presented here (Our Lady is discussed in Chapter Four; St. Michael in Chapter Six).

St. Joseph

Though he was poor on earth, St. Joseph is rich in heaven, ready to help all who request his intercession. Among his many patronages is the last, great favor of a happy death, the grace to die bravely and in peace with God and man.

St. Joseph himself may have died as a relatively young man. At the crucifixion, Jesus gave Mary into the keeping of the beloved disciple, indicating that His own foster father had already died. Legends declare, and we are permitted to believe, that St. Joseph died with Jesus and Mary nearby to comfort him. Thus, for those whose devotion to the saint emulates his humble work as an instrument of Divine Providence, his humility, his purity, his justice, his charity, then St. Joseph will be with them at the hour of their death. He will guide them to their homeland in heaven. As head of the Holy Family, St. Joseph could summon Jesus and Mary. He will surely call them again to the side of his special friends at the hour of their death (*St. Joseph Today*, p. 28).

It is a custom of Italian-Americans of Sicilian descent to save some of the blessed bread from the St. Joseph's altar built on his feast day. These pieces of bread are kept in houses and automobiles and in times of danger St. Joseph is invoked to protect the petitioner from harm. Sicilian-Americans say that those who bring St. Joseph into their lives and keep something of him with them will not suffer a violent death.

In Mexico, the laying out of a dead child has a special ritual of its own. If the child is a boy, he is often dressed as St. Joseph, patron of a happy death.

Prayer to St. Joseph for a Happy Death

St. Joseph, guide me on my way. Protect my soul from harm. And if this journey ends today, please come with Mary and her Son and take me to your Home to stay.

Pope St. Gregory I the Great — Gregorian Masses

Pope St. Gregory I the Great (c. 540-604), from whose reign stemmed the beautiful Gregorian chant, is also the pope from whose time we received the custom of saying thirty successive Masses for a dead person. The legend tells that one of the monks of his abbey, Justus, had received and kept for himself three gold pieces. This was a sin against his vow of poverty and on the discovery of his actions, he was excommunicated. He died, however, in a true spirit of repentance. St. Gregory, in order to impress the monks with a true hatred of the sin of avarice, did not withdraw the sentence of excommunication, so Justus was buried apart from the other monks and the three pieces of money were thrown into his grave. Some time later, the holy abbot decided that the scandal was sufficiently repaired and, moved with a spirit of compassion for the soul of Justus, told the brothers that out of charity they would offer a Mass every day in order to deliver him from purgatory. On the thirtieth day, the deceased appeared to one of the brothers to tell him joyously that on that very day he had been delivered and admitted into the society of the saints.

St. Odilo — Commemoration of All Souls

St. Odilo (962-1049) was one of the four great abbots of the famous Abbey of Cluny in France. Born in Auvergne in 962, Odilo entered the Abbey of Cluny to follow his vocation as a monk of the Benedictine order. By the time he was thirty-two, he was elected abbot; he served in this capacity for fifty years until his death in 1049.

A small man of insignificant appearance, Abbot Odilo was blessed with a forceful character. He was greatly devoted to the Incarnation and to Our Blessed Mother.

In order to maintain the proper monastic discipline at Cluny and in the monasteries under his direction, he visited all of them periodically. He mingled his authority with humility and love and brought great stability to monastic life by his leadership.

The saintly abbot was particularly devoted to the poor. During the famine of 1033 he sold many holy treasures of the monastery, using the proceeds to help the poor and suffering.

From the beginning, the Church has always prayed for her departed children, but there was no particular feast to commemorate the souls of all the dead until the time of St. Odilo. He issued a decree that all monasteries of the congregation of Cluny were annually to keep November 2 as a "day of all the departed ones" (*Omnium Defunctorum*). The decree ordered that on November 1, after Vespers, the bell should be tolled and afterward the Office of the Dead be recited; on the next day all priests had to say Mass for the repose of the souls in purgatory.

This observance was soon adopted by other Benedictines and by the Carthusians. Pope Sylvester II (1003) approved and recommended the feast. From the eleventh to the fourteenth centuries, it gradually spread throughout Europe until, in the fourteenth century, Rome placed the day of the commemoration of all the faithful departed in the official books of the Western church.

The Feast of All Saints had been celebrated on November 1 for several centuries. November 2 was chosen for the Feast of All Souls in order to celebrate on two successive days the memories of all departed souls, and thus to reinforce the Christian belief in the communion of saints. In the Byzantine Rite, the commemoration of the faithful departed was held on the Saturday before *Sexagesima* Sunday and called the "Saturday of the Souls" (*Psychosabbaton*). The Armenians celebrated on Easter Monday with the solemn Office of the Dead and a Mass of the Resurrection. The Syrian-Antiochene Rite celebrated on three separate days: on Friday before *Septuagesima* they commemorated all departed priests; on the Friday before *Sexagesima*, all the faithful departed; and on Friday before *Quinquagesima* "all those who died in strange places, away from their parents and friends" (Weiser, 1952, p. 309).

In 1927, Cardinal Mundelein commissioned Father William Roberts to establish a new parish in Berwyn, Illinois, under the patronage of St. Odilo. He officially honored the church as the "National Shrine of the Souls in Purgatory."

St. Nicholas of Tolentino — Patron of the Holy Souls

Nicholas of Tolentino (1245-1305) was an Italian Augustinian priest famous for eloquent preaching and as a confessor. An ardent pastor and lover of the poor, his fame spread because of the many miracles he worked in his lifetime. The recipients of his benevolence were told by the saint, "Say nothing of this. Give thanks to God, not to me. I am only an earthen vessel, a poor sinner." The confidence of the faithful placed great trust in his intercession for the souls in purgatory. Many years after his death, he was officially designated Patron of the Holy Souls.

Toward the end of his life, the saint was suffering from a prolonged illness when the Blessed Virgin appeared to him in a vision and told him to ask for a small piece of bread, dip it in water, and eat it. She promised he would be cured by his obedience to her wishes. In gratitude for his immediate cure, he began blessing small pieces of bread and giving them to the sick. This custom is continued even today at the shrine of the saint.

Forty years after his death, the incorrupt body of the saint was exposed to the faithful in the wooden urn in which it was first buried. During this exhibition the arms of the saint became detached from his body, beginning the strange history of the bleeding arms.

There is no documented proof concerning the identity of the person who amputated the arms of the saint, although legend says it was a German monk named Teodoro who wanted to take the arms as relics to his native country. A large flow of blood had followed the sacrilegious act. The guilty monk was apprehended and the body reburied. When exhumed a hundred years later, the arms were still intact and imbued with blood, although the body of the saint had completely decomposed. The remains were again reburied beneath the pavement of a chapel adjoining the church where the body had first been buried, and the arms were encased in beautifully crafted silver reliquaries.

Toward the end of the fifteenth century, fresh blood again began to spill from the arms. This effusion was repeated twenty times until 1699.

At one point, the community of Tolentino discovered the bones of the saint had disappeared. Several recorded meetings were held between 1475 and 1515 regarding the mysterious disappearance, but the motive and the location of the bones was not discovered. Five hundred years later, in 1926, the bones were located buried far beneath the pavement of the chapel. The bishop immediately petitioned the Vatican to examine the relics and in 1929 a Papal decree declared the authenticity of them (Cruz, 1977, pp. 96-98).

The Fourteen Holy Helpers

During the time of the Black Death, which devastated most of Europe between 1346 and 1349, devotion to a group of fourteen saints became popular, with the feeling that the most powerful of these saints were those who in some way assisted at the hour of death. The devotion is probably Germanic in origin, and a series of apparitions in Germany during the fifteenth century strengthened it.

The fourteen saints traditionally grouped together are: Sts. George, Blaise, Erasmus (Elmo), Pantaleon, Vitus, Christopher, Dennis, Cyriacus, Achatius, Eustace, Giles, Catherine, Margaret, and Barbara. All but one of these are martyrs.

In Germany, the fourteen are called *Die Vierzehn Heiligen Nothelfer*, the Fourteen Holy Helpers in Time of Need; occasionally another saint was included in the group. In France a fifteenth helper, the Blessed Virgin, was included.

Until the time of the plague, each of the saints had been invoked separately for a specific disease or danger. Invoking them as a group is an example of the medieval popular tendency to honor the saints more for what they would do for their devotees than for what they had been in their earthly lives. During the panic and horror of the plague years, invoking the saints as a group seemed to provide a blanket coverage against all afflictions. The cult spread widely over Europe, although it never became popular in England. Churches and hospitals were named after the Holy Helpers and their feast was permitted in various places, usually on August 8. The feast is still observed in a few places in Germany (Thurston, pp. 287-288). The devotion traveled to the New World and became popular throughout Latin America.

Those Holy Helpers who were invoked for exceptional assistance at the time of death are: Giles, who ensures a good confession; Achatius, who dissipates the fear of death; Christopher, who guards against sudden death; and Barbara, who protects against violent death (Lange, "The Art of Private Devotion," p. 66).

Barbara's patronage against sudden death undoubtedly stems from the legend that, after she was murdered by her father, he was killed by lightning. In medieval times she was universally invoked with prayers and hymns to grant a peaceful and well-prepared death. She is invoked against storms, fire, lightning, explosions, and other forms of death so sudden that victims have no time to receive the sacraments.

The legends of St. Christopher inspired many devotions. The faithful believed that by praying before his icon in the morning, no harm would come to them that day. It became a custom to hang his picture over the door of the house or to paint it on an outside wall so that others could also venerate him. Although coins imprinted with his picture date from an earlier time, today's use of the medals and plaques that many people carry on key chains or in their cars began in the sixteenth century. Their original purpose was to serve as a picture of the saint for travelers to gaze on in the morning to protect them from sudden death each day. An ancient rhyme tells of Christopher's protection: "If thou the face of Christopher on any morn shall see, Through the day from sudden death thou shalt preserved be." (Ball, 1993, p. 109).

Blaise is invoked against diseases of the throat. Pantaleon is a popular patron for medical men because of his legendary occupation as a court physician. Vitus was called on as a patron against chorea and epilepsy. Giles is a special patron of cripples.

Blessed Ana of the Angels — Victim for the Souls in Purgatory

Blessed Ana de Monteagudo de Ponce de Leon (1595-1686), better known as Ana of the Angels, was born high in the Andes mountains in Arequipa, Peru. The daughter of a noble family, at the age of fourteen she went against her family's wishes by refusing to take a husband. Her father refused her permission to enter a convent and would not give her a dowry, so she fled to the Dominican monastery of St. Catherine, where she resisted her father's attempts to drag her home. Her solid piety led to her eventual election as prioress but her zeal for reform caused her not to be reelected. Her special charisma was a consuming love for the Poor Souls and their patron saint, Nicholas of Tolentine.

In a mystical vision, the great Augustinian showed Ana a vision of purgatory and deputed her as a patron, promising his assistance. Her acceptance led to an infusion of gifts of the Holy Spirit including prophecy, bilocation, and miracles.

In 1676, Ana offered herself as a victim soul for the souls in purgatory. For the next ten years, she experienced physical and mystical sufferings combined with heavenly illuminations. She bore all her afflictions for love of her beloved souls, whom God permitted to visit her on occasion. She died gently at the age of ninety. God placed the seal of divine approval on her sanctity by granting miracles of healing to those who sought her intercession. When her body was exhumed ten months after her death, it was found incorrupt and fragrant. She was beatified by Pope John Paul II in 1985.

Blessed Mother Mary of Providence — Foundress of the Helpers of the Holy Souls

"With one hand I would empty purgatory, and with the other fill it with souls snatched from the brink of hell." Eugenie Smet (1825-1871) is a saint for our own times. With a twin vocation of providence and purgatory, she established a new society in the Church for the deliverance of souls from purgatory.

"Let us help souls to attain the end for which they were created," she repeated to her first companions. Her vocation and that of her society found itself at the crossroads of the indivisible church. Through trust in providence and by their efforts in charitable works of mercy, the Helpers of the Holy Souls expend themselves for the good of the souls in purgatory.

For herself, Mary of Providence felt intensely the mystery of the Cross, becoming a victim soul and suffering both spiritual aridity and physical pain from the cancer that caused her death at the early age of forty-five. In the midst of all her trials, she radiated joy, serenity, and confidence in Divine Providence. Her daughters in religion are not bound to any one form of particular apostolate; they endeavor to adapt themselves to the needs of souls wherever the service of the Church calls them.

The inspiration of the life of this holy foundress can help us lift our eyes towards the invisible and build our courage on faith and charity.

Other Heavenly Patrons

Tradition has assigned specific roles regarding the sick, dying, dead, and their caretakers to a wide variety of heavenly patrons. Many of these patronages are of medieval origin, stemming from the times of the plagues that swept across Europe. Additionally, a great number of these patrons are early saints and martyrs of the church. For some, other than the fact of their martyrdom, little is known of their life other than the legends or allegorical tales told of them. A partial list of these patronages is given below.

Acceptance of Death in the Family — Our Lady of the Rosary
Admission to Heaven — Peter the Apostle
Against Effects of Death in the Family — Our Lady of Sorrows
Against Fearful Deaths — Bartholomew (Nathaniel)
Against Impenitence at Death — Christopher
At Wakes for the Dead — Rosalia of Palermo
Condemned Prisoners — Quentin; Zita
Children's Nurses — Concordia
Compassion — Pantaleon
Consolation in Bereavement — Our Lady of Solitude
Conversion of Sinners — Mary Magdalen
Cripples — Giles
Death of the Unborn — St. Raymond Nonnatus
Deliver Souls from Purgatory — Our Lady of the Rosary; Our Lady of Mt Carmel; Our Lady of Light; Nicholas of Tolentino; Bl. Ana of the Angels; Bl. Mary of Providence
Doctors — Cosmas & Damian; Pantaleon; Raphael
Druggists — Cosmas & Damian
Dying patients — John of God
Feeble People — Camillus de Lellis
Good Death — Ursula
Heal Animals — Blaise; Roch
Happy Death — Joseph; Peter the Apostle
Holy Death — Andrew Avellino; Joseph; Paul
Hospitals — Camillus de Lellis; John of God
Impossible Cases — Jude

Incurable Diseases — Valentine
Invalids — Roch
Nurses — Agatha, John of God; Raphael
Oppose the Devil — Michael the Archangel
Pardon from Sins and Punishment — Roch
Physicians — Luke
Protectress from the "Ditch of Perdition" — Teresa of Avila
Repentance of Sin — Our Lady Refuge of Sinners; Dismas;
    Ignatius Loyola
Sick Animals or People — John of God
Social Workers — Frances of Rome
Solace for Those Condemned to Death — Cosmas & Damian
Souls in Purgatory — Gertrude the Great
Strength to Cope With Physical Handicaps — Bede
Sudden Death — Andrew Avellino; Christopher
Surgeons — Cosmas & Damian; Luke; Roch
Those Who Care for the Sick — Camillus de Lellis
Those Who Suffer for the Sins of Others — Lydwina
Violent Death — Barbara
Widows — Felicitus

The Korean Martyrs

It is the strength and the honor of the Catholic Church that it has possessed sons and daughters who, in all situations and in every country, have given their lives to proclaim and sustain their faith. Truly the seeds of our faith have been watered by the blood of the martyrs. Nowhere is this more evident than in the Catholic Church in Korea. A number of severe persecutions, no less horrifying than those of the early Christians, brought forth glorious martyrs whose lives and deaths vividly proclaimed the faith.

Although the reasons for the persecutions were varied and complicated, the tinder that lit the flames of martyrdom in Korea was the fact that the Christians *did not worship their dead*!

Ancestor worship was an established practice in Korea in the late 1700s, when the first Christian communities in the country began. When one's parent (or family member) died, one was expected to observe the customary funeral rites and to set up memorial tablets. Here one worshiped one's ancestors. Food and other offerings

**Father Leslie Blowers, M.M., officiates at a Korean
funeral service, c. 1965.**

were presented at the tablets. These obeisances were to be observed
for five generations.

Early in their history, Koreans believed the sun was the "Heavenly lord" and communication between God and man was possible
atop mountains. A primitive belief composed of sun worship, mountain worship, and ancestor worship guided their lives. This religion
is called animism, or shamanism, and it is based on the concept that
spirits reside in natural forces and inanimate objects. The shaman
was the tribal magician or priest who attempted to mediate with the
spirits, preventing natural disasters and curing illnesses.

Throughout the Orient, the introduction of sophisticated religions
did not result in the suppression of animism. Neither Buddhism nor
Confucianism considered itself in conflict with the rites relating to
local nature spirits, nor did these two major religions seriously con-
tradict each other. It became an ingrained Korean habit to hold si-
multaneous religious beliefs (*Korea*, pp. 47-48). Even today, Catholic customs in Korea are heavily influenced by the native culture.

The first Christians in Korea were self-taught. A group of scholars had obtained some Christian books on a trip to China, and after
studying them concluded that the Christian religion was the true

religion. By the time the first missionary entered the country, there were 10,000 Catholics waiting for him.

In 1790, the Christians appealed to the bishop in Peking to send a priest as soon as possible to the fledgling Korean church. In the same letter, written on silk so as to be more easily concealed and smuggled out of the country, the Christians inquired about the traditional rites of ancestor worship and other difficult points of the faith. In the bishop's reply, he declared the practice of the traditional ancestor worship to be heretical.

The Martyrdom of Paul Yun Chi-ch'ung

Paul Yun Chi-ch'ung and James Kwon Sang-yon were the first martyrs in the persecution that was touched off by the Confucianists and politicians, who used the ban on ancestor worship as their pretext. This is known as the Chin-san incident and was the beginning of the persecution of 1791.

Paul Yun was converted about the age of 25 after reading the writings of Father Matteo Ricci. He became a devout Christian. At the height of the previous persecution, he had burned some of his religious books, although he steadfastly retained his faith in secret. His mother died, so he put on the traditional mourning dress and carried out the funeral ceremony, but he did not bow before his mother's memorial tablet as the rite prescribed. His loyal cousin James Kwon followed his example in refusing to perform the act of worship to the dead.

Later, Paul buried the tablets of his parents under his house. This action triggered a thunderstorm of horrified denunciation from his neighbors. On hearing of it, a violent anti-Christian wrote a long letter to the Counselor of the Left, Ch'ae Che-Kong, requesting the death penalty, and at the same time demanded that the local magistrate arrest Paul and conduct a search of his house. The magistrate complied and when a search of the house revealed that there was no memorial tablet for Paul's mother, he ordered the arrest.

When warned, Paul and James fled, so the magistrate arrested Paul's uncle as a hostage. When the cousins heard of their uncle's arrest, they turned themselves in. Paul wrote notes of the interrogations, so we have, in his own words, the record of his defense of Christianity against ancestor worship:

Once having recognized God as my Father, I cannot allow myself to disobey His orders. The tablets in use in the homes of the nobles being prohibited by the religion of the Lord of Heaven, I cannot, since I belong to this religion, do anything but obey and conform to what it prescribes. The Fourth Commandment orders us to honor father and mother so that if in fact our parents were in these tablets every man who professes religion would have to honor them. But these tablets are made of wood. They have with me no relationship of flesh, blood or life. They took no part in the labors of my birth and education. The soul of my father and my grandfather, once having left this world, cannot remain attached to these material objects. Now, the name of father and mother being so great and venerable how could I dare to take an artificial thing made by a workman and make it my father or my mother and treat it as such?

As for the offerings of meat and wine to the dead or to their tablets, that is also a thing forbidden by the religion of the Lord of Heaven. In fact, when the Creator first made the different kinds of creatures, it was His will that material creatures should use material things and spiritual creatures should use spiritual things. That is why virtue is the food of the soul as material aliments are the food of the body. No matter how excellent the wine or the meat, it cannot nourish the soul for the reason that an immaterial being cannot get nourishment from material things. No matter how pious a man may be toward his parents, he doesn't try to offer them food while they are asleep because the time of sleeping is the time when one cannot eat. For the same and stronger reasons, when they are sleeping the long sleep of death, to offer them food is a vain thing and a false practice. How can a child honor his parents with vain things and false practices? (Kim, pp. 36-37)

Paul went on to martyrdom, one of thousands whose blood watered the seeds of faith in Korea. Today there is a thriving Catholic community in Korea. Here, Christianity has achieved and maintained a degree of influence out of all proportion to its actual number of converts.

Part Three:

FUNERAL CUSTOMS
AROUND THE WORLD

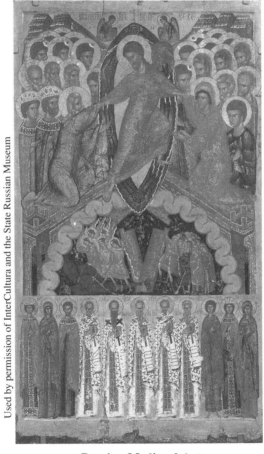

Used by permission of InterCultura and the State Russian Museum

Russian Medieval Art

Chapter Nine

Death and Burial in the Catholic Byzantine Churches

by Rev. Anselm Walker

D eath in the Byzantine Rite Churches, both Catholic and Orthodox, is dominated by the Resurrection. In fact, during the Paschal Season the beautiful canon for Easter Matins, or of the Resurrection, is sung in its entirety at funerals for adults. This is one long paean of lyrical praise of the risen Christ and his effect on the cosmos, the human race, and the individual. One hears often the recurring Paschal troparion "Christ is risen from the dead, by His death He has trampled upon death and to all in the tomb He has granted life." Outside Paschal time these specific words are missing, but there is a constant reminder that death is not final and that life will conquer in each of us as it did in Christ, our head.

The liturgical books of the Byzantine Rite contain formulas for the burial of ordinary folks, for children, and for those in monastic vows as well as those in holy orders. Basically these services are constructed similarly, with variations to fit each one. The constitutive elements are psalms, *tropars* (a sung commemoration for a saint), *kondaks* (a *tropar* containing a summary of the subject of a feast), and scriptural readings, interspersed with the ever-recurring *ektenias* (litanies) that give any Byzantine service its popular and pathetic appeal. In the services for the dead, the petitions are sung in a minor tone and the responses take on a supplicating tone filled with bathos.

The wake service, known in Greek as *Parastas* and in Slavonic as *Panikidy,* has a short and an extended form. The short form includes: the Beatitudes; the Lord's Prayer; a portion of the funeral canon of St. John of Damascus; the *ektenia* for the deceased, ending in the ancient prayer, "O God of the spirits of all flesh"; then another ode of the funeral canon ending with the soulful and haunting "Memory eternal." In the extended form of the *Parastas*, psalms, scriptural readings, *ektenias, tropars,* and *kondaks* are included.

This service is also celebrated on the five Saturdays of the departed, four during Lent and one on the Saturday before Pentecost. On these occasions *koliva* is prepared and blessed — a mixture of boiled wheat, currants, raisins, and chopped nuts, over which is poured honey or powdered sugar. This rests on a table generally in the center of the church with lighted candles around it. The icon of the Resurrection is present, as well as, perhaps, the individual's photograph. In some Byzantine usages flowers may also decorate the table. The priest, not fully vested and most often in a light color, swings the censer continually during the service.

On Saturdays the priest reads out the names of the departed submitted by the people while the congregation in a kind of undertone continually sings "Lord, have mercy." The *koliva* rests in a tray and three candles are placed upright in it, which burn during the service. At the end these are extinguished and each worshipper receives a small portion of the *koliva*. The sweetness of the *koliva* has a twofold purpose. It reminds us of the departed and prepares us for the joy of heaven.

The Divine (Eucharistic) Liturgy is also celebrated for the deceased in church with appropriate *tropars, kondaks,* and scriptural lessons. Each day of the week has its own Gospel for the departed. After the liturgy, the full funeral canon of St. John of Damascus may be sung. This exquisite piece of liturgical poetry was composed by St. John to comfort one of his fellow monks who had lost his brother. It is during this canon that the worshipers are called to give the last kiss to the departed, a practice that in some cases — as in times of plagues — tended to spread contagion. Today, a small icon of metal is placed on the chest of the corpse and is the recipient of the last kiss. Among the Russians, the head of the corpse is adorned by a ribbon tied around the forehead, on which appears the *trisagion* (Thrice-Holy Hymn recited during the Divine Liturgy): "Holy God, Holy Mighty, Holy Immortal, have mercy on us."

In Russia it was customary for a person to be buried in a shroud bought in Jerusalem. Pilgrims to the Holy City, after purchasing a shroud, would go to the Jordan to the site of the Lord's Baptism and swim in the shroud; or, he or she might buy several and ring them out in the Jordan and take them home for the folks back there. These shrouds were also often slept in until one's death, so as to accustom one's self to the long sleep until the general resurrection. Other peoples had similar customs using coffins.

At the grave, parts of the wake service — or all of it — would be repeated. Perfumed oil would be poured into the coffin (sometimes on it) and the priest would empty the ashes from the censer into the grave. Clerics were buried in their proper vestments, but a priest or bishop had his face covered with the "air" in the large veil that covers the chalice and the diskos during the Divine Liturgy. In a monastic funeral a meal is generally served for all the attendees.

In the next year the *Panikidy* and Divine Liturgy are celebrated periodically for the departed. In fact, in the Syrian or Antiochene jurisdiction this reminds us of the custom of the pre-Vatican II Latin Rite. The above-mentioned services were celebrated each month and after that, yearly. According to this tradition the soul does not go directly to its particular judgment but makes its way slowly up through the "toll" stations, at each of which it undergoes scrutiny by angelic inspectors (called "*archons*"); it is during these scrutinies that prayers by the faithful on its behalf are especially needed. The remote origins of this belief may well be Gnostic but became Orthodox in time. It is well known that our non-Catholic Oriental brethren do not accept the concept of purgatory, even though their fervor and intensity in interceding for the dead puts us to shame.

Another custom that originated in Russia during the Communist oppression, when churches were closed and priests were scarce, was to bury a dead Christian with whatever prayers a layman was allowed to use. In some places the laity adopted quasi-monastic practices, like the continuous reading of the Gospels or the Psalter until internment. Then a small amount of dirt would be taken from the grave and sent to the nearest "working church," where the priest would celebrate the funeral liturgy over the dirt, then send it back to be reinserted into its original spot in the grave.

A practice that is used by some of our Orthodox brethren is the canonization of saints (glorification is their term for it). The process begins with the regular requiem service (*Panikidy* in Slavic, *Parastas* in Greek) wherein prayers are offered for the repose of the person who is to be canonized. Somewhere near the middle of the service a change is made from praying *for* the candidate, to praying *to* him or her to intercede for us sinners. (The service then becomes a *Paraklesis*, a service modeled on Matins, often considered as the equivalent of the Latin Novena.) Canonization or glorification can be made by any of the autocephalous churches (that is, a jurisdictional entity that is self-governing and that has a hierarchy of at least three bishops). Even an individual monastery may glorify a saint, but others, as they become convinced of the justice of the candidate's cause, will begin to celebrate his or her feast day. Thus St. John Maximovitch was first glorified by one Orthodox monastery, but others have taken up his cause. St. John was the former Russian Synodal Archbishop of San Francisco, California. Earlier he had been the Archbishop of Shanghai. He went barefooted and was much given to prayer. By all accounts he was a holy hierarch. His tomb is in the crypt of the beautiful and synodal cathedral "Our Lady Joy of All the Sorrowing" on W. Gary Ave. in San Francisco.

Chapter Ten

Latin American Customs

In the prayers of the offices for the dead, the Christian community expresses its faith and intercedes for adults who have died so that they may enjoy eternal happiness with God. This is the happiness that deceased children, already made children of God through baptism, are believed to enjoy already. Prayers are offered for the parents of these infants, as for the relatives of all the dead, so that in their sorrow they may experience the consolation of faith (NCCB, p. 14). In the burial ritual for unbaptized children, the infant is commended to God's mercy.

Los Angelitos

In Mexico, there is a traditional set of customs and rituals concerned with the death of children. Dead children are known as *angelitos* (little angels) and the customs surrounding their burial rites emphasize true Christian joy that the soul of the little one is secure in eternal happiness. The rituals connected with child death attempt to convert grief into joy, and to celebrate the entrance of a pure soul into a new life. The expression "child death" refers to the Mexican cultural phenomenon by which a recently deceased child is no longer thought of as a child, but instead as a little angel — *angelito* — and as such their death is celebrated, rather than mourned. (Note: the ritual of child death is also practiced to some extent in other Latin American countries, most notably Argentina and Guatemala.) The children are considered innocent, free from all eternal misery, and their death is a joyful birth into another world. Parents who have lost a child experience the normal grief for their loss, but the grief is tempered with the joy of knowing the child lives forever.

The joy in child death is a concept hard to assimilate by many persons. It is, however, closely aligned to the cult of the Virgin Mary; both are Christian rituals which involve immaculate beings destined for life after death (Lacy, *Artes de Mexico*, p. 83).

Beginning in the eighteenth century, when the child of a wealthy family died, the parents had a memorial portrait painted of the child. These effigies helped the parents to forget them as children of flesh and blood and to remember them as *angelitos*. The earliest of these portraits usually showed the child as older than he or she actually was at the time of death. The eyes would be open, and were it not for inscriptions and floral tokens held in the child's hands, we would not know the child was dead. The early pictures included many objects in the background, such as the child's toys, religious symbols, etc. Later, the background was simplified and the face of the child took on more importance. More and more, parents wanted a faithful reproduction of their dead child to help fix in their memory an image as close to reality as possible.

These pictorial manifestations of death were an attempt by the parents to accept their loss, since the portraits would join the family gallery, where places were kept for the departed. This sentimental romanticism also resulted in miniature portraits painted on ivory and set in brooches, which served as permanent reminders of the loving bond between the bereft mother and child. The mother kept alive the memory of the child each time she clipped the brooch to her bosom (Aceves, *Artes de Mexico*, p. 89). The tradition continues even today, and a number of artists from the 1920s to date have continued the theme in artwork using their own beautiful and plastic language.

Around the turn of the century, portrait photography gave the ritual a great popular appeal. The tradition is carried on by local photographers in a number of towns throughout Mexico. The rise of photography allowed families of more modest means to afford to preserve the child's image and memory until the time came for the final reunion in the life after death. The photographic portraits of the dead child, surrounded by religious symbols and family members, helped the family reaffirm their belief in the Resurrection and to deal with their grief.

From the turn of the century through the 1930s there was an extremely high rate of infant mortality in Mexico. For every thousand births, there were nearly 300 deaths; about one of every three children died in infancy. The visual reminders of the *angelito* and the special rituals of his or her funeral helped the parents to overcome their feelings of impotence at their failure to prevent their child's death.

The following description of a funeral in the Ameca region of Jalisco gives us an idea of the way child death is treated throughout Mexico.

When the parents feel the death of their child is close, they notify the godparents, who play a large part in the ritual. After the death, the godparents first dress the child, then lay him or her out for burial. A little boy is usually dressed to represent St. Joseph or the Sacred Heart of Jesus, and the girls are dressed as the Immaculate Conception. Infants are usually dressed all in white, or in their best clothes. Little gold paper sandals are placed on the child's feet, and a spray of flowers made of palm leaves, orange blossoms, spikenards, or lilies is put in the child's hands. A floral wreath for the child's head is presented by the godmother. The clothing emphasizes the holy and innocent state of the child. Sometimes gilt or silver wings are added.

In addition to providing the clothing and the wreath, the godparents also shoulder the costs for items such as fireworks, mariachis, or other expenses the parents may not be able to afford.

For the wake, the child is laid on a table spread with a white sheet or tablecloth, and the friends and relatives encircle the body with flowers brought from their homes. Pots of flowers surround the table.

The high point of the wake is the coronation. The godparents set the wreath of spikenards on the tiny head, and fireworks are set off to announce the death to the community.

Prayers sung at the wake are called *Alabanzas*, and they express devotion to the Virgin Mary, comparing her virtues and qualities with those of the *angelito*.

Throughout the night, coffee, an alcoholic cinnamon drink, and bread are served.

The following day, the body is placed in a small white coffin adorned with angelic symbols. In earlier times, a stretcher covered with tissue paper was used to transport the body, which was later laid in the coffin.

Before leaving the home, the prayer "Farewell to *Angelitos*" (known in some regions as *Parabienes*) is recited. This is the only prayer used in the region specifically for infant funerals.

A procession of children carrying flowers, accompanied by *mariachis* (strolling musicians) playing waltzes, walks to the graveyard. Until the 1960s, the children in the procession dressed in white, the same way they dressed for processions in May honoring the Virgin.

At the cemetery, the procession halts briefly in front of the chapel, then proceeds to the spot where the child will be buried. As the coffin is lowered, the godparents throw in ritual handsful of dirt, then the tiny coffin is covered with flowers. A farewell song and a last burst of fireworks draw the ceremony to its close. At last, someone recites a prayer on behalf of the child, in which the child bids farewell to his family and his home. In the prayer, the mother is consoled for giving her child up to heaven, and a narrative describes the child's entry into glory, where he or she becomes a mediator in

Used by permission of Artes de México

An example of *Los Angelitos* from the early nineteenth century.

this florid death, which provides access into paradise (Aceves, *Artes de Mexico*, p. 84).

In Malinalco, near the Federal District, the wake of a child is more colorful and playful than in other areas of the country. The wake lasts longer than a few hours; sometimes, the celebration goes on for nearly two days. Friends and relatives come and go to contribute to the celebration of this celestial passage, rather than to offer condolences and tears. Almost like a noisy fair, the house is filled with flowers, decorations, and the music of guitars and violins. Food and drink are dispensed liberally. All ages join in the traditional "celestial death" games, about twenty of them, that celebrate the child's passage to the other world.

During the games, the child's body is laid out on a table surrounded with paper decorations and flowers. The child is dressed in the costume of a saint, some of the more popular being St. Augustine, St. Joseph, St. Francis, St. Monica, and St. Theresa. The games, which are in reality children's games, are played for hours, with some of the guests playing while others drink and eat. An alcoholic coffee drink with pieces of bread, and *Catarino*, an *atole* (or corn starch) drink, are among the popular refreshments. Bottles of *aguardiente* (brandy) and cigars are given as favors to those who attend the funeral.

At last, the child is accompanied to the cemetery with music provided by the godparents. The child is buried with music, fireworks, and joy, in order to return to God the child in the same joy with which the child was received (Schneider, *Artes de Mexico*, pp. 92-93).

Dia de los Muertos

Dia de los Muertos — Day of the Dead. The All Souls' Day celebration in the Hispanic cultural tradition is not a day of sadness and mourning. Instead, it is a joyful affirmation of the very heart of our religion — life everlasting.

Very Rev. Virgil Elizondo, Rector of San Fernando Cathedral in San Antonio, Texas, reminds his parishioners that "just because we bury people, we do not abandon them. On the Day of the Dead, we laugh and play and joke with death; for us, it is an affirmation of the ultimate life, and our celebrations can deepen this aspect of our faith.

On this day, we combine the pain of death with the joy of our loved one's life in God and in us. *Dia de los Muertos* is an enrichment of the doctrine of the communion of saints, a personalization of our own household saints."

Dia de los Muertos is celebrated in a number of Spanish-American countries, in various ways. The Mexican tradition has crossed the border into the United States, and the cathedral in San Antonio has adapted it with their own traditional liturgy and celebration. The cathedral celebration honors Hispanic heroes of the parish and of the city, as well as commemorating the dead of the parish families.

The Day of the Dead is one of the most sacred and revered days in the Mexican cycle of feasts. It stems from the ancient pre-Colombian belief that as long as one was remembered by family and friends, one continued to live. In celebrating the dead, they are maintained as alive; thus, the day is actually a day of the living.

San Fernando is the oldest cathedral sanctuary in the United States. It was founded by Canary Islanders in 1731. Thus, the Day of the Dead has been celebrated in the parish for over two hundred years.

In the celebrations of today, there is a roll call at the Mass. The families and friends gather and when the name of their honoree is intoned, a candle is lit on the *altar de los muertos*. Large photos of these heroes and heroines, affixed to crosses, are presented during the procession. All who attend the Mass are invited to write a message to the dead of their own families, which will be placed in a gaily-decorated coffin in front of the special altar. Pictures of all the previous bishops of San Antonio are also placed in front of this altar.

After the Mass, the parishioners and guests attend a reception. *Pan de los muertos* (bread of the dead) and bone punch are served. Mrs. Janie Dillard, Father Elizondo's assistant, created the recipe for the punch from traditional fruit juice ingredients. Pieces of sugar cane, the "bones," float in the punch.

Father Elizondo and a number of others in the parish feel that many Hispanics don't think enough of their roots and the heroes of their culture. The *Dia de los Muertos* observance is an opportunity to remember those who have been a good example for all to follow, and those who inspire young people to create a better world.

Rev. John Boscoe, C.S.B. recalls the *ofrendas* he saw during his nine years in the central and southern Mexican missions of his

Basilian order. He says, "Praying for the dead begins with remembering the dead. The *ofrenda* is a visual way to bring the dead to mind in order to pray for them."

In Mexico, the celebration begins on November 1, when the souls of the *angelitos* — children — are remembered. On November 2, deceased adults are honored. Folklore has it that the spirits of the dead return to earth to visit, so elaborate preparations are made to welcome them with deep reverence — and a great deal of warmth and humor. In some parts of Mexico, on October 27 offerings of bread and water are hung outside the houses or placed in a corner of the church for the spirits which have no one to greet them and no home to visit.

The *ofrenda*, or altar of the dead, commemorates the family dead. They are constructed in homes and sometimes in the *camposanto*, or cemetery. At this time of year, families go to the cemeteries and clean and weed them. They decorate with flowers. The two most traditional flowers are the *cempasuchil* and the *terciopelo*, similar to our marigolds and coxcomb. The streets near the cemetery are sometimes literally paved with blossoms. Flower wreaths, or *coronas*, are placed on every grave. Candles are numerous, to light the way for the souls of the dead to come and visit with their family. In some parts of the country, the church bells toll all afternoon on the first to signal the welcoming of the adult souls. Families sometimes hold an all-night vigil with their family dead at the cemetery. The men talk and drink and the women sit by the grave and pray. The people spend the next day at the cemetery in the company of their dead, but also enjoy the company of the living. *Mariachis* play favorite music and the people talk, eat, and drink.

The custom of the home *ofrenda* is observed in many Spanish-American homes in the United States. As in Mexico, these commemorative altars are covered in black cloth and decorated with *papel picado*, or cut paper. The altars include flowers, food, and anything special to the dead ones. Usually, pictures of the dead are set on the altar. Special toys and images of skeletons abound. Anything that is a special reminder of, or was much loved by, the family's dead may be put on the altar. Traditional foods include *mole*, a spicy chicken dish, and *pan de muertos*. This bread is usually made in the shape of a skull and crossbones, a volcano spewing tears, or in the shapes of men and women. For the children who have died young, there are special toys such as tiny coffins from which a skeleton emerges when a string is pulled, or puppets and masks.

Calaveras, or skulls, are in many sizes. Skulls made of sugar candy are decorated fancifully with glitter and icing. Names are sometimes written on them. Later, these candy skulls are exchanged as presents.

Calaveras, a word with the double meaning of "skulls" and "scatterbrain," is also the word for satirical poems. Another traditional Mexican and Mexican-American activity is the passing of these poems from one friend to another, much as we give valentines on St. Valentine's feast day. The calaveras often poke fun at politicians or other professionals and are elaborately illustrated with pictures of skeletons laughing and having a good time. Unlike the ghosts on Halloween which we view with fear, the *calaveras* draw us closer to the dead.

Jose Guadalupe Posada (1852-1913) was a Mexican artist with a great talent for illustrating the life and character of his countrymen. Although he died relatively unrecognized, he was the inspiration for a number of Mexico's most famous modern artists. He and his publisher were fearless crusaders who fought for reforms, and whose scathing caricatures of dishonest politicians constantly kept them in hot water. Posado is particularly famous for his illustrations of the *calaveras* filled with grinning, dancing cadavers miming every conceivable activity in human existence.

In Spain, three Masses are celebrated on All Souls' Day. Mission sermons are preached with special hymns composed for the occasion. *Septenario de Albas* is observed — seven days of prayers said at dawn for the repose of the dead souls.

In El Salvador, on November 1, the people "*Enflorar a los Ninos*," literally, "Flower the children." Either natural or paper flowers are taken to the cemetery and placed on the graves of children. On the second, the flowers are placed on the graves of the adults. A favorite custom is to make wreaths of cypress tree branches. The people go in *caravanas*, or groups, to the cemetery and the priest says Mass there. After the visit to the cemetery, the people often stop to buy traditional foods such as *pasteles* or *pupusas* (pastries) from the *champitas*, vendors who hawk their wares from grass huts with thatched roofs.

Father Elizondo feels that it is important for families to celebrate the memory of their loved ones. Far from simply being "sanitized witchcraft," the Hispanic-American celebration of *Dia de los Muertos* is a joyful affirmation of our faith.

This Is the Day — An *Alabanza*

> This is the day, the day of the dead.
> This is the day we remember our dead.
> We remember the happy times.
> We remember the days of happiness before our loved ones
>   passed away from us.
> We remember the good days with gratitude to our God who
>   loved us enough to give our loved ones time with us.
> This is the day, the day of the dead.
> This is the day we remember the goodness of God.
> This is the day, the day of the dead.
> This is the day we remember that because of the goodness of
>   God, our dead continue to live.
> Our beloved loved ones continue to live.
> They live in God, and they live in our hearts.

The author's home *ofrenda* on All Souls' Day. The statue in the center is the child Jesus, Infant of the Atocha.

Chapter Eleven

A Good, Old-Fashioned Irish Wake

The waking of the dead is an ancient custom throughout the world. Extant records of wakes in Europe go back over a thousand years. The practice has largely died out on most of the continent within the past century, although remnants of the customs remain in Ireland today.

Wakes held before the mid-1800s in Ireland, as in much of Europe, were a mixture of Christian devotion, traditional magic, ritual observance, and festive celebration. In 1778, Thomas Campbell observed, "These wakes are meeting of merriment and festivity, to which they resort from far and near. The old people amuse themselves in smoking tobacco, drinking whiskey and telling stories in the room with the corpse; whilst the young men, in the barn or some separate apartment, exhibit feats of activity; or, inspired by their sweethearts, dance away the night to the melodious pleasing of a bagpipe." In 1838, John Donaldson complained that wakes were the scene of "different kinds of diversions, tricks and pastimes quite unbecoming in such a place" (Connolly, p. 148).

At the ancient festive wake, the diversions mainly consisted of party games. There were competitions involving riddles, tongue twisters, and extempore versifying; games of competition involving feats of strength, agility, or endurance; and elaborate practical jokes which could end with the victim being drenched with water, tossed onto a dunghill, or otherwise maltreated.

At times, the jokes went so far as to include the corpse. Reports tell of cases in which the deceased, usually laid out on a table and in full view, was dealt a hand of cards, had a pipe inserted in his mouth, or was taken onto the floor for a dance (Connolly, p. 150).

Impoverished members of the lower classes were willing to endure extra hardships in life to set aside enough money for a "proper wake" when their time came. Funds were needed for food, tobacco and pipes, snuff, and plenty of Irish whiskey. Festive wakes of this type existed in most of Ireland in the late eighteenth and early nineteenth centuries, with the only exception being the southwest parts of Cork and Kerry, where the only entertainment known to have existed at such gatherings was storytelling (Connolly, p. 150).

Some wake games took the form of a mime. One particularly scandalous mime was called "Drawing the Ship Out of the Mud"; the men who engaged in this activity presented themselves before the rest of the assembly in a state of nudity. Particularly condemned by the Church were mimes involving fake weddings, where couples paired off and a man pretending to be a priest "married" them; mock confessions, where a man representing the priest listened to caricatured confessions and imposed ludicrous penances; and other satires directed at the Catholic clergy and aspects of Catholic teaching and religious practice.

A game called "Frimsy Framsy" was particularly popular. A man sat on a chair or stool placed in the middle of the room and called out to his sweetheart or the prettiest girl in the house. She came forward and kissed him, whereupon he returned to the circle and she took his place. "Come now, fair maid, frimsy framsy, who's your fancy?" he would call. She then designated a young man, who came over and kissed her. They exchanged places and the game continued with the participants smacking away for a couple of hours.

This game was singled out for special mention in clerical condemnations of wakes on at least three occasions during the eighteenth century, being denounced as a "most disgraceful ceremony and the cause of a multitude of sins" (Connolly, p. 153). Other repeated condemnations by the church authorities were against obscene songs, scurrilous talk, and excessive consumption of alcohol. The record of church condemnations paints a picture at wakes of a general atmosphere of ribaldry and heightened sexual awareness.

How can we understand this apparently incongruous practice of marking a death with a festive social gathering?

As Prim, an Irish historian, has written, "The people who took part in these games had no idea of outraging propriety or religion in their performance, holding an unquestioning faith in the old traditions that such observances were right and proper at wakes whilst under any other circumstances they would shrink with horror from such indelicate exhibitions." Prim points out that many of the activities at the festive wakes were remnants of pagan rites (Connolly, pp. 154-155).

Sean O'Suilleabhain argues that the festive wake was primarily intended to comfort and placate the spirit of the deceased person with a last great feast, at which he was present as the guest of honor. The main force behind the liveliness of the wake was a fear of the dead person himself, who was conceived as still present in the company and possessed of power to harm the living. Part of the vigor of the festive wakes undoubtedly also was an assertion of continued vitality in the face of a sudden reminder of universal mortality, and of continuity in the face of the abrupt removal of one of its members from a close-knit community (Connolly, p. 152).

Although celebration and festivity were the aspects of the wake which attracted most attention from contemporary observers, the wakes also involved a recognition that the occasion was for mourning. One way this was brought out was by the Irish "keen," an eulogy in verse on the qualities of the dead person and a lament for his passing, interspersed with loud wailings and cries of grief. The keen was performed at intervals over the corpse, first at the wake and later during the funeral procession and burial.

Although a keen could be performed by a friend or relative of the deceased, as late as the nineteenth century it was a frequent practice to hire specialist keeners, and keening appears to have developed into an art. Cries and wailings accompanied the verbal lament, and its affecting cadences, as reported by one observer, were "filled with a melancholy sweetness" (Connolly, p. 157).

The festive wake was a body of procedures which enabled the community to come to terms with the death of one of its members. By the display of vitality and gaiety, the members of the community responded to a reminder of general mortality; by the keen, the bereaved found a means to express their feelings in a controlled and manageable form (Connolly, p. 159).

By the end of the eighteenth century, the opposition of the Church to the practices of the festive wake had a long history. Public penances were imposed on those who engaged in lewd songs, games, or profane tricks. Time and again the church condemned the practice of distributing alcoholic drink at funerals. Young persons, especially the unmarried, were charged not to attend.

The main reason for the clerical opposition was practical, rather than ideological. The Church did not condemn the wake because it was a pre-Christian practice or as a ritual response to death, but rather because it was seen as an occasion of undesirable behavior. There was a marked hostility to keening based on the commands of St. Paul, who had forbidden displays of immoderate grief for the dead. In 1806, Archbishop Bray of Cashel condemned "all unnatural screams and shrieks and fictitious tuneful cries and elegies at wakes, together with the savage custom of howling and bawling at funerals" (Connolly, p. 163).

Many references to excessive funeral drinking can be found. In the 1600s, hundreds of horsemen and twice that many on foot would attend funerals and join in the feasting that sometimes impoverished the relatives of the dead person. A description of a 1778 wake mentioned that guests came from far and near to pass the time smoking and drinking whiskey. In 1841, a Mrs. S.C. Hall reported that at wakes "disreputable things occurred as there was no shortage of whiskey and both men and women drank to excess."

Older people of our own day bear testimony to the amount of drinking at wakes they attended in their youth, and at the high incidence of drunkenness. It is no wonder that the attention of the Church came to be directed on the use of alcohol at wakes and funerals and that every effort was made to curb the abuses (O'Suilleabhain, pp. 18-19).

The drinking of alcohol did not stop at the wake. In some places, a man stood with a bottle of whiskey at the entrance to the graveyard. He offered the funeral participants a drink as they passed by, if they wished (Harte, p. 13).

By the early decades of the nineteenth century, clerical prohibitions began to have an effect on wake practices. Toward the end of that century, a trend toward Anglicization changed many attitudes and many of the old Gaelic customs passed into history. Although wake games were still being played as late as the 1920s in some counties, today's wake is generally more sedate, with talking, visiting, and storytelling replacing the more boisterous recreations. The keen gradually was replaced by hymns and Gregorian chant. The use of alcohol at wakes and funerals has never been completely stamped out in Ireland, but today its use is more moderate and there is less condemnation needed because of drunkenness (Connolly, pp. 164-166).

Whatever the old ideas concerning the dead and their continued presence among the living that gave rise to wake customs, today's wakes retain little in their outward character that indicates a doctrine radically different than that of the Catholic Church (Connolly, p. 166).

As recently as twenty years ago, many traditional customs remained in the wakes and funerals of Ireland that seem odd or superstitious to today's American observers. Even today, remnants of these can be found in wakes held in the Irish countryside.

According to Irish actor and storyteller Eamon Kelly, when chided about these superstitions, or *piseoga*, the people murmur, " `Tis the custom and it is a brave man indeed who would defy them beyond the teeth."

In one of his presentations, Kelly outlines part of the ritual of an Irish funeral and the accompanying traditions. A certain man had died on a Saturday, and "an awful awkward day to die at that time, for you couldn't open a grave on Monday. Nothing but bad luck would come out of it. Of course, you can get round the piseog by turning one sod of the grave on Sunday, and that is what was done. Only those closely connected with the dead man's family would open the grave.... as it would be considered highly disrespectful to the dead for a stranger to have hand, act or part in the proceedings."

Molly Donovan, the local midwife, also helped lay out the dead. "The poor man that died was hardly inside the Golden Gates above when Molly was in the door and fortified with whiskey, she'd wash the corpse, put on the habit, put the pennies on the eyelids, the prayer book under the jaw and fold the arms with the rosary beads entwined around the fingers. The only case where she might look for assistance was the shaving. And a fellow helping her out one time had a ferocious shake in his hand. He was full of apologies after for not having the corpse look his best.

"'Yerra,' says Molly dusting the badly shaven face with flour, 'he's all right. he'll do. It isn't to America he's going.'

"Give Molly Donovan her due she carried out everything according to custom. The clock was stopped and the looking glass turned to the wall. The sad news was told to the bees, and in some places a crepe was hung on the hive. Bees were considered part of the family that time and they should be told what was going on.

"When Molly Donovan had the bed draped with starched linen, brought up over the foot and the head of the bead, a couple of boards under the corpse to keep him well os cionn clair, his Third Order habit on him with the white cord (traditionally, people were buried in a brown shroud or a blue Child of Mary Sodality cloak [Harte, p. 8]), and he nicely groomed and serene for himself no Pope that was ever laid out in the Vatican would look half as well. Of course, we didn't have the custom here of tapping him on the head with a hammer to see if he was dead!" (Kelly, pp. 11-12).

The advent of funeral homes has changed the character of Irish wakes in cities, and it has become a solemn occasion in most areas, which people attend to pray for the dead and console the grieving. Gradually, wakes are being replaced by social gatherings after the funeral in the home or in a local hotel. Relatives from different parts of Ireland often only meet at funerals, and friendships and family bonds are renewed and strengthened here. There is a warm, friendly atmosphere in spite of sorrow (Harte, p. 8). Grief, yes, but also a sense of a social occasion and of celebration of life and close bonds, especially if the deceased has lived a long life.

Death and the Mass in Ireland

Death and the Mass are closely associated in Ireland. When a person dies, many people give an offering to the priest and ask him to say a Mass for the soul of the deceased. They ask the priest to sign a Mass card, which they present to the bereaved family. The cards are placed in an envelope on top of the coffin, or in a small basket beside it. At the beginning of November, a novena of evening Masses for the dead is the custom in many parishes. Many people write a list of deceased family members, place it in an envelope with a small offering, and hand it in at the sacristy. The lists are placed on the altar for the novena, and the people listed are included in all Masses for the entire month. Also during this month dedicated to the dead, on a Sunday afternoon the priest goes to the graveyard to say a rosary and prayers, and to bless the graves.

The "month's mind" is the custom of having a Mass offered, with the family attending, one month after the death of a family member. Each year on the anniversary of the death of a family member, many families ask for a Mass to be said which they also attend, if possible. Often, notices of these anniversaries are printed in the local paper, sometimes with poetry or comments included. On Saturday and Sunday at all Masses, anniversaries of deaths are announced, if the family has requested it. Many people still follow this custom, sometimes for many years.

Mortuary or memoriam cards have long been a custom in Ireland. The name and details of the dead person, short prayers, and sometimes a small photo of the deceased are included on the cards, which are distributed at funerals. When Catholics used to carry missals to church, they would often be full of these cards, which the people used to remember to pray for their dead at Mass. Although not used as frequently as before, these cards are still popular in many places in Ireland today (Harte, pp. 9-11).

The Apparition at Knock

On August 21, 1879, fifteen witnesses saw an apparition of the Blessed Virgin Mary, St. Joseph, and St. John the Evangelist, which appeared at the south gable of the parish church at Knock (*Cnoc Mhuire*), County Mayo, Ireland. Beside them, and a little to the right, was an altar with a cross and the figure of a lamb around which angels hovered.

The witnesses, young and old, stood and watched the apparition for two hours in pouring rain, reciting the rosary. Unlike other Marian apparitions, Our Lady at Knock did not speak.

This apparition occurred immediately after the parish priest, Archdeacon Kavanagh, finished celebrating a series of one hundred Masses for the holy souls. Many people see a connection and believe the apparition at Knock was a sign of heavenly approval and of gratitude of the holy souls. To them, the presence of the altar and the lamb seems to indicate the Holy Sacrifice of the Mass (Harte, p. 22).

An Irish Night Prayer

Jesus, Mary and Joseph, I give you my heart and my soul.
Jesus, Mary and Joseph, assist me in my last agony.

Jesus, Mary and Joseph, may I breathe forth my soul in peace with you.

Into your hands O Lord I commend my spirit.

This replica of the Consoler of the Afflicted of Luxemburg is located at the Shrine of Our Lady, Carey, Ohio.

Chapter Twelve

Korean Funerals Today

Today's Korea is changing constantly, becoming more Westernized all the time. Many of the traditions of the culture have been simplified and modernized with the encouragement of the government. Korean funerals, however, still have a complicated etiquette that is carried out by the families in much the same manner as a century ago.

The French foreign missionaries developed the Christian faith in Korea. Because of the prohibition against ancestor worship, they tried to change the funeral rites as much as possible, although maintaining many of the traditional customs in a modified form. They simplified the Christian burial rite and substituted the litany of the saints for long Korean chants. To the Koreans, who were used to days of ritual wailing, these chants and litanies were comfortable substitutions and became very popular. The chants form an important part of the Catholic funeral rite that is conducted in the home of the deceased.

With their history of filial respect to ancestors, the Koreans have always emphasized funerals. The ceremonies used to last four or five days, although today the government has pushed for shorter funerals and the average now is only three days. After death, the corpse is washed, especially the hands, face, and feet. This ritual washing is distasteful to most Koreans and there are usually a couple of parishioners who perform this service as a special ministry, for which the family is very grateful. After the body is washed, it is dressed in new clothes, the hands are wrapped with a band of cloth, and special socks are used to cover the feet. The face is covered and the simple wood coffin immediately closed.

Just as in European wakes, the family sits up with the body all through the nights before burial. The coffin is usually hidden from view, covered with a large folding screen. Some parishes have beautiful screens with Christian scenes on them, which are borrowed for the wake. A large number of friends and relatives come to the house to pay condolence calls and to eat, drink, and say the *Yondo* prayers (psalms from the Psalter). These are chanted in a rectotonal chant, a crying sound of an old Korean melody. Men and women alternate the verses.

There is no furniture in a traditional Korean home, other than one closed cabinet. The floor is heated. A low table is placed in front of the funeral screen, on which is always placed a large photo portrait of the deceased, with a jar of sand to hold incense in front of it. Candles are lighted, and occasionally blessed holy water in a bowl is dipped out with a twig to sprinkle over the coffin. New arrivals light an incense stick using the candles and place it in the pot in front of the photograph.

The traditional Korean mourning costumes are unique. Family members wear special funeral clothes made of bleached hemp with a rough weave. The use of the rough-cut fabric with crude stitching is to symbolize simplicity and heartfelt grieving (Yang, p. 70). White is the color of preference for funerals. The large, hempen, basket-like headgear worn by the men completely covers their face. (Because of its disguising capabilities, the first missionaries to Korea were able to sneak into the county by dressing in mourning attire.)

The coffin is carried to the burial site on an elaborate hearse on poles carried by men, although in the cities buses are now sometimes used. Flags and a drummer also form part of the procession. Mourners chant a wailing cry to express sorrow.

In keeping with their ancient traditions, Koreans today are still very choosy about the burial site, even the Catholics. A large horseshoe-shaped mound is built around the burial site. After the coffin is interred, a mound of earth is built up over it. The Church has allowed food to be placed at the burial mound, although the people know the food is not for the spirits but is rather a gesture of familial love. The food is eaten by the mourners.

A Mass is said on the anniversary of the death for several years.

There is an annual memorial day in the fall set by the lunar calendar. Families have a picnic at the grave site of their ancestors.

There is always a bowl of rice set out in honor of the deceased. The Korean Church gave its blessing to a community Mass offering for this special day. Candles, incense, and photographs of family dead are placed in front of the altar for this Mass. Fruit is piled around and the celebration has a festive air.

A 1960s-era Korean funeral procession.

Chapter Thirteen

The Japanese Can Be Catholic and Cremated

Until recent years, the Church's ban against the practice of cremation, and its slow incorporation of meaningful symbols of the Japanese culture into its own rites, sometimes formed a stumbling block for missionaries in Japan.

The intrepid Basque Jesuit, St. Francis Xavier, opened the first Christian mission in Japan about 1547. During his ten years in the missions, he traveled the greater part of the Far East, leaving behind him flourishing churches. He gladly faced the peril of death for the love and service of God, and instructed his fellow Jesuits to bear themselves lovingly toward the people and to constantly visit each of the new Christian families.

These early missionaries were faced with attempting to convert a people whose society for over eight hundred years had practiced ancestor worship and had burned, not buried, their dead.

The Background of Cremation

Whether a society practiced inhumation or cremation largely depended on its religious beliefs. Cremation was the normal custom in the ancient civilized world, except in Egypt, Judaea, and China. It was repugnant to the early Christians because of the belief in the resurrection of the body.

Early Christian beliefs regarding the disposal of their dead were based on the ideas of the Hebrews as expanded by the teaching of Christ. Like other Semites, the Hebrews believed the soul led a shadowy afterlife in a netherworld called *Sheol* and that both the righteous and the wicked would be raised from the netherworld at the day of the last judgment for their final rewards and punishments. In all historical periods the Jews interred their dead; cremation was considered an indignity to the corpse.

Jesus preached the infinite and equal value of every human soul, which is both spiritual and immortal. The soul is not annihilated in death; there is a resurrection of a glorified body.

In spite of the assurances from St. Paul, the earliest Christians often held onto a superstitious dread that they could not have any part of the resurrection of the flesh if their bodies did not rest in the grave.

According to Paul, the disposition of the body after death is largely a matter of indifference; the resurrection is a miracle of God and bodies buried, burned, or lost at sea share equally in the miraculous transformation (cf. Romans 8:23; Philippians 3:21).

The Church, however, held it revolting that the body, once the "temple of the Holy Spirit," should be burned except in well-defined cases of need when it was necessary to prevent the spread of disease. Customarily then, Christians buried their dead, and during the reign of Constantine cremation was prohibited. In 789, Emperor Charlemagne made it a capital offense in the New Christian Empire to cremate a body according to the ancient pagan rite.

The practice of cremation was forbidden for centuries because it was believed that to do so was a sign of disbelief in the immortality of the soul and an act of disrespect for the body. However, the Church never declared that the practice was intrinsically wrong.

Eastern Practices

In the Orient, the custom of cremation began in India about 900 B.C. The disciples of Gautama Buddha (Prince Siddhartha) burned his body when he died in 483 B.C. With the spread of Buddhism as a world religion, the practice of cremation spread throughout the Far East (Lally, 1994).

The first cremation in Japan was that of the Buddist *bonze* (monk), Dosho, in 700 A.D. As Buddhism spread throughout Japan, blending with the indigenous religion, Shinto, cremation became the normal means of disposing of the dead (Lally, 1994).

When Christianity entered the country in the sixteenth century, at first it spread rapidly. However, in the last four centuries it has not reached its initial promise. Part of the impediment to its spread has been its refusal to adapt and inculcate native practices into its own rites, insisting instead on its European-based rites and celebrations.

In 1886, the Sacred Congregation of the Holy Office forbad cremation in response to suspected materialistic and anti-Christian sentiments of those who proposed it. However, instructions to missionaries were much milder in tone, allowing a greater tolerance of the practice in foreign lands.

In the 1917 *Code of Canon Law*, Canon 1203 condemned cremation and required that Christian bodies be buried. Canon 1240 forbade ecclesiastical burial for those who ordered their bodies to be cremated. In 1926, an instruction of the Holy Office characterized the proponents of cremation as "enemies of Christianity" (Lally, 1994).

By the 1960s, many proponents of cremation felt that modern funeral customs were unchristian because of their great emphasis on the importance of the body and the luxurious burial paraphernalia used. This view was shared by many Catholics (Lally, 1994).

In 1963, the July 5th instruction of the Holy Office virtually repealed the penalties of Canon 1240. It allowed for cremation as long as it is not done in contempt of Catholic doctrine. Although funeral rites were not permitted at the place of cremation, a priest or deacon was allowed to go there to offer prayer. Under the new *Code*, Canon 1184 lists the only three types of people to whom funeral rites are to be denied: (1) notorious apostates, heretics, and schismatics; (2) persons who have chosen cremation for reasons opposed to Catholic faith (for example, as a denial of the Resurrection); and (3) other manifest sinners for whom ecclesiastical funeral rites cannot be granted without public scandal to the faithful. When there is any doubt, the local bishop must be consulted (Sheedy, *Our Sunday Visitor*, March 14, 1993).

One of the major concerns of Vatican II was that it be an ecumenical council, global in its concerns. Its decree on the missions pointed to areas of the world, especially in Asia and Africa, whose diverse cultures had not yet been penetrated by the Gospel. This decree emphasized the need for the Church to adapt to local conditions. It suggested that young churches examine the customs and traditions of their native peoples in order to draw from their wisdom, their learning, and their arts and sciences all those things which could contribute to the glory of their Creator. Further, it charged that Episcopal conferences in each major sociocultural territory unite to pursue this program of adaptation with one mind and with a common plan (Abbot, pp. 612-613).

That the Japanese Bishops understood this message of the great council is shown by the fact that in 1971 the bishop of Urawa, Most Rev. Lawrence Satoshi Nagai, as Chairman of the Japanese Bishops' Liturgical Committee, approved the Catholic funeral rites, which take into account the national custom of cremation. Bishop Nagai became famous during Vatican Council II as a leader in the movement to accommodate the European Catholic liturgy to national customs (Lally, 1994).

In 1983, in the amended *Ordo Exsequiarum*, the Congregation for the Sacraments and Divine Worship teaches that Catholic funeral rites are to be granted to those who have chosen to be cremated. The model used in the region should be followed and rites usually held at the grave may be held even in the crematory room (Lally, 1994).

Other Japanese funeral customs are gradually being incorporated into the Japanese Catholic church.

The ancient leave-taking ceremony, *Kokubetsu-shiki*, is a part of the Catholic funeral liturgy. In this ceremony that bids farewell to a person who has died, the closest male relative gives a brief history of the deceased, his accomplishments, and the details of his death. He then thanks the mourners for their friendship and prayers. Often a few mourners, facing the coffin, will read a farewell address to the deceased, using heartfelt words of praise for their goodness, and thanks for their friendship (Lally, 1994).

Joss is burned before the coffin and the grave at Catholic services. "Joss" is a corruption of the Portuguese word "*Deos*," meaning "God," and these incense sticks have been burned before the Chinese idols for centuries. At a Japanese funeral service, invariably a photograph of the deceased is placed in front of the casket, facing the mourners, and the joss sticks are placed in a container near this. Called *senko* in Japanese, the incense is lit as a prayer for the dead (Lally, 1994).

Nokotsudos (ossuaries, mausoleums, or columbariums) are commonly attached to a Catholic Church or built as a separate facility nearby. These hold the cinerary urns of cremains. *Columbariums* are found in ancient Rome as subterranean sepulchres with niches in the walls for the urns. Today's *columbaria* are generally chapels or outdoor garden walls with boxlike private lockers for the cremated remains (Lally, 1994).

As other cultural traditions of the Japanese are drawn slowly into the Church, perhaps the directives of Vatican II regarding examining the wisdom of other societies to draw forth good things to contribute to the glory of the Creator will result in other patterns that also enhance mankind's life on earth.

A single example (from many possible) is the Japanese treatment of the elderly. Ancestor worship is, of course, heretical. The honor bestowed on the elders, however, is not. Nor is the remembrance of our beloved dead; this is particularly charged to faithful Catholics. We Americans who annually build old folks' homes to accept our family elders could benefit by an examination of the Japanese treatment of the older members of their family.

Father Campion Lally visits the graves of the early French missionaries of Tokyo.

Chapter Fourteen

Native American Culture Blends With Catholicism

Native American Catholics in many instances have successfully blended a strong, traditional, cultural identity with their Catholicism.

For centuries herbs have been used and valued by mankind as medicines to heal the sick and wounded. In Europe, much herbal knowledge was preserved in the gardens of the medieval monasteries and given a Christian orientation. The treatment of human illness, from the example of St. Basil, became an extension of Church teaching.

European immigrants brought their folk medicine to America. In the New World, it blended with the natural healing practiced for centuries by native Americans. In many rural areas of the United States, people today still use traditional botanical home remedies.

The *curanderos, curanderas*, and native American medicine men of the Southwest do a brisk business in herbal remedies even today. The useful properties of plants such as manzanilla, aloe vera, garlic, mint, and peppers, for example, have been known and used for centuries by native American healers.

Physicians at the Indian Hospital of the U.S. Public Heath Service on the Papago Reservation in Arizona work side by side with Papago Indian medicine men, and the hospital is open to these traditional healers (Dobelis, p. 72).

A Southwestern Faith Healer

One of the best-known figures in Southwest folklore is Don Pedrito Jaramillo, a *curandero* and faith healer who came to South

Texas from Mexico in 1881. Over the course of twenty-five years he treated thousands of people.

People came from near and far for his healing, often camping for two or three days. Don Pedrito not only gave them remedies, he also fed many of them without charge.

Known as the Healer of Los Olmos, there is a large but simple marker at his grave site that tells his story. In part, it reads, "Unlike other faith healers, he claimed no power of his own, but said God's healing was released through faith." He did not charge for his services; patients gave or withheld as they chose. But whatever was given voluntarily he often gave to the poor — food as well as remedies.

As the story goes, when he was a young man Don Pedrito was riding a horse and was hit in the face by a mesquite limb, which broke his nose and tore his face. In great pain, he stumbled to a nearby pond and put his face in the mud. Immediately the pain stopped. That night he had a vision, in which he was told he could heal the sick through faith. The vision told him to cure only in God's name and to give as his prescription whatever came to mind immediately. From that point he began his healing ministry, always telling the afflicted that not he, but their own faith in God's power, would heal them.

Don Pedrito Jaramillo has been acclaimed as a popular, or folk, saint by the people, many of whom believe it is only a matter of time before the Church canonizes him. Even today, his grave is treated as a shrine and visited annually by many who light candles, pray, and leave numerous *ex votos* such as photos or expired driver's licenses in thanksgiving (*San Antonio Express News*, p. 1).

Kateri Tekakwitha, Saintly Indian Patroness

Cardinal John O'Connor of the New York Archdiocese pointed out in a homily at St. Patrick's in 1989 that Native Americans have struggled through the years to overcome numerous injustices that have deprived them of their true heritage. He also underscored the respect and reverence for the environment that has been a hallmark of Native Americans throughout their history (*Lily of the Mohawks*, p. 1). The "Lily of the Mohawks," Blessed Kateri Tekakwitha, is a sterling example of how successfully Native American cultural heritage can blend with Catholicism.

Born in 1656 near Auriesville, New York, where St. Isaac Joques and his companions were martyred, Kateri was the daughter of a captive Christian Algonquin mother and a pagan Mohawk father, both of whom died while she was still an unbaptized child.

Baptized by missionaries at the age of eighteen, Blessed Kateri was persecuted by her relatives, who claimed her Christianity caused her to forsake their ancestral beliefs. She escaped to Laprarie, Canada, and while living at the Indian mission became a model of prayer, of love for the Holy Eucharist, and of the Blessed Virgin. In 1679, she was the first of her people to make a vow of virginity.

At the beginning of Holy Week, 1680, Kateri, who had been stricken a year before with an ailment that left her with a low fever and chronic stomach pains, took to her fur mat. Inconveniently an invalid, Kateri was left alone with a plate of cornbread and a little water within reach. On Tuesday she began to sink and, when the priest brought Our Lord to her, received Holy Viaticum with conscious fervor. She had borrowed a friend's tunic as she felt hers was too shabby in which to receive her God. She encouraged her friend to keep the Christian faith. On Wednesday, she kept an Algonquin silence, laying on her fur mat on the floor of the lodge. She was anointed with the holy oils, then entered her gentle agony. Her final words were spoken softly: "Jesus, I love you."

The Indians at the mission were generally buried on a board with their faces greased and covered. Kateri, however, was buried in a coffin made for her by two Frenchmen. Although one of the priests wanted to bury her on the chapel grounds, Father Cholonec disagreed, and she was laid to rest in the Indian cemetery where some time before she had pointed out a spot to one of her friends.

The process for Kateri's beatification was begun in 1884; she was beatified by Pope John Paul II in 1980. Over four hundred Native Americans attended the beatification Mass in St. Peter's Basilica in Rome.

Annie Marie Pablito — Zuni and Catholic

Among the Zuni Indians of New Mexico, as a sign of respect to the local culture, much of the ceremony that surrounds the death and burial ritual remains silent. The priest is sometimes called the night before burial for a rosary, but there is generally no funeral

Mass. The dead are not embalmed, but are wrapped simply in a blanket without the use of a casket, and buried within twenty-four hours. A wake, held in the family home the night before burial, centers around the body of the departed, which is placed in the middle of the floor. The wake lasts all night. In the morning, six or seven Zuni religious men take the body to the cemetery and perform the burial in private, with no one else present.

The old Zuni Mission church, first built in 1629 and restored in 1970, is still in use today. The cemetery in front of the church is full, with some bodies only a few feet underground. Therefore, a new cemetery was built nearby in the early 1900s. Markers in the old cemetery are simple, small wooden crosses or markers made of pottery. Some of the graves are not marked at all. Deceased military personnel are the only ones with stone markers. Visitations to the cemetery itself are not common.

In Memoriam
Annie Marie Pablito
1981 – 1993

An exception to the Zuni practice of not holding a funeral mass was made in the 1993 death of Annie Marie Pablito, a well-loved twelve-year-old who attended a mission school. The photo on the memorial card at left displays pride in her Indian heritage. The little Zuni girl is shown in her native American clothing holding an ear of corn.

Eternal rest grant unto her, O Lord,
and let perpetual light shine upon her.
May she rest in peace. Amen.

Stories and Customs From Around the World

A Page From a Missionary's Diary

Father Richard Antall, a priest of the Cleveland diocese on mission in El Salvador, described his work among the poor at the mission in La Libertad. Death and dying are familiar subjects at the mission because of the war-torn condition of the country. This is his story about two funerals held on a single day (from *Our Sunday Visitor* newspaper, November 8, 1992):

Five people stood at the door of the apartment in the school where the missionary priests live. Two of the women wanted funerals.

In this country, the priests rarely wait more than twenty-four hours for a funeral. Instead of a wake, nine days of prayer are conducted after the death of a person. The people are so poor that many cannot afford a coffin. At first, the missionaries attempted to help the neediest cases. Later, they realized they were better off making the coffins.

The first funeral was held out in the country. The brother of one of the mission parishioners had been killed by thieves. One of the friends who visited the woman did not stay for the Mass because he had to attend another funeral, that deceased also a victim of violent crime.

The second funeral was for a woman killed by a car. Her sister was more tearful than is usual at the mission funerals. Here the bereaved are often fatigued by an all-night vigil or are injected with tranquilizers to help resist the rigor of emotion. This woman had lost another sibling in a similar accident and was overwhelmed with grief. The mission church has no lights and it is dark in the tropics very early so the 6 P.M. Mass was held with candle and flashlight.

The Cross of Life

In Spanish Colonial times in the New World, one Easter Week prop found in most churches was a wooden cross painted green. The color symbolized the merciful, life-giving qualities of the cross and emphasized the fact that the crucifixion is not a negative event, sorrowful though it is, but rather a positive one, giving divine life to the faithful.

In 1595, after a vision of Christ was seen by one of the Indians, the natives of the town of Esquipulas, Guatemala bonded together to accept the Christian faith. The bishop's provisor ordered an image carved for these faithful. A Portuguese sculptor named Quirio Cantano, living in Antigua, was given the commission. A mystic as well as an artist, he was able to project both the pain and the compassion of Our Lord dying on the cross. But the cross was not a symbol of death. Cantano placed the miraculous black Christ on a living cross; it is covered with leaves and sprouting vines to symbolize the life of the Resurrection.

The Raising of the Cross

In earlier times in Mexico, after a person had received the last sacraments, a linen cloth was placed on the floor and a cross of ashes was drawn on it. The sick person was placed there until death.

By this means, the dying person was reminded that death is the natural conclusion of life and that his preparation for death was of utmost importance. To support him, the priest and relatives gathered around and prayed. The prayers stressed repentance and trust in the Lord.

Among other rituals, the priest would make the sign of the cross on the chest of the dying person. He would repeat the words used at the imposition of ashes at the beginning of Lent: "Remember, man, that you are dust, and unto dust you shall return."

Although this ancient custom is no longer practiced, in some regions they place a cross of ash or lime in the place where the body of the deceased was attended.

After finishing a novena of prayer, there is a special ceremony called *Lavantamiento de la Cruz*, the raising of the cross. A cross made of wood or iron is taken to the church, blessed, then taken to the cemetery to conclude the rites and prayers which accompany the death of a beloved one.

This raising of the cross is a reminder that death is something provisional. A day will come when there will be no death, no tears, or suffering for all those who have made the effort to live well.

Descansos

A death-related aspect of folk art exists in many places of the Southwest in the form of *descansos* (resting places) that relate to ancient custom among Mexican Americans. In the old days, when the body was carried to the cemetery, the pallbearers had to stop and rest several times, as the distance was often over a mile. The places where they put down their load were called *descansos* and were often marked in some way, as were ritual stopping places inside the cemeteries. The custom was later extended to include the marking of the spot where death had occurred, if it was a highway death or death by violence. The name of Las Cruces (the crosses), New Mexico, indicates the antiquity of this custom. The city received its name from the crosses, erected in earlier times, to commemorate the deaths of persons killed by the Indians, who were later buried by the people who came on the site. The folk art *descansos* of today are crafted of many materials. Some are even made of the parts of the car or bicycle that was in the accident (West, pp. 238-239). Memorial markers and lonely graves along the miles of fencing line the highway between George West and Laredo, Texas.

Travelers who stop to pray or to examine the markers merely from curiosity may receive an unexpected bonus. Behind many of these markers is a plastic bottle of water. Whether left there for later use at the marker or grave, or for the use of travelers along this lengthy strip of highway unbroken by any service station, more than one motorist has blessed the provident hand that left the water there. Weather, highway crews, and vandals take their toll on these monuments of folk art.

On the other side of the Mexican border, however, the *descansos* take more the form of roadside shrines. The *descansos* are sometimes cut into the rock on the hilly side of the highway; some are elaborate enough to form a space for a person to kneel inside. Others are *gruttas* (grottos) formed of native stone. These generally

**An example of *descansos*, the marking of the spot
where death has occurred, in this case by a highway.**

include a statue or tile picture of the Virgin or one of the saints. That
people still stop and pray at these shrines is indicated by the large
number of *miraglos*, or tiny ex-votos, left there.

Icons — Eyes on Eternity

The entire history of Russian art covers a span of only a little
more than a thousand years. The conversion of the Grand Prince
Vladimir in the eleventh century brought *Kievan Rus* into the cultural orbit of Byzantium. The visual legacy of this earliest period of
Russian history is usually known as Old Russian art, and it corre-
sponds to what we in the West term medieval.

In the secular world we live in, we often consider art to be merely
entertainment, but Russian icons were created to be more than works
of beauty; they functioned as windows to eternity. The art of Russian medieval Christendom not only had aesthetic qualities; it also
had a spiritual and metaphysical nature. Their art was a ritual art,
created for public or private devotion (Petrove, p. 6).

The word "icon" is derived from the Greek word for image —
eikon. Visible things are revealed images (*eikones*) of invisible things.

The icon is not confined to the created world. St. Paul, in his Epistle to the Colossians (1:15) asserts that Christ Himself is the image (*eikon*) of the invisible God (Averintsev, p. 11).

Two icons point out some of the medieval Christian ideas of Heaven and Hell.

The icon "The Vision of the Heavenly Ladder" illustrates a text by St. John Klimakos of Sinai, a treatise on the spiritual perfection of monks. According to this saint, the constant memory of death assists and supports people in their spiritual ascent to heaven.

The image of a heavenly ladder is of ancient origin. An Egyptian belief held that by such a ladder the dead ascended to heaven. A vision of a ladder was sent to Jacob (Genesis 23:10-12), who saw angels ascending and descending between heaven and earth. In the lower-left corner of the icon, we see St. John reading to the monks. Paradise is behind a massive wall, which is portrayed behind the saint. Monks are slowly climbing the steps of a ladder, each figure giving the impression of a desire to ascend. Christ extends his hand to the monk who has mounted the final step, in order to assist him in entering the open gate of paradise. The Virgin, St. John the Baptist, and the archangels meet the new entrant, and a golden nimbus circles his head. Paradise is painted in white to symbolize spiritual purity and attained perfection. Near the entrance to paradise, groups of saints on clouds praise the Creator.

Not all the aspirants reach paradise, however. Many fall and are taken by the mischief and artifice of demons. In the lower right corner the icon depicts a bare rock, under which we see the abyss in the darkness of passion where a red monster symbolizes death and hell (Shalina, pp. 201-202).

A sixteenth-century Vologda icon, "The Descent Into Hell," is from the Church of St. George. In it, Christ is represented in luminous clothing against a large, round mandorla. His shining robes are symbolic of his bringing light and salvation to the dead. Divine rays stream from Christ to those resurrected from the underworld. In his hands, Christ holds a scroll representing the sins of the human race, which he has destroyed. Adam is shown rising from the shadow of death, holding his arms out to the Savior. Christ stands on a cross, whereby the artist links the crucifixion to the symbolic descent into hell. Around the central figures of Christ and Adam are Old Testament figures and the righteous dead. At the center of the abyss is a large keyhole and the Archangel Michael, keeper of the keys to paradise, is standing to its left with the key hanging from his hand. He has opened paradise to those who have been saved (Shalina, p. 206).

By contemplating these beautiful icons, legacy of the medieval world, those of us living in the twentieth century may be able to recover at least a part of the perfect harmony between heaven and earth to which the Russian artists and patrons aspired.

Bread of the Dead

Special breads are used in many parts of the world to celebrate All Souls' Day. Called *Pan de Muerto* (bread of the dead) in Mexico, *Ossi Dei Morti* (bones of the dead) in Italy, *Dirge cakes* (donuts) in Central Europe, and *Seelenbrot* (soul bread) in Germany, all are made and eaten in honor of the souls of the faithful departed.

Chung Yeung

In Hong Kong, Chinese Christians follow the ancient custom of visiting the tombs of their relatives twice a year at *Ching Ming* and on Double Nine Day, September 9th. This day is called the festival of *Chung Yeung*. The families sweep and clean around the tombs and place flowers and food there. They burn joss sticks. Then the family has a picnic at the cemetery, or takes the food home for a feast.

A Consoling Modern-Day American Custom

After her daughter's tragic death, Pat O'Brien made a journal filled with pictures of her daughter, friends, and family. The journal was placed in a plastic box at the cemetery. A note on the box invites all who visit to write in the journal. On the anniversary of her death, the family went to Mass, then to the coastal town where her daughter had lived. They bought flowers and took a walk on the boardwalk, scattering the flowers in the ocean. Then they went for lunch to one of their daughter's favorite restaurants. Instead of a down, depressing day, the family made it a hopeful and positive one, even in the midst of their sadness.

Funeral Herbs

A number of plants throughout history have found a place in the legend and lore of the dead.

Parsley was known as a funeral plant to the Greeks. It was later consecrated to St. Peter in his role as heavenly gatekeeper.

Rosemary, a symbol of love and fidelity, was often worn at weddings. St. Thomas More wrote that he let this herb run all over his garden, to please his bees and because it was the symbol of memory and friendship. He also pointed out that it was the chosen emblem of English funeral wakes and burial grounds. In France, rosemary was carried by mourners at funerals and thrown into the open grave.

In England, an elder bush trimmed in the shape of a cross was planted on a new grave. If the bush bloomed, the common folk said the spirit of the deceased was happy. Green branches of the plant were also buried in the grave to protect the occupant from demons. Funeral hearse drivers often carried a whip of elder.

Part Four:

Praying for and to the Dead

"The Sorrowful Mother" at prayer.
Il Sassoferrato, 1605-1685.

Chapter Sixteen

Prayers for the Sick and Dying

Pray for those who are sick and dying, little sisters. If you only knew what goes on! How little it takes to lose control of oneself! I would not have believed this before.

I am not dying; I am entering into life.

Jesus, allow me to save very many souls; let no soul be lost today; let all the souls in purgatory be saved.

— St. Therese Lisieux

Say a Prayer

"Say a little prayer for me," you say.
And I reply, "Of course I will."
And of course I shall — but perhaps the words are not
The standard, traditional words you may expect.
How tempting to say, "God, let him live. Reduce the pain.
Let him stay with us a bit longer. Heal his body."
How difficult to say, "Your Will be done, not ours."
When love is strong, it's hard to let go.
So in this case, my little prayer begins,
"Lord, let my brother see Your face.
For when he looks through your eyes,
Fear will be replaced by certainty."
I'm not asking, Lord, for an overwhelming vision,
Or a burning bush.
Just let my brother look about this beautiful world
And see Your imprint on even the tiniest of things.
Then, Lord, perhaps he will see

That the same power that could create the known
Was only showing us a foretast
Of the more beautiful days ahead.
Divine Mercy,
Allow him the courage of stoic acceptance;
May he joyfully touch the outstretched hand
Of our blessed Sister Death, when she comes.

For the Sick

Most compassionate Heart of Christ, You loved during Your life on earth to soothe and to console, to comfort and to heal the sick of body and mind. Dearest Lord, hear our prayers for all who are now on beds of pain, afflicted with various illnesses, in great need of Your mercy and compassion. Give them patience, sweet Jesus, to bear their sufferings for love of You. Alleviate a little, by Your almighty power, the sharpness of their pain. Send them kind friends who will comfort and instruct them. Teach them, by Your grace, how to pray and to offer all their sufferings for the love of You. Heal their souls, good Jesus, though it is Your will that they shall endure sickness of the body.

Make them understand that You hurt them but to cure them, that You let them suffer now so that you may spare them hereafter. Hear, Lord, the prayers of all Your angels and saints, and in particular those of Your blessed Mother, in behalf of the sorrowful and the distressed. We pray not alone for those sufferers who are known and dear to us, but we beseech You as well for all whom we do not know and who perhaps have few to pray for them here on earth. Pity them all in Your loving mercy. Bring them, purified by their sufferings and afflictions, to the peace and joy of everlasting life in heaven with You, forever and ever. Amen.

— Rev. Edward Garesche, S.J.

To the Child of the Atocha — Prayer for a Mother and an Unborn Child During a High-Risk Pregnancy

Most Holy Infant of the Atocha, this child is Yours to demand what honor you wish. I understand he belongs to the True God, in Whom we live and have our being. Through Your love for Your mother, to whom You could refuse no request, protect this mother and this child and keep them from all harm. Santo Nino, I beg you, allow him breath and time to greet his earthly parents in this life, and keep him in Your Sacred Heart now and in the afterlife.

Prayer for Those in Their Agony

O most merciful Jesus, Lover of souls: I pray Thee by the agony of Thy most Sacred Heart, and by the sorrows of Thy Immaculate Mother, cleanse in Thine own Blood the sinners of the whole world who are now in their agony and are to die this day. Amen. Heart of Jesus, once in agony, pity the dying.

For the Dying

Jesus, saviour and Lover of souls, by the memory of Your own agonizing death on the cross, have mercy upon all the dying. At every instant, sweet Jesus, some poor souls are trembling on the threshold of eternity, about to appear before Your awful judgement. Have mercy on them all, with a most tender mercy, at this the hour of their greatest need.

Remember dear Jesus, the awful price which You have paid for their redemption. Remember the anguish of Your agony in the Garden, the bloody sweat with which You bedewed the ground, the pang of Your betrayal, the insolence and cruelty of Your executions, the mocker of Your trial, the torture of Your scourging, the weariness and suffering of Your Way of the Cross! Oh, by these holy memories, help the souls of the dying!

Remember, most good and merciful Jesus, the anguish of Your crucifixion, the bitterness of Your dereliction, Your thirst and sufferings, and Your agonizing death, and help and heal the souls of the departing. Give them strength, dear Lord, at the last hour. Give them love and sorrow. Sustain them by Your holy graces; deliver them from the attacks of the enemy. We ask it of You through the intercession of the Blessed Virgin, Your Mother, and of all Your angels and saints. Amen.

— Rev. Edward Garesche, S.J.

Prayer for Mercy — Isaiah 14:1

For the Lord will have mercy on Jacob, and will yet choose Israel and set them in their own land: and the strangers shall be joined with them, and they shall cleave to the house of Jacob.

Mercy. Lord God have mercy on Your people. You will, won't You?

You are a just God, But none desire justice! Justice is right but all desire mercy!

And Lord, you told Faustina to tell us To pray, "Jesus, I trust in You." And, Lord, you reminded us of Divine Mercy.

You will have mercy on Jacob And will yet choose Israel. You will know Your own And will take us with the strangers And mercifully bathe us in Your Blood And hold us in Your Heart Forever.

For All The Dying

Almighty and merciful God, who hast bestowed upon mankind saving remedies and the gift of everlasting life, look graciously upon us Thy servants and comfort the souls which Thou hast made, that in the hour of their passing, cleansed from all stain of sin, they may deserve to be presented to Thee, their Creator, by the hands of the holy angels. Through Christ our Lord. Amen.

— Roman Missal

Daily Prayer for the Dying

O most merciful Jesus, lover of souls, I beseech Thee by the agony of Thy Most Sacred Heart and by the sorrows of Thine Immaculate Mother, wash clean in Thy Blood the sinners of the whole world who are now in their agony and who are to die this day. Amen.

Heart of Jesus, who didst suffer death's agony,

Have mercy on the dying.

To Mary, Mother of the Dying

O Mary, conceived without sin, pray for us who have recourse to thee; O refuge of sinners, Mother of the dying, forsake us not at the hour of our death; obtain for us the grace of perfect sorrow, sincere contrition, the pardon and remission of our sins, a worthy receiving of the holy Viaticum, and the comfort of the Sacrament of Extreme Unction (Anointing of the Sick), in order that we may appear with greater security before the throne of the just but merciful Judge, our god and our Redeemer. Amen.

For the Dying

Remember also, most merciful and loving Father, all who are sick and dying, and grant that in the solitude of suffering each may truly "come to himself," and like the Prodigal of the Gospel may at last discover Thy love and return to a Father's heart. That most bountiful Heart has given them joy of life and youth, hope and desire; and from it all good and pleasant things, all enduring comfort and true delight, descend in copious benediction. Feed them before they die with the Body and Blood of Thy beloved Son, that nothing may be wanting to Thy love nor to their eternal beatitude. Amen (O'Connell, p. 138).

Gravesite of a child. Note the toys.

Chapter Seventeen

Prayers for the Dead

Memento of the Dead

Remember also, O Lord, your servants [names] who have gone before us with the sign of faith, and rest in the sleep of peace. To them, O Lord, and to all who rest in Christ, we entreat you to grant a place of comfort, of light and peace.

— from the Roman Canon, Eucharistic Prayer I

The Rosary for the Dead

My friends, let us pray much and let us obtain many prayers from others for the poor dead. The good God will return to us a hundredfold the good we do them. Ah! If every one knew how useful to those who practice it is this devotion to the holy souls in Purgatory, they would not be so often forgotten; the good God regards all we do for them as if it were done for Himself

— St. John Vianney, Curé d'Ars

In the mid-nineteenth century, Abbé Serre of the Chapel of the Hotel Dieu at Nismes, France, composed the Rosary for the Dead for the benefit of the poor suffering souls in purgatory. The chaplet was promoted by the Archconfraternity of Notre Dame du Suffrage.

The chaplet consists of four decades of ten beads each which commemorate the forty hours Christ spent in limbo, where He went for the purpose of delivering the souls of the holy persons who died before Him. The rosary has a cross and a medal of the Archconfraternity, representing the souls in purgatory. The chaplet may also have five introductory beads as found on the Dominican rosary.

The *De Profundis* (Psalm 130) is said upon the cross, at the beginning, and the ending of the chaplet. Anyone who is not familiar with that prayer may substitute an Our Father and a Hail Mary. The *Requiem Eternam* ("Eternal rest grant unto them," etc.) and the Acts of Faith, Hope, and Charity are said on the large beads, and on the small beads is said, "Sweet Heart of Mary, be my salvation."

In Ireland, a similar chaplet was known as the Beads of the Dead. It was said in the same manner as listed above except that on the small beads the people repeated, "Lord Jesus grant them eternal rest." Here, each decade was ended by saying, "Eternal rest grant to them, O Lord, and let perpetual light shine upon them. May they rest in peace. Amen."

Prayer for the Faithful Departed

Eternal rest grant unto them, O Lord. And let perpetual light shine upon them. May their souls and the souls of all the faithful departed, through the mercy of God, rest in peace. Amen.

Adieu, My Friend

Adieu, my friend. Adieu.... to God I commend you ... Goodbye ... God be with ye ... Farewell ... words spoken at parting. Adieu, my friend, we part for now, But not forever.

Sorrow? Not sorrow, my friend; Yet grief and sadness are my lot For now and a while. Grief and sadness Are my companions briefly, For you are not here.

Peace and joy creep in, my friend. Peace and joy to take their turn. And whirl my mind To memory Of the joy you knew, and the Joy you sought And by your life taught.

Rejoice! Rejoice, my friend. Your eyes closed briefly Ere they opened again From joy to Joy. Rejoice, my friend. Now and forever.

Psalms

Two psalms, the 50th and the 129th, are prayed as indulgenced prayers for the souls in purgatory.

The Miserere — Psalm 50

This psalm, composed by David after his sin with Bathsheba, is a beautiful act of contrition, confession, and supplication by a repentant sinner. David offers to God the sacrifice of a humble and contrite heart, and in reparation promises to lead others back to God by telling them of the ways of divine justice.

> Have mercy on me, O God, in Your goodness; in the greatness of Your compassion wipe out my offense.
>
> Thoroughly wash me from my guilt and of my sin cleanse me.
>
> For I acknowledge my offense, and my sin is before me always:
>
> "Against You only have I sinned, and done what is evil in Your sight" —
>
> That You may be justified in Your sentence, vindicated when You condemn.
>
> Indeed, in guilt was I born, and in sin my mother conceived me;
>
> Behold, You are pleased with sincerity of heart, and in my inmost being You teach me wisdom.
>
> Cleanse me of sin with hyssop, that I may be purified; wash me, and I shall be whiter than snow.
>
> Let me hear the sounds of joy and gladness; the bones You have crushed shall rejoice.
>
> Turn away Your face from my sins and blot out all my guilt.
>
> A clean heart create for me, O God, and a steadfast spirit renew within me.
>
> Cast me not out from Your presence, and Your holy spirit take not from me.
>
> Give me back the joy of Your salvation, and a willing spirit sustain in me.
>
> I will teach transgressors Your ways, and sinners shall return to You.
>
> Free me from blood guilt, O God, my saving God; then my tongue shall revel in Your justice.
>
> O Lord, open my lips, and my mouth shall proclaim Your praise.
>
> For You are not pleased with sacrifices; should I offer a holocaust, You would not accept it.
>
> My sacrifice, O God, is a contrite spirit; a heart contrite and humbled, O God, You will not spurn.
>
> Be bountiful, O Lord, to Sion in Your kindness by rebuilding the walls of Jerusalem;
>
> Then shall You be pleased with due sacrifices, burnt offerings and holocausts; then shall they offer up bullocks on Your altar.

De Profundis — *Psalm 129*

Here, the psalmist cries out because of his sense of sin and tells God that no man could be forgiven if strict justice were demanded. Since God is forgiving and merciful the psalmist hopes for redemption.

As Christians, we are far more aware of God's loving mercy to sinners than the ancient Israelites were. Thus, we may pray this psalm with far greater trust in God.

Out of the depths I cry to You, O Lord; Lord, hear my voice!

Let Your ears be attentive to my voice in supplication:

If You, O Lord, mark iniquities, Lord, who can stand?

But with You is forgiveness, that You may be revered.

I trust in the Lord; my soul trusts in His word.

My soul waits for the Lord more than sentinels wait for the dawn.

More than sentinels wait for the dawn, let Israel wait for the Lord,

For with the Lord is kindness and with Him is plenteous redemption;

And He will redeem Israel from all their iniquities.

The Holy Souls in Purgatory

The holy souls are those who have died in the state of grace, but who are not yet free from all punishment due to their unforgiven venial sins and all other sins, already forgiven, for which satisfaction is still to be made. They are certain of entering heaven, but first they must suffer in purgatory. The holy souls cannot help themselves because for them the night has come, when no man can work (John 9:4). It is our great privilege of brotherhood that we can shorten their time of separation from God by our prayers, good works, and especially the Holy Sacrifice of the Mass (O'Connell, p. 83).

Invocation

Eternal rest grant unto them, O Lord; and let perpetual light shine upon them. May they rest in peace. Amen.

For the Souls in Purgatory

My Jesus, by the sorrows Thou didst suffer in Thine agony in the Garden, in Thy scourging and crowning with thorns, in the way to

Calvary, in Thy crucifixion and death, have mercy on the souls in purgatory, and especially on those that are most forsaken; do Thou deliver them from the dire torments they endure; call them and admit them to Thy most sweet embrace in paradise.

*****

O Lord, who art ever merciful and bounteous with Thy gifts, look down upon the suffering souls in purgatory. Remember not their offenses and negligences, but be mindful of Thy loving mercy, which is from all eternity. Cleanse them of their sins and fulfill their ardent desires that they may be made worthy to behold Thee face to face in Thy glory. May they soon be united with Thee and hear those blessed words which will call them to their heavenly home: "Come, blessed of My Father, take possession of the kingdom prepared for you from the foundation of the world."

For All the Deceased

By Thy resurrection from the dead, O Christ, death no longer hath dominion over those who die in holiness. So, we beseech Thee, give rest to Thy servants in Thy sanctuary and in Abraham's bosom. Grant it to those, who from Adam until now have adored Thee with purity, to our fathers and brothers, to our kinsmen and friends, to all men who have lived by faith and passed on their road to Thee, by a thousand ways, and in all conditions, and make them worthy of the heavenly kingdom.

— From the Byzantine Liturgy

For the Souls in Purgatory

O Queen of Heaven, cause that the ardent longing of the souls in Purgatory to be admitted to the Beatific Vision quickly may be fulfilled. O Mother, we pray thee especially for the souls of Priests, for the souls of our kindred, for the souls of those who were zealous for thy veneration, for the souls of those who helped others and wept with those who wept, and finally for the forgotten souls. Cause that in due time, reunited in heaven, we may be happy in the possession of God, in the joy of thy sweet presence, in the communion of the saints, and eternally may thank thee for thy many benefits, O our mother, our unfailing help.

— Rev. James Cashman

Prayer for the Poor Souls

O God the life of those who live, the hope of those who die, the salvation of all who trust in Thee: mercifully grant that the souls of Thy servants and handmaidens being freed from the chains of our mortal nature, may by the intercession of Blessed Mary, ever a Virgin, rejoice together with Thy saints in everlasting light. Amen.

— The Dominican Missal

For the Dead

Be mindful, O Lord, of Thy servants who on departing this life were found unfit to enter into Thy joy, and are therefore now being prepared by suffering for that final beatitude. Grant that the claims of Thy justice may be satisfied, and the debts of these helpless sinners be fully paid by their loving Lord and Master, Jesus Christ Thy son, the one Mediator of all mankind. Amen (O'Connell, p. 147).

For Friends in Purgatory

My God, pour forth thy blessings and Thy mercies upon all persons and upon all souls in purgatory for whom, by reason of charity, gratitude and friendship, I am bound or desire to pray. Amen.

Prayers for Each Day of the Week

Sunday

O Lord God omnipotent, I beseech Thee by the Precious Blood, which Thy divine Son Jesus shed in the Garden, deliver the souls in purgatory and especially that one which is the most forsaken of all, and bring it into Thy glory, where it may praise and bless Thee for ever. Amen.

Our Father, Hail Mary, Eternal rest, etc.

Monday

O Lord God omnipotent, I beseech Thee by the Precious Blood which Thy divine son Jesus shed in His cruel scourging, deliver the souls in purgatory, and among them all, especially that soul which is nearest to its entrance into Thy glory, that it may soon being to praise Thee and bless Thee for ever. Amen.

Our Father, Hail Mary, Eternal rest, etc.

Tuesday

O Lord God omnipotent, I beseech Thee by the Precious Blood of Thy divine Son Jesus that was shed in His bitter crowning with thorns, deliver the souls in purgatory, and among them all, particularly that soul which is in the greatest need of our prayers, in order that it may not long be delayed in praising Thee in Thy glory and blessing Thee for ever. Amen.

Our Father, Hail Mary, Eternal rest, etc.

Wednesday

O Lord God omnipotent, I beseech Thee by the Precious Blood of Thy divine Son Jesus that was shed in the streets of Jerusalem whilst He carried on His sacred shoulders the heavy burden of the Cross, deliver the souls in purgatory, and especially that one which is richest in merits in Thy sight, so that, having soon attained the high place in glory to which it is destined, it may praise Thee triumphantly and bless Thee for ever. Amen.

Our Father, Hail Mary, Eternal rest, etc.

Thursday

O Lord God omnipotent, I beseech Thee by the Precious Body and Blood of Thy divine Son Jesus, which He Himself on the night before His Passion gave as meat and drink to His beloved Apostles and bequeathed to His Holy Church to be the perpetual Sacrifice and life-giving nourishment of His faithful people, deliver the souls in purgatory, but most of all, that soul which was most devoted to this Mystery of infinite love, in order that it may praise Thee therefor, together with Thy divine Son and the Holy Spirit in Thy glory for ever. Amen.

Our Father, Hail Mary, Eternal rest, etc.

Friday

O Lord God omnipotent, I beseech Thee by the Precious Blood which Jesus Thy divine Son did shed this day upon the tree of the Cross, especially from His sacred Hands and Feet, deliver the souls in purgatory, and particularly that soul for whom I am most bound to pray, in order that I may not be the cause which hinders Thee from admitting it quickly to the possession of Thy glory where it may praise Thee and bless Thee for evermore. Amen.

Our Father, Hail Mary, Eternal rest, etc.

Saturday

O Lord God omnipotent, I beseech Thee by the Precious Blood which gushed forth from the sacred Side of Thy divine Son Jesus in the presence and to the great sorrow of His most holy Mother, deliver the souls in purgatory and, among them all, especially that soul which has been most devout to this noble Lady, that it may come quickly into Thy glory, there to praise Thee in her, and her in Thee through all the ages. Amen.

Our Father, Hail Mary, Eternal rest, etc.

Prayer to Our Lady of Pity

Oh Lady of Pity, consoler of the afflicted and mother of all who believe, look mercifully on the poor souls in Purgatory who are also your children and more worthy of your pity because of their incapacity to help themselves in the midst of their ineffable sufferings. Pray, dear Co-redemptrix; intercede for us with the power of your mediation before the throne of divine mercy and in payment for their debt offer up the life, passion and death of your divine Son, together with your merits and those of all the saints in Heaven and the just on earth, so that, with divine justice completely satisfied, they may come into Paradise soon to thank and praise you forever and ever.

Amen.

— St. Alphonsus

Prayer for Departed Parents

O God who didst command thy people, saying "Honor thy father and thy mother," of thy loving kindness have mercy on the soul(s) of my father (mother) and forgive *them* all *their* sins. I humbly pray thee that thou wouldest grant unto me to behold *their* face(s) in the glory of eternal felicity. Through Jesus Christ Our Lord. Amen.

— St. Augustine's Prayer Book

For a Mother Who Has Lost Her Baby

Almighty, ever-living God, lover of holy purity, who has called this woman's child into Your heavenly kingdom; Lord, let her also experience Your merciful kindness. Comfort her with Your love, help her bravely to accept Your holy will, and so find sweetness in her sorrow. Comforted by the merits of Your passion, and aided by

the intercession of Mary ever virgin and of all the Saints, may she
be united at last with her child for all eternity in the kingdom of
heaven: who lives and reigns, God, forever and forever. Amen
(O'Connell, p. 105).

Prayer for the Murdered Unborn

O God, through the merits of the blood of the Holy Innocents,
martyred for your son, I beseech you to turn your face to the mil-
lions of unborn, murdered in their mothers' wombs. Count these
innocents as martyrs of choice. Trusting in your infinite mercy, I
beg you to take these souls to sing Your glory. Amen.

Prayer for the Unborn

O God, flood with your infinite Mercy the souls of the unborn
children who, through no fault of their mothers, have died in the
womb. Majestic Creator of mankind, you have made these souls; let
them sing your praise in glory forever and ever, Amen.

My Angel

An angel came.
It did not stay.
It fluttered in my womb,
Then went away.
A mortal, I
Must question why:
So little time to be,
And then goodbye.
But life was there
Of him and me.
And now in Heavenly grace
It waits for me.
My angel child
At Jesus' feet
Sings songs of love and praise
Until we meet.

Prayer on the Death of a Child

O merciful Father, whose face the angels of the little ones do
always behold in heaven; Grant us steadfastly to believe that this

thy child hath been taken into the safe keeping of thine eternal love; through Jesus Christ Our Lord. Amen.

— The Book of Common Prayer

To All Parents

I'll lend you for a little time a child of Mine, He said,
For you to love the while she lives and mourn for when she's dead.
It may be six or seven years, or twenty-two or three,
But will you, till I call her back, take care of her for Me?
She'll bring her charms to gladden you, and shall her stay be
    brief
You'll have her lovely memories as solace for your grief.
I cannot promise she will stay, since all from earth return,
But there are lessons taught down there I want this child to learn.
I've looked the wide world over in my search for teachers true
Now will you give her all your love, nor think the labor vain,
Nor hate Me when I come to call to take her back again?
I fancied that I heard them say: Dear Lord, Thy will be done.
For all the joy Thy child shall bring, the risk of grief we'll run.
We'll shelter her with tenderness, we'll love her while we may,
And for the happiness we've known forever grateful stay;
But shall the angels call for her much sooner than we'd planned,
We'll brave the bitter grief that comes and try to understand.

— Anonymous

In Memoriam at Easter

This season takes on a special meaning
Since it will be without my wife.
I think Heaven will be kinder to her
Than this world was, or even I.
One day, we will meet again
And I will know as she does now
What the resurrection truly is.
Now it is a mystery; then a revelation.

— C. Henry Kropf

A Prayer to Our Lady of Consolation for Beloved Dead

Mary, please pray with me this day for all my loved ones who have died. I wish to pray for them because I loved them so much while they were on this earth. Now I love them and their memory, and pray for their eternal happiness in heaven. Dearest Mother of Consolation, you who knew the death of your only Son, of your beloved husband, Joseph, you know my heart. You know the affliction of the loss of a loved one from your life. Strengthen me, guide me and pray with me now for these loved ones. My hope, dear Mary, is in the Resurrection. My trust is in your beloved Son. My calm and peace is ever in His Gospel, and in your loving prayers. Amen.

— Brother Jeffrey, OFM Conv.

Kontakion

With the saints, O Christ, give rest to Your servant(s) where there is no pain, sorrow, nor mourning, but life everlasting.

Chapter Eighteen

Prayers for Those Who Mourn

Prayer for Those Who Mourn

Almighty God, Father of all mercies and giver of all comfort, deal graciously, we pray thee, with those who mourn, that casting every care on thee, they may know the consolation of thy love, through Jesus Christ our Lord.

— Book of Common Prayer

For Widows

Immaculate Mother of God, most pure and faithful spouse of the meek St. Joseph, have pity, we beg of you, on all widows, who have been bereaved of their husbands whom they loved, and who, therefore, are now in special need of your holy and compassionate intercession. Be pitiful, most dear Mother, on those in particular who are most afflicted with loneliness, who are in need of the necessaries of life, or who suffer in some special way from their bereavement.

Obtain for them singular graces from almighty God, so that they may live a holy life and abound in good works, making of their widowhood, a time of prayerful service to your Divine Son. If they have children, aid them to take also the place of a father so that they may faithfully guide and shepherd their little flock.

Bring them to practice always deep and sincere piety, and teach them to imitate your holy example and to be devout and charitable and fervent in the service of God. Plead for them all to your Divine Son. Bring them all, through the sorrows of this life, to the glory of heaven, where your Jesus, with the Father and the Holy Ghost, lives and reigns,

one God, the joy and glory of all the just, world without end. Amen.
— Rev. Edward Garesche, S.J.

Prayer of a Widower

O Lord, governor of heaven and earth, in whose hands are embodied and departed spirits, if thou hast ordained the souls of the dead to minister to the living, and appointed my departed wife to have care of me, grant that I may enjoy the good effects of her attention and ministration, whether exercised by appearance, impulses, dreams, or in any other manner agreeable to thy government; forgive me my presumption, enlighten my ignorance, and however meaner agents are employed, grant me the blessed influences of thy Holy Spirit, through Jesus Christ our Lord.
— Samuel Johnson

Lord, Lift Us Up

The absence of that presence is everywhere.
I smother, Lord, in my despair.
So blind, my God, I did not see,
Nor draw him gently close to Thee.
From pain and sorrow let me rest
My weary head upon Your breast.
My earthly cares to You I yield.
Say but the word, and I am healed.
Lord, you lift us up when we fall.
Lord, have mercy.
Lord, you love us, even when we do not love ourselves.
Christ have mercy.
Lord, you love us and forgive us, even when we have sinned.
Lord, have mercy.
To mercy, Lord, I now appeal.
Say but the word, and I will heal.

Life Is Eternal

Life is eternal and love is immortal, and death is only a horizon, and a horizon is nothing save the limit of our sight. Lift us up, strong Son of God, that we may see further. Cleanse our eyes that we may see more clearly.
— Bede Jarrett, O.P.

Chapter Nineteen

Prayers for Ourselves

Swing Low

Swing low, sweet chariot, coming for to carry me home.
I looked over Jordan, and what did I see?
A band of angels, coming after me.
If you get there before I do,
Tell all my friends I'm coming, too.
I'm sometimes up and sometimes down;
But still my soul feels heavenly bound.
Swing low, sweet chariot, coming for to carry me home.

— traditional African-American hymn

Let No One Fear Death

Let no one fear death, for the Savior's death has set us free. For Christ, having risen from the dead, has become the first fruits of those who have fallen asleep.

— St. John Chrysostom

Prayer for Serenity

God, grant me the serenity to accept the things I cannot change,
The courage to change the things I can,
And the wisdom to know the difference.

Living one day at a time,
Enjoying one moment at a time;
Taking as Jesus did,
This sinful world as it is,
Not as I would have it;

Trusting that You will make all things right if I surrender to
   your will;
So that I may be reasonably happy in this life
And supremely happy with you forever in the next.
   — Reinhold Niebuhr

The Jesus Prayer

Lord Jesus Christ, have mercy on me, a sinner.

This short, meaningful prayer can be said alone or with the use
of a sacramental known as the Jesus beads. This chaplet consists of
a string of one hundred beads joined at the end with a crucifix.

Aspiration to the Providence of God

Providence of God, shown forth by the Heart of Jesus, have mercy
on us.
   — from the manual of the Sisters of Providence

Prayer to St. Elena (Helen) to Overcome Distress

May this burden of grief, sorrow, and suffering be lifted from my
aching heart. Replace these afflictions with the healing love which
will lift me out of my despair. Banish bitterness from my mind and
turn my sad thoughts toward happy memories, gratitude for the good
which remains in my life, and the serenity with which to go forward
to a truly happier future (Rivas, p. 88).

Ejaculations for a Happy Death

Jesus, Mary, Joseph, I give you my heart and my soul.
                    *****
Jesus, Mary, Joseph, assist me in my last agony.
                    *****
Jesus, Mary, Joseph, may I breathe forth my soul in peace with
   you.
                    *****
From a sudden and unprepared death, deliver us, O Lord!

Prayer to the Blessed Virgin for Fidelity and Final Perseverance

Virgin Mother of god, mediatrix of all graces, we plead for your
most powerful intercession to obtain for us the great and perfect gift

of fidelity to god's inspirations and of final perseverance. Never was it heard, most loving Mother, that anyone ever asked your help without finding an answer worthy of the love and tenderness of your motherly heart.

With the most childlike confidence and perfect trust we rely on you to win for us, by your perpetual pleadings with the Sacred Heart of your Divine son, a complete and persevering faithfulness to God's holy graces, and above all, a happy and holy death, so that we may enjoy forever the delights of your children in heaven. Most sweet Mother, let us not be lost on whom your Divine Son has poured forth the saving treasure of His precious Blood.

Help us at the hour of our death, most mighty Mother. Save us then, most powerful Virgin, deliver us then, most faithful Patroness. Bring us safe to the glory of your heavenly home, there, for all eternity, to behold Jesus, your Divine Son, living and reigning forever, with the Father and the Holy Ghost, one god, the life of all the blessed, world without end. Amen.

— Rev. Edward Garesche, S.J.

For a Happy Death and for a Happy End

Divine Jesus, mighty Saviour, Conqueror of death and sin, the time is swiftly approaching when we shall each one be summoned to pass through the dark doors of death into Your kingdom of eternity. May the prayers of Your own Sacred Heart, of the Immaculate Heart of Your Virgin Mother, and of all the angels and the saints in heaven and the just on earth, together with the mighty efficacy of all Holy Masses rise up forever in petition for us for a holy and happy death. Amen.

Remind us frequently, dear Lord, to pray for the dying and for our own happy death. Accept all our thoughts and words and actions, in union with Your Sacred Heart and with the Immaculate Heart of Your holy Mother, in petition for this great boon. May our death and that of each one for whom we are bound or wish especially to pray, be serene and tranquil, guarded round by all the holy angels, protected by our patron saints. May our hearts, at that supreme moment be full of the pure love of You, may our souls be clean from every stain. Make our faith, then, perfect and untroubled, our hope most bright and strong, and our love pure and mighty, when we go forth to meet You, our Saviours and our Judge. Multiply, great

Lord, at that tremendous moment, Your effective graces. Thus may we praise You, sweet Jesus, and thank You throughout all ages of eternity, where You live and reign, with the Father and the Holy Ghost, one Eternal God, the peace and joy of all the blessed, world without end. Amen.

— Rev. Edward Garesche, S.J.

For a Happy Death

O my dear Lord Jesus Christ, I do most humbly beseech Thee by those bitter pains Thou didst suffer for us in Thy cruel Passion, particularly in that hour wherein Thy divine Soul passed forth from Thy blessed Body, that Thou wouldst take pity on our souls in their last agony and passage to Eternity. And do Thou, O compassionate Virgin Mother, remember how thou didst sadly stand by thy beloved Son dying on the Cross; by thy grief and thy son's death assist us at our death and conduct us to a happy eternity. Amen (O'Connell, p. 140).

To St. Joseph, Patron of a Happy Death

Eternal Father, by the love Thou bearest toward Saint Joseph, who was chosen by Thee from among all men to exercise Thy divine fatherhood over Thy Son made Man, have mercy on us and upon all poor souls who are in their agony.

Our Father, Hail Mary, Glory be, etc.

Eternal Son of God, by the love Thou bearest toward Saint Joseph, who was Thy most faithful Guardian upon earth, have mercy on us and upon all poor souls who are in their agony.

Our Father, Hail Mary, Glory be, etc.

Eternal Spirit of God, by the love Thou bearest toward Saint Joseph who guarded with such tender care most holy Mary, Thy beloved Spouse, have mercy on us and upon all poor souls who are in their agony.

Our Father, Hail Mary, Glory be, etc.

For a Holy Death

O my adorable Creator, I ask of Thee the greatest of all Thy graces, that is to say, a holy death. No matter how greatly I have hitherto abused the life Thou gavest me, grant me the grace to end it in Thy holy love.

Let me die, like the holy Patriarchs, forsaking this valley of tears without sadness, to enter into the joy of eternal rest in my own true country.

Let me die, like the glorious Saint Joseph, I the arms of Jesus and Mary, repeating in turn each of these sweet Names which I hope to bless throughout eternity.

Let me die, like the immaculate and blessed Virgin, in the purest love, and desire to be reunited to the only object of my love.

Let me die, like Jesus on the Cross, with the most lively sentiments of hatred for sin, of charity toward Thee, O Heavenly Father, and of perfect resignation in my agony. Holy Father, into Thy hands I commend my spirit. Be merciful unto me.

Jesus, who didst die for me, grant me the grace of dying in an act of perfect love for Thee.

Holy Mary, Mother of God, pray for me now and at the hour of my death.

My Guardian Angel, my holy Patron saints, forsake me not at the hour of my death.

Saint Joseph, obtain for me the grace of dying the death of the just. Amen.

O my God, sovereign Lord of life and of death, who, by an immutable decree for the punishment of sin, hast determined that all men must die, behold me humbly kneeling before Thy dread Majesty, resigned and submissive to this law of Thy justice. With all my heart I detest my past sins, by which I have deserved death a thousand times; and for this cause I accept death in reparation for my sins and in obedience to Thy holy will. Yes, great God, send death upon me where Thou wilt, when Thou wilt, and in what manner Thou wilt. Meantime I shall avail myself to the days which it shall please Thee to bestow upon me, to detach myself from this world and to break every tie that holds me in bondage to this place of exile and to prepare myself to appear with sure confidence before Thy judgement seat. Wherefore I surrender myself without reserve into the hands of Thy fatherly Providence. May Thy divine will be done now and for evermore!

Amen.

For Mercy in the Last Hour

O Lord, my god, I now, at this moment, readily and willingly accept at Thy hand whatever kind of death it may please Thee to send me, with all its pains, penalties and sorrows.

O Lord Jesus, God of goodness and Father of mercies, I approach to Thee with a contrite and humble heart; to Thee I recommend my last hour, and that which then awaits me.

When my feet, now motionless, shall admonish me that my mortal course is drawing to an end;

Merciful Jesus, have mercy on me.

When my hands, trembling and benumbed, no longer able to hold Thy crucified Image, shall let it fall from their feeble grasp upon my bed of pain;

Merciful Jesus, have mercy on me.

When my eyes, dim and troubled at the horror of approaching death, shall fix on Thee their languid and expiring looks;

Merciful Jesus, have mercy on me.

When my cheeks, pale and living, shall inspire the beholders with pity and dismay; and my hair, bathed in the sweat of death, and stiffening on my head, shall forbode my approaching end;

Merciful Jesus, have mercy on me.

When my ears, soon to be forever shut to the discourse of men, shall open to hear Thy voice pronounce the irrevocable decree which shall decide my lot for eternity;

Merciful Jesus, have mercy on me.

When my imagination, agitated by horrid and terrifying phantoms, shall be sunk in mortal anguish; when my soul, affrighted at the sight of my iniquities and the terrors of Thy judgements shall have to fight against the angel of darkness, who will endeavor to conceal Thy mercies from my eyes, and plunge me into despair;

Merciful Jesus, have mercy on me.

When my poor heart, oppressed with the pains of sickness, and exhausted by its struggles against the enemies of its salvation shall be seized with the pangs of death;

Merciful Jesus, have mercy on me.

When the last tears, forerunners of my dissolution, shall drop from my eyes, receive them as a sacrifice of expiation for my sins, that I may die the victim of penance; and in that dreadful moment,

Merciful Jesus, have mercy on me.

When my friends and relations, encircling my bed, shall shed the tear of pity over me, and invoke Thy clemency in my behalf; Merciful Jesus, have mercy on me.

When I shall have lost the use of my senses, and the world shall have vanished from my sight; when I shall groan with anguish in my last agony and in the sorrows of death;

Merciful Jesus, have mercy on me.

When my last sighs shall summon my soul to go forth from my body, receive them as the effects of a holy impatience to fly to Thee, and in that moment,

Merciful Jesus, have mercy on me.

When my soul, trembling on my lips, shall bid adieu to the world, and leave my body lifeless, pale and cold, receive this separation as a homage which I willingly pay to Thy Divine Majesty; and in that last moment of my mortal life,

Merciful Jesus, have mercy on me.

When at length my soul, admitted to Thy presence, shall first behold with terror Thy awful Majesty, reject me not, but receive me into Thy bosom, where I may for ever sing Thy praises; and in that moment when eternity shall begin to me.

Merciful Jesus, have mercy on me (O'Connell, p. 144).

Prayer to Be Sinless at the Hour of Death

Lord Jesus Christ, who willest that no man should perish, and to whom supplication is never made without the hope of mercy, for Thou saidst with Thine own holy and blessed lips: "All things whatsoever ye shall ask in My name, shall be done unto you"; I ask of Thee, O Lord, for Thy holy name's sake, to grant me at the hour of my death full consciousness and the power of speech, sincere contrition for my sins, true faith, firm hope and perfect charity, that I may be able to say unto Thee with a clean heart; Into Thy hands, O Lord, I commend my spirit: Thou hast redeemed me, O God of truth, who art blessed for ever and ever. Amen.

— St. Vincent Ferrer

Against a Sudden Death

O most merciful Lord Jesus, by Thine agony and sweat of Blood, by Thy precious death, deliver us, we beseech Thee, from a sudden and unprovided death. O most kind Lord Jesus, by

Thy most sharp and ignominious scourging and crowning with thorns, by Thy holy Cross and bitter Passion, by Thy loving-kindness, we humbly pray that Thou wouldst not suffer us to die unprovided with Thy holy Sacraments. O dearly beloved Lord Jesus, by all Thy labors and sorrows, by Thy Precious Blood and sacred wounds, by those Thy last words on the Cross: "My God, my god, why hast Thou forsaken me?" and those others: "Father, into Thy hands I commend my spirit," we most earnestly beseech Thee to deliver us from a sudden death. Grant us, we pray, room for repentance; grant us a happy passing in Thy grace, that so we may be able to love Thee, praise Thee and bless Thee forever. Amen.

Newman's Prayer for a Happy Death

O my Lord and Savior, support me in that hour in the strong arms of Thy Sacraments, and by the fresh fragrance of Thy consolations. Let the absolving words be said over me, the holy oil sign and seal me, Thine own Body be my food, and Thy Blood my sprinkling. Let Thy sweet Mother Mary come to me, my angel whisper peace to me, Thy glorious saints and my own dear Patrons smile on me; that in them all, and through them all, I may receive the gift of perseverance, and die, as I desire to live, in Thy Faith, in Thy Church, in Thy service and in Thy Love. Amen.

— Cardinal Newman

Prayer at the Approach of Death

God of God, true God of true God, we know that Thou art goodness itself. Assist us in Thy benevolence. Protect us, lest we some day share with Satan the pains of hell. Spread over us the wings of Thy mercy.

We acknowledge Thee as the light; we are but servants in Thy hands. Permit not that the evil one wrest us from Thee forever and that we rebel against Thy sovereignty.

We know that Thou art just; be for us justice, O Lord. We know that Thou art our Savior; deliver and preserve us from evil. We proclaim Thy holiness; sanctify us with Thy Body and Blood. May the elect, who have eaten Thy flesh and drunk Thy Precious Blood, sing Thy glory.

Grant us pardon, O God of goodness, who art merciful to sinners. Amen.

— St. Ephrem the Syrian

Prayer to the Trinity for Final Perseverance

Father, Son and Holy Ghost, Eternal Trinity, I beg of You by the life, passion and death of Jesus Christ, and by the merits of the Blessed Virgin and of all the angels and saints, give to me the grace of final perseverance, of a happy death and a blessed eternity. May the last moments of my life, my God, be the best and holiest. Provide for me a time of repentance and atonement, the grace to be fortified at my death with Your holy sacraments, protection from yielding to temptation in my last hour, and the grace of loving and serving You even to the end of my life.

I wish this prayer to be the constant intention of all my thoughts and words and actions, of all Masses and Communions, of all the merits that I am able to gain in Your sight, during all the days of my life. Divine Father, You have created me, please have pity on me at the moment of my death. Divine Son, You have redeemed me, please have mercy on me at my last hour. Holy Spirit, You have sanctified me, please keep me holy at the last. And you, my blessed Mother, and all you saints and angels of God, I rely on you all to aid me at my last hour, and to bring me safe, by your prayers, through the darkness of death, to the light and glory of your eternal home. Amen.

— Rev. Edward Garesche, S.J.

Prayer for a Good Death

O Mary, conceived without stain, pray for us who fly to thee. Refuge of sinners, Mother of those who are in their agony, leave us not in the hour of our death, but obtain for us perfect sorrow, sincere contrition, remission of our sins, a worthy reception of the sacraments, so that we may be able to stand with safety before the throne of the just but merciful Judge, our God and our Redeemer.

Act of Acceptance of Death

O Lord my God, I now, at this moment, readily and willingly accept at Thy hand whatever kind of death it may please Thee to send me, with all its pains, penalties, and sorrows. Amen.

Chapter Twenty

Special Circumstances

Baptism in an Emergency

Where there is danger of death, baptism may be lawfully administered by any person who observes the essential conditions. Outside of the danger of death, it would be wrong for a lay Catholic to presume to baptize. However, where the danger does exist, the person baptizing may be a man or a woman, a Catholic or non-Catholic, even a non-believer. What is important is (1) that the person pour the water on the head or face of the one to be baptized; (2) that he pronounce the following formula while pouring the water: "I baptize thee in the name of the Father, and of the Son, and of the Holy Ghost"; (3) that he intend to baptize the person, or at least, that he intend to do what the Church does when administering the sacrament.

If possible, two witnesses should be at such a private baptism, in order that the ceremony may be attested to and its validity assured.

Since the valid baptism of anyone with the use of reason requires the intention to be baptized, it would be necessary in the case of a dying adult either to baptize conditionally or to have foreknowledge of, or a sign of, the person's desire for the sacrament.

The Heroic Act of Charity

The Heroic Act of Charity in behalf of the souls in purgatory consists in a voluntary offering, made by any one of the faithful in their favor, of all works of satisfaction done by him in this life, as well as of all suffrages which shall be offered for him after his death. By this act he deposits all these works and suffrages into the hands of the Blessed Virgin, that she may distribute them on behalf of those holy souls whom it is her good pleasure to deliver from the pains of purgatory and at the same time he declares that by this personal offering he only foregoes in their behalf the special and personal benefit of these works of satisfaction; so that, if he is a priest, he is not hindered from applying the Holy Sacrifice of the Mass according to the intention of those who give him alms for that purpose.

Selected Bibliography

Abbott, Walter M., S.J. *The Documents of Vatican II*. New York: Guild Press, 1966.

Aceves, Gutierre, coordinator. *Artes de Mexico,* special edition, "*El Arte Ritual de la Muerte Nina.*" Mexico, D.F.: *Consejo National para la Cultura y las Artes. Libro Trimestral Numero 15, primavera de 1992.*

Alberione, Rev. James. *Mary, Mother and Model.* Boston: Daughters of St. Paul, 1962.

Antall, Richard, "A Day in the Life...." *Our Sunday Visitor*, November 8, 1992.

Appleton, George, ed. *The Oxford Book of Prayer*. Oxford: Oxford University Press, Inc., 1986.

Aries, Philippe. *The Hour of Our Death*. New York: Alfred A. Knopf, Inc., 1981.

Attwater, Donald. *The Avenel Dictionary of Saints*. New York: Avenel Books, 1981.

Ball, Ann. *A Litany of Mary*. Huntington, IN: Our Sunday Visitor Publishing, 1987.

Ball, Ann. *Catholic Traditions in Cooking*. Huntington, IN: Our Sunday Visitor Publishing, 1993.

Ball, Ann. *Handbook of Catholic Sacramentals*. Huntington, IN: Our Sunday Visitor Publishing, 1991.

Barnett, Carol, "Tansy, a Bitter Taste of Immortality," *The Herb Quarterly*, Winter, 1992.

Blaher, Damian J., O.F.M., intro. *The Little Flowers of St. Francis, The Mirror of Perfection, The Life of St. Francis*. New York: E.P. Dutton and Co., Inc., 1951.

Book of Blessings. New York: Catholic Book Publishing Co., 1989.

Boss, Gayle, and Hellner, Cheryl. *Santo Making in New Mexico: Way of Sorrow, Way of Light*. Washington, D.C.: Potter's House Press,1991.

Bowen, Brownyn, "Cemetery Talk," unpublished notes, 1994.

Clement, Clara Erskine. *Angels in Art*. Boston: Colonial Press, 1898.

Coffey, Thomas J., S.J. *Blessed Kateri Tekakwitha*. Auriesville, New York: Tekakwitha League, 1982.

Connolly, S.J. *Priests and People in Pre-Famine Ireland*. New York: St. Martin's Press, 1982.

Cruz, Joan Carroll. *Miraculous Images of Our Lady*. Rockford, IL: TAN Books, 1993.

Cruz, Joan Carroll.*The Incorruptibles*. Rockford, IL: TAN Books, 1977.

Delaney, John J., ed. *A Woman Clothed With the Sun*. Garden City, NY: Image Books, 1961.

Delaney, John J. *Dictionary of Saints*. Garden City, NY: Doubleday and Co., 1980

De Leonardis, Rev. Gerard, OFM Cap, "Feast of the Assumption," *Capuchin Visitor*, Vol. 8 No. 2, August 1993.

Dobelis, Inge N., ed. *Magic and Medicine of Plants*. Pleasantville, NY: The Reader's Digest Assn., 1990.

Doerner, David L., S.A., "A Problem for the Catholic Church in Japan," *Japan Press*, April, 1976.

Every, George. *Christian Mythology*. London: Hamlin Publishing Group, 1970.

N.A. "Falfurrias Shrine Recalls Cures of Curandero," *San Antonio Express News*, Saturday, September 26, 1981.

Farb, Peter. *The Land, Wildlife, and Peoples of the Bible*. New York: Harper and Row, 1967.

Frazer, James C. *The Golden Bough*. New York: Grammercy Books, 1993.

Garesche, Rev. Edward F. *Moments With God*. Milwaukee: Bruce Publishing Co., 1942.

Gavitt, Rev. Loren, ed. *Saint Augustine's Prayer Book*. New York: Holy Cross Publications, 1974.

Giffords, Gloria Frasier. *The Art of Private Devotion: Retablo Painting of Mexico*. Austin: InterCultura, 1991. (Essays by Yvonne Lange, Virginia Armella de Aspe, and Mercedes Meade.)

Gilmour, Peter. *Now and At the Hour of Our Death*. Chicago: Liturgy Training Publications, 1989.

Graham, Joe S. ed. *Hecho en Texas*. Denton, TX: University of North Texas Press, 1991.

Green, Louisa Meigs. *Brother of the Birds*. Philadelphia: David McKay Co., Inc., 1929.

Grierson, Roderick, editor. *Gates of Mystery: The Art of Holy Russia*. Milan: InterCultura, 1993. Includes articles by Evgeniia Petrova, Sergei Averintsev, and Irina Shalina.

Grieve, Mrs. M. *A Modern Herbal*. New York: Dover Publications, Inc., 1981.

Guarducci, Margherita. *The Tomb of St. Peter*. New York: Hawthorn Books, 1960.

Habenstein, Robert and Lamers, William. *The History of American Funeral Directing*. Milwaukee: National Funeral Directors Association, 1981.

Harte, Catherine, "Irish Catholic Funerals and Customs," unpublished notes, 1993.

Jeffrey, Brother, O.F.M. Conv. *Prayers to Our Lady of Consolation for Each Day of the Week*. Carey, OH: Basilica and Shrine of Our Lady of Consolation, no date.

Kalberer, Augustine, O.S.B. *Lives of the Saints, Daily Readings*. Chicago: Franciscan Herald Press, 1975

Kelly, Eamon. *According to Custom*. Dublin: The Mercier Press, 1979.

Kelley, Sister Eileen Ann, archivist, and Borntrager, Sister Rosemary, archivist assistant, "Customs of the Sisters of Providence of St.-Mary-of-the-Woods," notes from the archives of the order, 1994.

Kim, Rev. Joseph Chang-mun. *Catholic Korea, Yesterday and Today*. Seoul: St. Joseph Publishing Co., 1984.

Knowles, Leo. Letter to the author, Aug. 16, 1993.

Korea, Your New Cultural Environment. San Francisco: USFK PAO Command Information Division, 1987.

Lally, Rev. Campion, OFM, "Oriental Christian Cremation and Burial Customs," unpublished notes, 1994.

Male, Emile. *Religious Art*. New York: Belgrave Press, 1949.

Martin, George, "The Graveyard of Jesus," *Catholic Digest*, April 1993, p. 7.

Mead, Jude, C.P. *St. Paul of the Cross: A Source/Workbook for Paulacrucian Studies*. New Rochelle: Don Bosco Publications, 1977.

Morganstern, Julian. *Rites of Birth, Marriage, Death and Kindred Occasions Amonth the Semites*. Cincinnati: Hebrew Union College Press, 1966.

"Native Americans Participate in Liturgy At St. Patrick's," *Lily of the Mohawks*. Auriesville, NY: Blessed Kateri Tekakwitha League, Vol. XLII No. 3, Summer 1989.

The New American Bible. Nashville: Thomas Nelson Publishers, 1971.

O'Connell, Rev. John P. and Martin, Jex, ed. *The Prayer Book*. Chicago: The Catholic Press, 1954.

O'Suilleabhain, Sean. *Irish Wake Amusements*. Cork: The Mercier Press, 1967.

Office of Christian Burial According to the Byzantine Rite. Pittsburgh: Byzantine Seminary Press, 1975.

Pellowe, William C.S. *Chuckles in the Cemetery*. Adrian, MI: Swenk-Tuttle Press, 1958.

The Raccolta. Boston: Benzinger Brothers, 1943.

The Roman Ritual, Rite of Funerals. New York: Catholic Book Publishing Co., 1971. (English translation approved by the National Conference of Catholic Bishops and confirmed by the Apostolic See.)

Riva, Anna. *Devotions to the Saints*. Toluca Lake, CA: International Imports, 1982.

Stravinskas, Peter M. J., ed. *Our Sunday Visitor's Catholic Encyclopedia*. Huntington, IN: Our Sunday Visitor Publishing, 1991.

St. Joseph Today. St. Louis, MO: Work of St. Joseph, 1974.

Schouppe, Rev. F.X., S.J. *Purgatory Explained by the Lives and Legends of the Saints*. Rockford, IL: TAN Books, 1986 (Reprint of the 1926 edition.)

Sheedy, Rev. Frank, "Burial Rites for Catholics," *Our Sunday Visitor*, March 14, 1993, p. 20.

Sloya, Virginia, ed. *A Sourcebook About Christian Death*. Chicago: Liturgy Training Publications, 1990.

Steele, Thomas J., S.J. *Santos and Saints*. Santa Fe: Ancient Press, 1982.

Sutter, John Wallace, custodian. *The Book of Common Prayer*. New York: Oxford University Press, 1952.

Thurston, Herbert, S.J., and Attwater, Donald. *Butler's Lives of the Saints*.

Ulanov, Barry. *Death: A Book of Preparation and Consolation*. New, York: Sheed and Ward, 1959.

Valabek, Redemptus, O.Carm. *Carmel in the World*. 1982.

Valente, Flaviano Amatuli. *Novenario de Difuntos*. Mexico City: Apostoles de la Palabra, no date.

Weigle, Marta. *The Penitentes of the Southwest*. Santa Fe: Ancient City Press, 1970.

Weigle, Marta. *Brothers of Light, Brothers of Blood*. Santa Fe: Ancient City Press, 1976.

Weigle, Marta, "Ghostly Flagellants and Dona Sebastiana: Two Legends of the Penitente Brotherhood," *Western Folklore*, Volume XXXVI, No. 2, April 1977.

Weiser, Francis X. *Handbook of Christian Feasts and Customs*. New York: Harcourt Brace and World, 1958.

Weiser, Francis X. *The Holyday Book*. New York: Harcourt Brace and Co., 1956.

West, John O. *Mexican-American Folklore*. Little Rock, AR: August House, 1988.

Wilder, Mitchell A. and Breitenbach, Edgar. *Santos: The Religious Folk Art of New Mexico*. Colorado Springs: The Taylor Museum of the Colorado Springs Fine Arts Center.

Will, George F. "Facing the Skull Beneath the Skin of Life," Newsweek, March 7, 1994, Vol. 123, No. 10. p. 74.

Wroth, William. *Images of Penance and Images of Mercy: Southwest Santos in the Late Nineteenth Century*. Norman, Oklahoma: University of Oklahoma Press, 1991.

Yang, Seung Mok. *Social Customs in Korea*. Seoul: Songmoonkak Publishing Co., 1969.

Thanks

M y sincere thanks to these and the many others who helped in the preparation of this manuscript.

Every effort has been made to determine the ownership of all texts and to make proper arrangements for their use. Any oversights that may have occurred, if brought to our attention, will gladly be corrected in future editions.

Rev. Eugene Beaudet, St. Philip of Jesus Church, Willsboro, New York

Rev. Carl Belish, Houston, Texas

Rev. Leslie F. Blowers, M.M., Maryknoll Fathers and Brothers, Cincinnati, Ohio

Rev. John Boscoe, C.S.B., Basilian Fathers of Mexico, Mexico City, D.F.

Gayle Boss, Washington, D.C.

Bronwyn Bowen, Abilene, Texas

Verna Burke, San Antonio, Texas

Heather and Glynn Burleson, Houston, Texas

Tim Cadogan, Reference Librarian, Cork County Library, Cork, Ireland.

Brother Joseph Candel, OFM Conv., Director, The National Shrine of Our Lady of Consolation, Carey, Ohio

Celeste Cottingham, Librarian, Corpus Christi Parish, Houston, Texas

Rev. John Catoir, Director, The Christophers, New York, New York

Rita Crabbe, Secretary, St. Basil's Center, Houston, Texas

Mary Pat Day, Director, Owings Dewey Fine Art, Santa Fe, New Mexico

Dra. Margarita de Orellana, Artes de Mexico, Mexico D.F.

V.P. De Santis, Department of History, University of Notre Dame, Notre Dame, Indiana

The Dismasians, Honolulu, Hawaii

Julie Douglas, Jacksonville, Texas

Rabbi Stuart Federow, Houston, Texas

Rev. Richard Flores, St. Rita's Church, Ft. Worth, Texas

Rev. James Gaunt, C.S.B., Sacred Heart Church, Manvel, Texas

Brother Hilary Gilmartin, F.S.C., Christian Brothers Center, Romeoville, Illinois

Anita Glasgow, Ord, Nebraska

Susan Hanson, Handmaids in Mary's Rosary Ministry, Millbury, Massachusetts

Catherine Harte, Newton, Rosscarbery, County Cork, Ireland

Sister Julia Hurley, R.S.C.J., Albany, New York

Rev. Dale Jamison, Mission Director, St. Anthony Zuni Indian Mission, Zuni, New Mexico

Sister Mary Jeremiah, Sister Mary of the Trinity, Sister Mary Roseanne, and all the nuns of the Monastery of the Infant Jesus, Lufkin, Texas

Sister Ann Joachim, Convent Station, New Jersey

Sister Maria Agnes Karasig, Sister Mary Antoninus Pelletier, and all the nuns of the Monastery of Our Lady of the Rosary, Summit, New Jersey

Sister Eileen Ann Kelley, Archivist, Sister Rosemary Borntrager, Assistant, Sisters of Providence Saint Mary of the Woods, Indiana

Leo Knowles, Manchester, England

Charles H. Kropf, Houston, Texas

Rev. Campion Lally, O.F.M., Gumma, Japan

Dr. Yvonne Lange, Santa Fe, New Mexico

John Laughlin, Huntington, Indiana

Chris Layton, Commonwealth Institute of Mortuary Science, Houston, Texas

Dr. Guillermo Lux, Southwest Historian, New Mexico State Library, Santa Fe, New Mexico

Francis X. Markley, Phoenix, Arizona

Brother Roger Mercurio, C.P., Passionist Community, Chicago

Rev. Michael Miller, C.S.B., Vatican Secretariat of State, Rome, Italy

Rev. Francisco Morales, O.F.M., Collegio S. Bonaventura, Rome, Italy

Virginia Murthough, Houston, Texas

Julie Nelson, American Funeral Service Museum, Houston, Texas

Arthur Olivas, Photographic Archivist, Museum of New Mexico, Santa Fe, New Mexico

Patricia O'Brien, Leonardo, New Jersey

Paul Pavletich, Jacksonville, Texas

Susan Pellowe, Chicago, Illinois

Rev.Basil Pennington, O.S.C.O., Trappist Monastery, Lantao Island, Hong Kong

Pat Rensing, Fountain Valley, California

Rev. Roderick, O.F.M., Franciscan Mission Associates, Mt. Vernon, New York

Orlando Romero, History Librarian, Museum of New Mexico, Santa Fe, New Mexico

San Fernando Cathedral, San Antonio, Texas

Rev. Kevin Shanley, O. Carm, *The Carmelite Review*, Darien, Illinois

Marcus Sloan, Director, InterCultura, Ft. Worth, Texas

Sister Marian Jose Smith, Sister Miriam Teresa League of Prayer, Convent Station, New Jersey

Mary Eunice Spagnola, Mary Productions, Middletown, New Jersey

Brother Deporres Stilp, M.M., Wilkes Barre, Pennsylvania

Brother David Tejada, F.S.C., Santa Fe, New Mexico

Rev. Paul Thomas, Patton, Pennsylvania

Rev. Paul K. Thomas, Archivist, Archdiocese of Baltimore, Baltimore, Maryland

Rev. Redemptus Valabek, O.Carm. Rome, Italy

Rev. Anselm Walker, St. Basil's Center, Houston, Texas

Marta Weigle, The University of New Mexico, Santa Fe, New Mexico

Bea Whitfil, Houston, Texas

Index

D

life after death 32, 149
"Life is Eternal" 203
limbo 191
"Lord, Lift Us Up" 203
Lord of Souls 109
Los Angelitos 122, 148, 151
Loyola, Ignatius   139
Luke 139
Luxembourg 90
Lydwina 139
lying in state 64

M

Maccabees 12, 15
Mary of Providence   137, 138
mausoleum 171
Memento Mori 52, 111, 113
Memento(es) of the Dead 77, 191
memorial 29, 41-42, 74, 77, 81, 95, 118, 139, 141, 149, 166, 176,
    179
memorialization 73-74, 77
Michael the Archangel 108, 139 *see St. Michael*
Middle Ages, the 44
Miller, Rev. J. Micheal C.S.B. 11
Miserere — Psalm 50 192
missionary 81, 92, 94, 141, 177
monkey spoons 66
monuments 29, 49, 50, 56, 57, 76, 111, 179
Mother of Mercy, Refuge of Sinners 85
Mourning Angels 111
mourning cards 71, 76, 77
mourning colors 40, 72
mourning costumes 166
mummers 62
"My Angel" 199
myrrh 36, 39
Mystical Death 106

N

National Shrine of Our Lady of Consolation 90, 220
National Shrine of the Souls in Purgatory 134
Native American 173, 174, 175-176, 218
nefesh 33
Newman, Cardinal 25, 211
"Newman's Prayer for a Happy Death" 211
Nicholas of Tolentino 138
Niebuhr, Reinhold 205
Novena for the Blessed Souls in Purgatory 124

O

ofrenda 9, 153-154, 156
"On the Death of the Nun Bernadette" 100
Ordo Exsequiarum 171
Osiris 28, 29
Our Lady at Knock 163
Our Lady of Consolation 88-90, 200, 217, 220
Our Lady of Herbs 97
Our Lady of Hope 87-88
Our Lady of Light 138
Our Lady of Mt Carmel 138
Our Lady of Mt. Carmel 90, 127
Our Lady of Pity 85-86, 198
Our Lady of Silence 163
Our Lady of the Rosary 138
Our Lady Refuge of Sinners 139
Our Lady's Thirty Days 97

P

Pantaleon 138
papal infallibility 96
"Papa's Funeral, 1941" 78
papel picado 154
Parastas 144, 147
Patron of the Holy Souls 110, 134
Paul 138 *see St. Paul*
Paul Yun Chi-ch'ung 141

pyramids 29

R

Raising of the Cross 178-179
Raphael (the archangel) 110, 127, 138, 139
Reformation 15, 43, 49, 60, 62
Requiem Eternam 192
Requiem Mass 40, 41, 45, 110, 116, 123
Retablo 123, 216
ritual wailing 165
Roch 138, 139
Roman Missal 189
"Rosary for the Dead" 191
Rosemary 51, 183

S

Sabbatine Privilege 92
sanctuary 34, 58-59, 153, 195
santero 114
sarcophagi 29, 50
Savonarola, Girolamo 54
"Say A Prayer" 186
scarab 30
Seelen brot 120, 182
Separate Organ Burial 55
sepulchre 31, 32, 34, 37, 40, 67, 73, 85, 96, 172
Serre, Abbé 191
Seven Sorrows of Mary 84
sexton 55, 66, 67
Sheol 33-35, 168
Sister Death 99, 103, 187
Sisters for the Dying 107
Sisters of Providence 105, 205, 217, 221
Social Functions of the Cemetery 58
soul food 120
St. Alphonsus 198
St. Augustine 14, 21, 88-89, 100, 152, 198, 216
St. Catherine of Alexandria 109
St. Christopher 136

Savor the Flavor

Catholic Traditions in Cooking

By Ann Ball
No. 0-87973-531-7, paper, $15.95, 180 pp.

This extraordinary cookbook is much more than a collection of recipes. It's a celebration of the rich heritage of the Catholic Faith.

Weave Catholic cooking and traditions into your family's commemorations of Advent, Christmas, Lent, Easter, Confirmation, Baptism, Feast Days of the Saints, and others.

Convenient indexes make it possible to add the flavor of Faith to an entire meal—from the proverbial soup to nuts.

Available at your local religious bookstore or use this page for ordering.

Please send me _____ of the above title. I am enclosing payment plus $3.95 per order to cover shipping/handling. Or, MasterCard/ VISA customers can order by telephone: 1-800-348-2440.

Name_____

Address_____

City/State_____ Zip_____

Telephone(_____)_____

Prices and availability subject to change without notice.

Our Sunday Visitor
200 Noll Plaza

More Favorites From Author Ann Ball

Qty. A Handbook of Catholic Sacramentals

( ) By Ann Ball

> No. 0-87973-*448*-5, paper, $7.95, 224 pp.
> Learn the history of sacramentals and their roles in contemporary
> Catholic spirituality. This carefully researched book looks at such
> revered practices as: the Stations of the Cross, the making of
> novenas, the Rosary, the wearing of scapulars, and much more.

( ) **A Litany of Saints**

> By Ann Ball
> No. 0-87973-*460*-4, paper, $8.95, 224 pp.
> Discover some of the world's most fascinating people. Unique facets
> of each saint are explored through art, devotional customs,
> sacramentals, and relics.

( ) **Holy Names of Jesus: Devotions, Litanies, Meditations**

> By Ann Ball
> No. 0-87973-*428*-0, paper, $7.95, 120 pp.
> Look at some of the well-known and not so well-known names of
> Jesus, along with the prayers and devotions designed to increase your
> Faith and enhance your prayer time.

( ) **A Litany of Mary**

> By Ann Ball
> No. 0-87973-*509*-0, paper, $7.95, 178 pp.
> Give homage to Mary with this beautiful collection devoted to
> honoring the Mother of God.

> Available at your local religious bookstore or use this page
> for ordering.

> Please send me the above titles. I am enclosing payment plus $3.95
> per order to cover shipping/handling. Or, MasterCard/VISA
> customers can order by telephone: 1-800-348-2440.

Name_____

Address_____

City/State_____ Zip_____

Telephone ( )_____

Prices and availability subject to change without notice.

 Our Sunday Visitor
200 Noll Plaza
Huntington, IN 46750

A53BBHBP

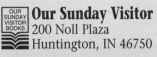

OUR SUNDAY VISITOR BOOKS

BEST SELLING BOOKS

CURRENT

Essentials of the Faith: . . . . 740-9 . . . . . . $ 9.95
A Guide to the Catechism of the Catholic Church
By Alfred McBride, O.Praem.

Pontiffs: Popes Who Shaped History . . . . 479-5 . . . . $16.95
By John Jay Hughes

A Pastor's Challenge: . . . . (cloth) . . . . 738-7 . . . . $19.95
Parish Leadership in an Age of Division,
Doubt, and Spiritual Hunger
By George A. Kelly

Marvels of Charity: . . . . (cloth) . . . . 648-8 . . . . $29.95
History of American Sisters and Nuns
By George C. Stewart, Jr.

Making Things Right: . . . . (English) . . . . 351-9 . . . . $ 3.95
The Sacrament of Reconciliation . . . . (Spanish) . . . . 349-7 . . . . . $ 3.95
By Jeannine Timko Leichner

Daily Roman Missal . . . . (bonded leather) . . . . . . 120-6 . . . . $59.95

Exploring The Teaching of Christ . . . . 624-0 . . . . $139.95
By Bishop Donald W. Wuerl

The Eager Reader Bible Story Book . . . . (cloth) . . . . 252-0 . . . . $15.95
Catholic Edition

A Guide to the Catechism of . . . . (blackline masters) . . . . 126-5 . . . . $29.95
the Catholic Church
By Alfred McBride, O.Praem.

Called to Serve: A Guidebook for . . . . (pkg. of 6) . . . . 663-1 . . . . $14.95
Altar Servers - Revised Edition
By Albert J. Nevins, M.M.

Lives of the Saints You Should Know . . . . 576-7 . . . . $ 7.95
By Margaret and Matthew Bunson

The Catholic One Year Bible (NRSV) . . . . (cloth) . . . . 231-8 . . . . $24.95
. . . . (kivar) . . . . 232-6 . . . . . . $18.95

Available at your local religious bookstore or use this page for ordering:

OUR SUNDAY VISITOR • 200 NOLL PLAZA • HUNTINGTON, IN 46750

Please send me the above title(s). I am enclosing payment plus
$3.95 per order to cover shipping/handling. Or, MasterCard/Visa customers
can order by phone **1-800-348-2440**.

Name _____

Address_____

City _____ State _____ Zip _____

Telephone ( ) _____

Prices and availability subject to change without notice.

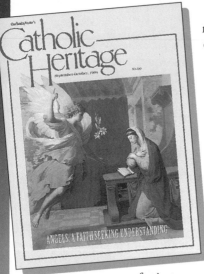